CW00344322

The story of a city,
through the eyes of its newspaper

In Love with Leeds

By Grant Woodward

Foreword by Barbara Taylor Bradford

Yorkshire Evening Post

CELEBRATING 125 YEARS OF THE YORKSHIRE EVENING POST

GREAT NORTHERN

Great Northern Books Limited
PO Box 1380, Bradford, BD5 5FB
www.greatnorthernbooks.co.uk

ISBN: 978-0-9933447-1-8

Design and layout: David Burrill

CIP Data
A catalogue for this book is available from the British Library

CONTENTS

In Love With Leeds

Grant Woodward

For

Rory and Skye

(this is what Daddy was doing all those late nights),

and the people of Leeds, past, present and future.

ACKNOWLEDGEMENTS

In compiling this book I am indebted to the *YEP*'s David Clay and his knack for tracking down the material that eluded me. The treasure trove that is the British Newspaper Archive – www.britishnewspaperarchive.co.uk – allowed me to delve into the *YEP*'s pages from a century and more ago. I am forever grateful to my parents and sister, and my wife Fiona for her patience. Sarah Freeman's proof-reading skills provided a welcome second pair of eyes, while David Burrill and David Joy of Great Northern Books also offered valuable assistance. Above all, however, this book owes its existence to all those journalists and photographers whose words and pictures have graced the Yorkshire Evening Post through the decades.

FOREWORD

Just imagine, for 125 years people have been reading the *Yorkshire Evening Post*. It's a fantastic achievement.

I will never forget the day I became a junior reporter on the *YEP*. It was in the late summer of 1949. I had worked in the typist pool of the newspaper for some months, but I'd always wanted to be a journalist. So I wrote some features off my own bat, simply dropped them on the sub-editors' table and hoped for the best.

I was thrilled when they appeared in the newspaper, even though my name wasn't on them. Later on, when the accounting department attempted to pay a girl called Barbara Taylor, they soon discovered she was a girl in the typist pool and not a stringer at all. The editor heard the story, was apparently intrigued, and sent for me.

Barry Horniblow was a talented Fleet Street journalist brought up to Leeds to revamp the *YEP*. He liked young people and wanted to encourage them, and eventually he had me moved to the reporters' room to be trained.

That Monday morning when I stood in front of the news editor's desk still remains in my mind. Ken Lemmon had been expecting me, but looked as if he didn't quite know what to do with me. In those days a girl in the midst of a bunch of tough northern newspaper men was unheard of. It was a man's world.

At last he spoke to me, announcing that if he sent me out to cover a wedding and the church burned down, I shouldn't come back and tell him there was no story because of the fire. That *was* the story. I nodded my understanding.

He beckoned to a young man who was standing nearby and introduced us. It was Keith Waterhouse, a seasoned reporter. Mr Lemmon explained that Keith was going to help me write proper newspaper copy. Keith led me to a desk in the reporters' room. He was kind, very reassuring and welcoming, told me it wasn't personal, that they men didn't want me there because they would have to watch their language, bite back swear words.

I grew up in that reporters' room. That lovely old building in Albion Street was the most exciting place to me, my whole world. Typewriters clattering, ticker-tape machines rattling, sub-editors shouting out headlines.

In my mind's eye I can still see all those friends I made there, and who set me on the right path: Keith, Madeleine McLaughlin, the women's page editor, Frank Metcalfe, Barrie Farnill and Frank Shire, the night news editor who took me under his wing.

When people ask me where I went to college, I tell them I grew up in a newspaper office and went to the best university in the world, the *Yorkshire Evening Post*.

Barbara Taylor Bradford, September 2016.

The Yorkshire Evening Post.

BUFF EDITION

No. 1. (Registered for Transmission Abroad.) LEEDS, MONDAY, SEPTEMBER 1, 1890. DAILY—ONE HALFPENNY.

READ "A FAMILY WITHOUT A NAME," A NEW STORY BY JULES VERNE, NOW APPEARING IN THE YORKSHIRE WEEKLY POST.

Public Notices.

INTERNATIONAL EXHIBITION, LEEDS. [illegible]

CLASSICAL LIVING STATUARY. [illegible]

INTERNATIONAL EXHIBITION, LEEDS. [illegible]

GRAND THEATRE, LEEDS. [illegible]

LEEDS HAREHILLS CYCLING CLUB. [illegible]

SCARBOROUGH. [illegible]

WHEN IN LEEDS CALL AT THE "VIADUCT" WHISKY BAR, COMMERCIAL COURT, BRIGGATE, IMMEDIATELY ADJOINING THE RAILWAY BRIDGE. [illegible] SCOTCH AND IRISH WHISKIES, ALL HIGH-CLASS, AND RANGING FROM FIVE TO TEN YEARS OLD. PARTICULARS AND QUOTATIONS ON APPLICATION. WEDDERSPOON & CO., THE "VIADUCT" WHISKY BAR, COMMERCIAL COURT, BRIGGATE.

GLASS! GLASS! CONFECTIONERS' JARS. [illegible]

Business Announcements.

MILLER'S.

THE GREAT POPULAR FURNISHERS. [illegible] LARGEST and MOST COMPLETE, [illegible] NEW GOODS for the COMING SEASON.

UNPARALLELED DISPLAY AT MILLER'S, PROVIDENCE HOUSE, 45, NORTH STREET, LEEDS.

NEW and ARTISTIC PRODUCTIONS IN DRAWING and DINING ROOM FURNITURE.

NEW DESIGNS in BRASS, IRON, and PARISIAN BEDSTEADS. MILLER'S.

NEW DESIGNS in BED and WINDOW DRAPERIES. MILLER'S.

NEW CARPETS in EVERY CONCEIVABLE MAKE and STYLE [illegible]

DINING-ROOM FURNITURE. [illegible]

DINING-ROOM SUITES.—MAHOGANY, WALNUT, or OAK. [illegible] MILLER'S.

DINING-ROOM SUITES.—[illegible] OAK, WALNUT, or MAHOGANY. [illegible] MILLER'S.

DINING-ROOM SUITE, POLLARD OAK, MAHOGANY or WALNUT. [illegible] MILLER'S.

NEW and ELEGANT DESIGNS in SIDEBOARDS. [illegible] MILLER'S.

NEW and ARTISTIC DESIGNS in DRAWING ROOM FURNITURE. MILLER'S.

DRAWING-ROOM SUITES in ENDLESS VARIETY. [illegible] MILLER'S.

DRAWING-ROOM SUITES, INLAID ROSEWOOD and CHIPPENDALE MAHOGANY. [illegible] MILLER'S.

DRAWING-ROOM SUITE (Novelty). [illegible] MILLER'S.

DRAWING-ROOM CABINETS.—Elegant INLAID ROSEWOOD and WALNUT CABINETS. [illegible] MILLER'S.

BAMBOO FURNITURE (Special).—New designs in [illegible] MILLER'S.

DRAWING-ROOM FANCY OCCASIONAL CHAIRS. [illegible] MILLER'S.

MILLER'S BEDROOM SUITES [illegible]

BEDROOM SUITE in solid HARDWOOD. [illegible] MILLER'S.

BEDROOM SUITE in SOLID WALNUT. [illegible] MILLER'S.

BEDROOM SUITE—THE PRINCESS. [illegible] MILLER'S.

THE GREATEST FACILITIES FOR INSPECTION.

SECOND-HAND DEPARTMENT. [illegible] MILLER'S.

SECOND-HAND SPANISH MAHOGANY DINING TABLE. [illegible] MILLER'S.

SECOND-HAND INLAID ROSEWOOD CABINET. [illegible] MILLER'S.

SECOND-HAND MAHOGANY SECRETAIRE BOOKCASE. [illegible] MILLER'S.

SECOND-HAND MAHOGANY DINING-ROOM SUITE. [illegible] MILLER'S.

SECOND-HAND 6ft. 6in. SIDEBOARD (Mahogany). [illegible] MILLER'S.

SECOND-HAND 4ft. WARDROBE. [illegible] MILLER'S.

SECOND-HAND SIDEBOARD, in rich cultivated Mahogany. [illegible] MILLER'S.

SECOND-HAND DECORATED BEDROOM SUITE. [illegible] MILLER'S.

SECOND-HAND BOOKCASE. [illegible] MILLER'S.

SECOND-HAND 6ft. MAHOGANY WARDROBE. [illegible] MILLER'S.

SECOND-HAND MAHOGANY DINING TABLE. [illegible] MILLER'S.

SECOND-HAND GASALIERS, three and four light. [illegible] MILLER'S.

SECOND-HAND AMERICAN ORGAN. [illegible] A GENUINE BARGAIN. CALL AND SEE IT.—MILLER'S.

GOODS ARE WAREHOUSED IN DRY ROOMS FREE OF CHARGE UNTIL REQUIRED.

COTTAGE FURNITURE. THE LARGEST STOCK IN THE COUNTY. CONTRACTS FOR REMOVALS.

NOTE THE ADDRESS— MILLER & CO., 45, NORTH STREET, LEEDS.

ROLLED IRON GIRDERS. LARGEST STOCK IN YORKSHIRE. EVERY SECTION KEPT IN STOCK, [illegible] CHAS. AUTY & CO., IRON WAREHOUSE, ASSEMBLY STREET, LEEDS.

HOWELL'S [illegible] WINDOW BLINDS and FITTINGS. [illegible] 100, ALBION STREET, LEEDS.

27 AND 29, ALBION STREET, LEEDS.

THE BEST FLOOR COVERINGS.

DENBY & SPINKS' SEAMLESS CARPETS.

DENBY & SPINKS supply the Best Styles, [illegible] 27 and 29, Albion Street. [illegible]

NEW CENTRAL CARPETS.

PRICE LISTS of all kinds of Central and Seamless Carpets [illegible] ALBION STREET, LEEDS.

DENBY & SPINKS' TURKEY CARPETS.

FOR DINING and DRAWING ROOMS.—[illegible]

SPECIAL TILE LINOLEUM.

LINOLEUM, FOUR YARDS WIDE. [illegible]

NEW AUTUMN CURTAINS.

DENBY & SPINKS have received their first delivery of New Autumn Window Curtains [illegible]

"LIBERTY" ART FABRICS.

SPECIALITIES.—DENBY & SPINKS are [illegible] "Liberty" Art Furnishings [illegible]

BEDSTEADS, SPRING MATTRESSES, BEDDING.

DENBY & SPINKS keep a large Stock of Brass and Iron Bedsteads [illegible]

THE LARGEST and MOST CONVENIENT CARPET and CURTAIN WAREHOUSE. DENBY & SPINKS, ALBION STREET, LEEDS. TELEPHONE 93.

FURNISHING IRONMONGERY.

BEST VALUE FOR CASH. C. M. BROWN & SON, 11 AND 12, KIRKGATE, LEEDS.

[illegible] IN GREAT VARIETY. [illegible]

C. M. BROWN & SON. CENTRAL IRONMONGERY STORES, 11 AND 12, KIRKGATE, LEEDS.

TERMS:—CASH. CLEANLY, DURABLE, CHEAP, SANITARY.

THORNTON & CO.'S GOLD MEDAL WATERPROOFS. [illegible]

THORNTON & CO. [illegible] LEEDS.

WANTED, WASTE PAPER, [illegible] WILLIAM BENSON, [illegible] QUARRY HILL, [illegible]

UNIVERSAL FURNISHING COMPANY.

FURNISH ON THE EASY PURCHASE SYSTEM, AT CASH PRICES.

THE UNIVERSAL FURNISHING COMPANY, THE OLDEST ESTABLISHED AND BY FAR THE MOST EXTENSIVE FURNISHERS ON THE EASY PURCHASE SYSTEM IN THE PROVINCES, SUPPLY EVERY REQUISITE FOR THE COMPLETE FURNISHING OF COTTAGE, HOTEL, OR MANSION CONSIDERABLY CHEAPER THAN THE MAJORITY OF THOSE FIRMS WHO SELL FOR CASH ONLY. THIS WE ARE ABLE TO DO THROUGH HAVING A VERY LARGE CAPITAL AT COMMAND, AND BEING THE BONA-FIDE MANUFACTURERS OF THE PRINCIPAL GOODS WE SELL.

IN THE EVENT OF ILLNESS, DULNESS OF TRADE, AND NON-EMPLOYMENT, NO FORCIBLE SEIZURES ARE MADE. LENIENCY, FAIRNESS, AND HUMANITY ARE ADHERED TO.

NO SECURITY REQUIRED,
NO EXTRA EXPENSES,
ON OUR EASY PURCHASE SYSTEM.

THE FAIR AND EQUITABLE MANNER in which our business is carried on, and our REASONABLE TERMS AND LOW PRICES [illegible]

GENERAL TERMS, [illegible] WEEKLY, MONTHLY, or QUARTERLY.

AMOUNT.	DEPOSIT.	WEEKLY PAYMENTS.
£5	10s.	2s.
£10	£1	4s.
£20	£2	6s.
£30	£3	7s.
£50	£6	12s.

AN INSPECTION OF OUR STOCK [illegible] BETTER VALUE [illegible] EASY PURCHASE SYSTEM [illegible]

ALL GOODS ARE DELIVERED FREE IN OUR OWN OR PRIVATE VANS, [illegible]

WE ALLOW NO COMMISSION, NOR DO WE EMPLOY AGENTS OR COLLECTORS, [illegible]

ONLY ONE UNIVERSAL FURNISHING COMPANY. [illegible]

UNIVERSAL FURNISHING COMPANY, 1, 3, 5, AND 7, NORTH STREET, (BOTTOM OF LOVELL ROAD ROW), LEEDS.

OYSTERS! OYSTERS!! OYSTERS!!! SEASON 1890-91.

NORTON'S OYSTER ROOMS, ALBION ST., LEEDS. ARE THE BEST-ADAPTED PREMISES IN YORKSHIRE. [illegible] F. NORTON.

CHADWICK'S COMPOUND BALSAM OF LINSEED AND HONEY. [illegible] A MARVELLOUS CURE FOR COUGHS, COLDS, HOARSENESS, ASTHMA, BRONCHITIS, WHEEZING, DIFFICULTY IN BREATHING, CONSUMPTION, [illegible] INFLUENZA, IT HAS NO EQUAL. [illegible]

THE PRINTERS, GOODALL AND SUDDICK, THE PRINTERS, LITHOGRAPHERS, and STATIONERS, COOKRIDGE STREET, LEEDS. ESTIMATES GIVEN FOR ALL KINDS OF WORK. TELEPHONE, 175. TELEGRAMS, SUDDICK, LEEDS.

THE EXCELLENCE OF BELL'S WATCHES IS UNDENIABLE. A. & J. BELL, WATCH MANUFACTURERS, ESTABLISHED [illegible] YEARS AT 106 AND 108, ALBION STREET, LEEDS. [illegible] RELIABLE SPECIALITIES. [illegible] WHOLESALE AGENTS FOR THE WALTHAM WATCH COMPANY. CLOCKS OF EVERY DESCRIPTION. [illegible]

J. BOND, [illegible]

ESTABLISHED 50 YEARS.

EDMONDSON'S STUFF WAREHOUSE. THE LARGEST STOCK OF DRESS GOODS IN THE KINGDOM.

NEW and FASHIONABLE FABRICS [illegible]

USEFUL and FASHIONABLE TWEEDS and CHEVIOTS [illegible]

INDIGO-DYED SERGES, [illegible] CELEBRATED "PLAINNOUGHT" SERGES [illegible]

NEW and FASHIONABLE FURS AT SUMMER PRICES. [illegible]

NEW FANCY and BROCADED CLOTHS [illegible]

SILK SEAL PLUSHES [illegible]

RICH SILKS in Faille, Merv, Satin, [illegible]

VELVETS and VEVETEENS [illegible]

15, ALEXANDER STREET, PARK LANE, LEEDS, [illegible]

RETURN TO SCHOOL.

HYAM & CO., LIMITED, [illegible] EVERY NECESSARY IN SCHOOL OUTFITS FOR BOYS RETURNING TO SCHOOL.

ETON, HARROW, AND RUGBY SUITS, READY MADE OR TO MEASURE.
OVERCOATS OF EVERY DESCRIPTION, READY MADE OR TO MEASURE.
NIGHT AND DAY SHIRTS, READY MADE OR TO MEASURE.
DRESSING GOWNS IN GREAT VARIETY, READY FOR IMMEDIATE USE.
GLOVES, COLLARS, FRONTS, and BRACES. UNDERCLOTHING, RUGS and UMBRELLAS.
BAGS, PORTMANTEAUS, and PLAY BOXES. TOILET REQUISITES.
FELT HATS, SILK HATS, and CAPS,
BOOTS, SHOES, and SLIPPERS, and
EVERY REQUISITE FOR SCHOOL OUTFITS.

PRICE LIST FREE ON APPLICATION.

HYAM & CO., LIMITED, 42 AND 43, BRIGGATE, LEEDS.

BY HER MAJESTY'S ROYAL LETTERS PATENT. BY APPOINTMENT TO H.R.H. THE PRINCE OF WALES, K.G.

SCAFE'S PATENT LEATHER and RUBBER COMBINATION BOOTS. [illegible]

HIGHLY RECOMMENDED by the MEDICAL PROFESSION, [illegible]

SPECIALLY ADAPTED for SHOOTING, FISHING, TENNIS, CRICKET, &c. 20, ALBION STREET, LEEDS, and 104, NEW BOND STREET, LONDON, 65 AND 66, CHANCERY LANE, LONDON.

S. TETLEY, CIGAR AND TOBACCO MERCHANT, 2, BOAR LANE, LEEDS.

BOYS' RETURN TO SCHOOL.

"LION" SCHOOL SUITS.
"LION" SCHOOL SUITS.
"LION" SCHOOL SUITS.
MOST DURABLE MATERIALS.
MOST SERVICEABLE COLOURS.
MOST ECONOMICAL PRICES.

THE "LION" IS IN KIRKGATE, LEEDS.

JONES, [illegible]

WATCHES, WATCHES, WATCHES.

FIRST AND GENUINE SALE.

ALTERATION AND EXTENSION OF PREMISES.

DYSON, WATCHMAKER AND JEWELLER, 24, 25, and 26, BRIGGATE, LEEDS.

DYSON'S SALE. NOW PROCEEDING. [illegible] Wedding, Birthday Presents. Sporting and other Prizes. Genuine Reduction of [illegible] ALL GOODS GUARANTEED.

DYSON'S SALE. IMMENSE SUCCESS. AN OPPORTUNITY SELDOM OFFERED. NOW DRAWING TO A CLOSE.

ALL GOODS GUARANTEED. ALL GOODS GUARANTEED. THIS CLEARANCE SALE [illegible] IN THE POUND. [illegible]

DON'T MISTAKE THE ADDRESS— TIME BALL BUILDINGS, THREE DOORS BELOW BOAR LANE. LOOK FOR THE PROJECTING CLOCK AND "FATHER TIME." (Registered Trade Mark.)

"E.Y.O." WHISKY.

"E.Y.O." WHISKY. "The Perfection of Scotch Whisky." It is supplied to The Royal Military Academy, Woolwich, many of the Nobility, Gentry, and Clergy, and numerous Clubs, Messes, and First Class Hotels throughout the Country, and may be obtained from Wine and Spirit Merchants, Hotel and Inn Keepers, and Licensed Grocers, in our Labelled and Capsuled Bottles. [illegible] Sample bottle will be sent by Parcel Post, carefully packed, on receipt of [illegible]

Samples and Quotations for Home and Export Trade on Application.

Sole Proprietors: COWBROUGH & CO., WHISKY MERCHANTS, LEEDS.

THE CHEAPEST HOUSE IN LEEDS FOR DRAPERS' CAP PAPER, GROCERS' CAP PAPER, STRAW BOARDS, CLEANING WASTE, SPONGE CLOTHS, TWINE, BROWN PAPER, GLAZED PAPER, BISCUIT CAP PAPER, GROCERS' PAPER, DRAPERS' PAPER, PRESS PAPER.

WILLIAM BENSON, MANUFACTURER OF ALL KINDS OF FELT PAPER, QUARRY HILL (Corner Regent Street), LEEDS.

W. BRIERLEY, BOOKSELLER, MERCANTILE AND FAMILY STATIONER, 2, BOND STREET, LEEDS.

WHITEHEAD & MILLER, PRINTERS, LITHOGRAPHERS, AND BOOKBINDERS, 129, KIRKGATE, LEEDS. MUSIC PRINTING: OLD AND NEW NOTATIONS.

G. TRELWELL & CO.'S SPECIALITIES. [illegible] WORTH'S CORSETS. 33, COMMERCIAL STREET, LEEDS.

JOHN O'BRIEN, GLOBE BILLIARD WORKS, [illegible] MANCHESTER. [illegible]

ECHOES.

Is life worth living? The old, weary, stale, time-honoured enquiry comes back to us in the autumn tide, when a young man's fancy lightly turns to thoughts of seaside resorts, excursion trains, boating flannels, and cheap cigars of Samson strength. "Partings and death and divisions make barren our lives." Do congresses, andconferences, and associations—religious, scientific, and philanthropic—make us any brighter, or happier, or more contented with our lot in this work-a-day world? I doubt it. I speak as a sceptic with small veneration for the antique and the historical. Vandal as I must appear, I confess to a sneaking sympathy with the gentleman moved to unutterable scorn by the enthusiastic demonstrations of an archæological party at the sight of a cromlech. "And what do you think it was?" asked my disgusted friend. "Two stones with another stone on top of them."

Times change, and scientific sections probably change with them. Still I cannot eradicate the vivid impression left on my mind some years ago when a highly influential and important association was holding its annual sittings in a certain town. The day was hot. The sun shone as it never seems to shine now. A pleasant hum of cheery voices was borne in by soft breezes from the sea. Flags were flying in the offing, and boatmen invited the reckless to take as many "miles of danger" as they chose at contract price. Local bigwigs were dispensing generous hospitality—the sort of medicine one never grows tired of, and local caterers arranged glorious excursions at prices putting dreams of avarice to shame. But science was inflexible. A section had been summoned to attend an expository discourse upon the collapsibility of boats. As a slave of duty I forswore the delights of the bright outer world and attended that meeting. What a rude awakening was that! The lecturer was there, the non-collapsible boat was there, but the audience consisted of one elderly lady, with a strong affection for acid drops, who would never have trusted her precious being in a boat if empires were offered as a reward. Yet she was recompensed for conscientious devotion. Her lukewarm brother and sister scientists who had gone cruising in the bay were overturned and nearly drowned. They have never forgiven themselves for their practical faith in the non-collapsibility of the common or garden licensed wherry.

A marvellous stimulus to archæological research—I speak from my own experience—is provided by a liberal marking down of intervals for needful refreshments. I travelled once with a highly cultured party in closely packed waggonettes for a distance of twenty miles or more. We had been visiting churches, Roman remains, and trifles of that description. A long delay was made in one spot by a couple of savants holding a protracted dispute whether the buttress on the north side of the church was built between 1160 and 1170, or between 1170 and 1185. No satisfactory decision has ever been arrived at, but the poignancy of my individual grief at the distressing uncertainty was considerably mollified when we halted at a baronial hall—hot and dusty with our ride—and were royally entertained upon viands, up to date, by a fine old English gentleman, one of the real good type. Even then everybody was not happy. A melancholy man surveying the moated roof, the mullioned windows, the tastefully laid out lawn, and the comfortable stables, groaned in anguish of spirit, as he exclaimed, "Oh, dear me, it's modern; I hoped it was a ruin." Possibly the proprietor might have held less rigid views.

The Dutch captured Holland many years ago. Holland captures London once a year. It—the brown variety—is the "only wear" now in the West End of town where we immediately take our credulous country visitor when we want to palm off upon him the precious falsehood that London is empty. The Metropolis is not such a "city of the plague" as some imaginative writers endeavour to make out. Parliament had risen several days, and all its members, we were told, packed off to various parts of the earth, when one evening I espied Mr. Speaker Peel swinging a bamboo cane and strolling down Parliament Street unnoticed, unhonoured, and unsung. Presently he disappeared into deserted Palace Yard, and probably went to bed earlier than he had done for six months before. You may meet Irish members daily in the Strand, and the highlands and islands have not drawn all the Scotch members out of London.

How much Sir Michael Hicks-Beach has improved in appearance! I was watching a brief allowance of ozone at the end of last week when I suddenly came across a happy-looking triumvirate in yachting suits. The President of the Board of Trade was the tallest, the smartest, and the most active of the lot. He wore no glasses, and was inspecting the local "lions" with brisk and active interest. In a physical sense Sir Michael is the most upright man in the House of Commons next to Mr. Gladstone, whose straightness of figure is amazing, remembering the old man's age. Mr. Balfour stoops. So does Mr. Goschen. Lord George Hamilton looks as if a dose of drill on board ship would make a new man of him. Sir Edward Clarke is upright enough. But then little men never stoop. There is not enough of them. Anyhow, I was rejoiced to see a sterling, honest, and capable Minister like Sir Michael Hicks-Beach showing such a wonderful improvement on the careworn figure he presented two years ago.

An affecting incident is reported from Cornwall. During the triumphal progress of Mr. Gladstone eighteen months ago, an unfortunate Wesleyan minister, rejoicing in the name of Josiah Jutsum, had the ill-luck to lose his watch and chain. He had mingled with the multitude which cheered for Home Rule, hooted the tyrannies of a violent and brutal Government, and clamoured for "Freedom" with leathern lungs. All this was, of course, very delightful and exceedingly gratifying. The Radical newspapers beamed with glowing descriptions of the magnificent doings in the land of Conybeare and early vegetables. In such a collection of pure and disinterested patriots a minister who was not a Wesleyan might have been pardoned for feeling that sense of security from robbery which a man can freely enjoy upon an American racecourse. It was a gathering of the masses and not of the classes, and the virtues of these estimable persons must have suffered a considerable drop in the reverend gentleman's estimation when he discovered that an ardent Home Ruler had determined to retain a permanent memento of the Grand Old Man's visit. As for the lost watch, its value was heightened by the fact of its being a presentation one. Verily, Mr. Josiah Jutsum was ill-used. But there is hope at last. A new timekeeper has now been presented to him, and his Liberalism will go as strong as ever.

The parson went out in the Cornish crowd,
He shouted long and he shouted loud;
For miles around Tre, Pol, and Pen
Hurrahed for the grandest of grand old men.
[illegible]
And wilder grew such furious shout
The moment that he commenced to spout,
But when the crowd dispersed from view
The parson's jewellery vanished too.
Old Father Time in his lending flight
The face of the parson renders bright;
May Jutsum keep THIS watch and chain
Till Mr. Gladstone speaks again.

BREVITIES.

DROWNED WHILE BATHING. A draper of Norwich, named Bullen, was d[illegible] while bathing on Saturday off Cortes, near [illegible]

RESIGNED.

DEATH OF A PIANIST.

SO LIKE THE RADICALS.

A KING PARDONED BY A QUEEN.

THE LAST OF THEM.

THAT SAD SOUDAN.

THE FASTEST PASSAGE FROM THE CAPE.

DEATH OF A FRENCH JOURNALIST.

CROFTING REDUCTIONS.

MOSCOVITE COURTESY.

A NEGRO CONVENTION.

THE CHANNEL SQUADRON.

ROYAL AUTHORS.

LONDON HOUSE-PAINTERS' DEMONSTRATION.

TITHE COLLECTING IN WALES.

THE ARMADA.

NO REFRESHMENTS.

RAILWAY RATES.

SHEEP WORRYING.

A NEW ANTIQUARY. [illegible]

IN THE BEGINNING

The last 125 years of Leeds' history have been chronicled in millions of words and pictures by the *Yorkshire Evening Post*. Decade after decade, the *YEP* has been there to report the city's news, its most memorable events, inspirational people and unforgettable sporting triumphs.

But what isn't so well known is that the paper's own story began amid personal tragedy. The idea for a new evening newspaper had been conceived by Charles Pebody, then editor of *The Yorkshire Post*.

But three days before its launch he collapsed and would never return to work. In his place, it was left to the *YEP*'s first editor, the young and relatively inexperienced Alexander Paterson, to steer the ship.

"This left me in a very awkward position," Paterson later recalled. "Still, we went on – and, of course, had mishaps and misadventures, both editorial and mechanical. But I have never been so happy as when I turned out the *Yorkshire Evening Post*, for it was my hobby and my life."

The Scotsman, then just 24, had worked as assistant sub-editor on the *Edinburgh Evening News* and been chief sub-editor of the *Dundee Courier* after graduating from the University of Glasgow. But, having moved to Leeds, the prospect of creating a readership for an evening newspaper at a time when it was still something of a novelty was a different matter entirely.

There had been signs that an appetite for an evening paper serving Leeds was growing, however. Eleven years earlier, public interest in the trial of notorious murderer Charles Peace at Leeds Assizes had reached fever pitch.

The Yorkshire Post duly responded to the clamour by publishing a special four-page evening edition containing a full account of the hearing, which only lasted a day and resulted in Peace, who had killed a policeman and his neighbour after becoming obsessed with the man's wife, being sentenced to death.

Working from the Albion Street offices of owners Yorkshire Conservative Newspapers, Paterson now set about capitalising on this potential new market for an evening digest of the day's events. The very first edition of the *YEP* was duly published on Monday, September 1, 1890, with a price of half a penny. In those days, a general labourer could expect to earn just £62 a year, while the annual salary of a teacher was around £133.

That first edition consisted of only four pages and the front page featured row upon row of tightly-packed text, much of which was occupied by adverts for companies such as Dysons, the famous watchmakers and jewellers on Briggate.

Long forgotten products being promoted included E.Y.O Whisky and Scafe's Patent leather and rubber combination boots. School uniforms from city centre store Hyam & Co were also

The front page of the first ever edition of the Yorkshire Evening Post, September 1, 1890.

The Leeds public's fascination with the trial of murderer Charlie Peace, pictured, was behind the decision to launch a new evening newspaper in the city.

advertised. A leading article meanwhile promised readers that "the prompt and accurate publication of news – news of all kinds – is the main business of the *Yorkshire Evening Post*".

The first week's news stories didn't quite match the fervour surrounding the trial of Charles Peace, but they at least showed that the paper would stay true to its word, providing a chronicle of events in the city, both good and ill.

The hosting of the annual meeting of the British Association for the Advancement of Science was considered a coup for Leeds and was accompanied by a sketch from Harry Furniss, the famous caricaturist whose work featured heavily in satirical magazine *Punch*. It showed a proud Leeds Mayor William Emsley greeting the visitors at a reception at the Town Hall.

From the courts there were stories of rioting on Briggate and fighting in Marsh Lane, for which the police blamed celebrations surrounding the annual Halton Feast. The collapse of the town reservoir at Castleford disrupted water supplies, while a man was fined 2s 6d for not having his dog properly muzzled. The promoters of the "new Yeadon railway" were unable to secure sufficient financial backing, leaving the project in deadlock amid fears the line wouldn't be completed.

Among the attractions at the International Exhibition held in Leeds that week was Mademoiselle Josephine's troupe of young ladies, who "showed

Opposite:

Top:
YEP newspaper boys with posters proclaiming the relief of Ladysmith during the Boer War, March 1900.

Bottom:
Newspaper vendors in 1901 show a series of bills for the Yorkshire Evening Post which followed the illness, death and funeral of Queen Victoria.

Evening Post
LADYSMITH
RELIEVED
NATIONAL

Evening Post
QUEEN'S
Evening Post
QUEEN:
SLIGHT
RALLY.
Evening Post
GRAVE
BULLETINS:
FAMILY
ASSEMBLED.
Evening Post
THE QUEEN
SINKING:
OFFICIAL.
DEATH
OF THE
QUEEN.
Yorkshire Post
The Times of the North
Evening Post
THE QUEEN'S
FUNERAL
TO-DAY'S
Evening Post
THE QUEEN'S
FUNERAL
IMPRESSIVE
AND AFFECTING
SCENES.
Evening Post
DATE OF
THE QUEEN'S
FUNERAL
Evening Post
THE DEAD
QUEEN:
Evening Post
DATE OF
THE QUEEN'S
FUNERAL:
Evening Post
THE KING'S
SPEECH TO
PARLIAMENT
Evening Post
Evening Post
SPEECHES
THE

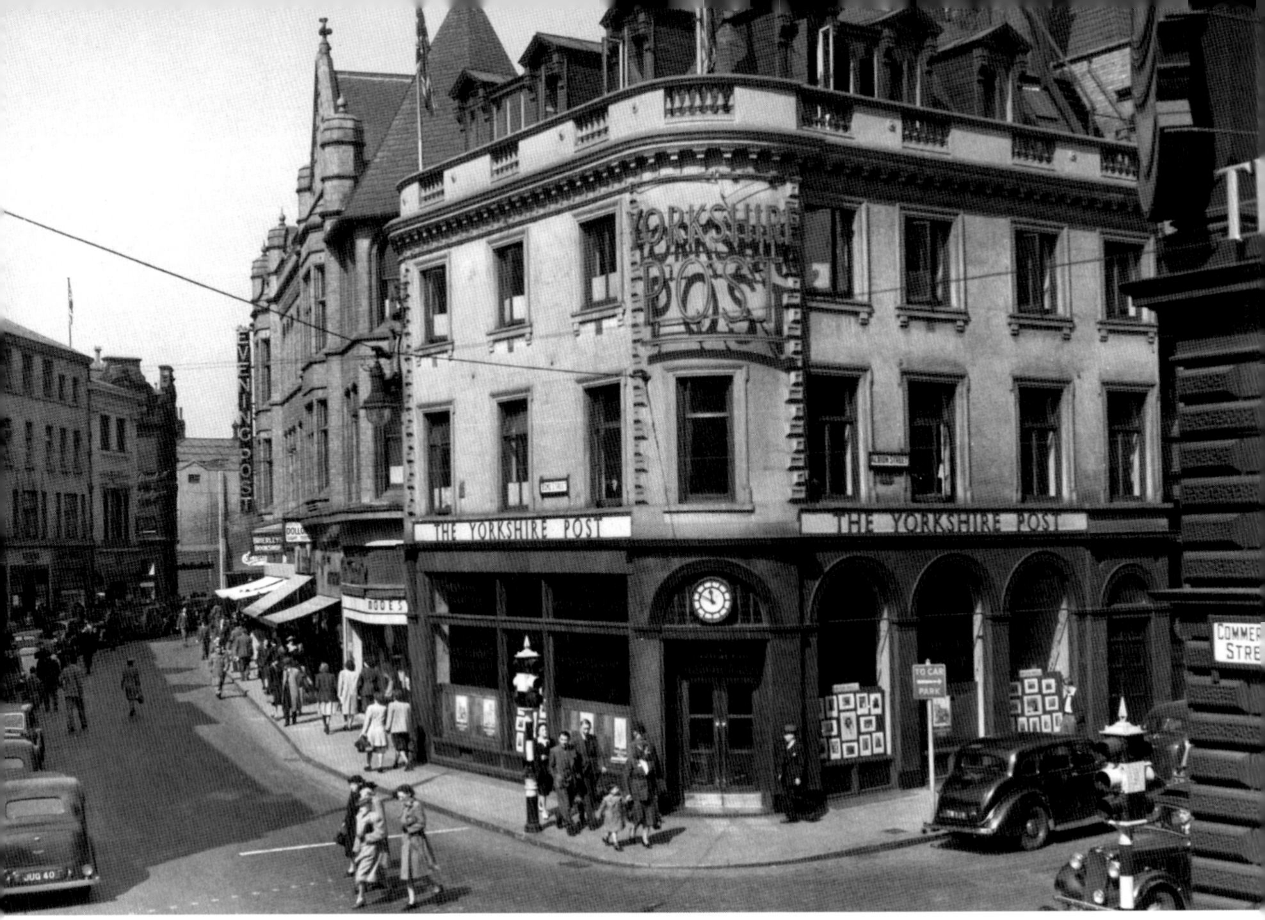
YORKSHIRE POST
EVENING POST
THE YORKSHIRE POST
THE YORKSHIRE POST
TO CAR PARK
JUG 40

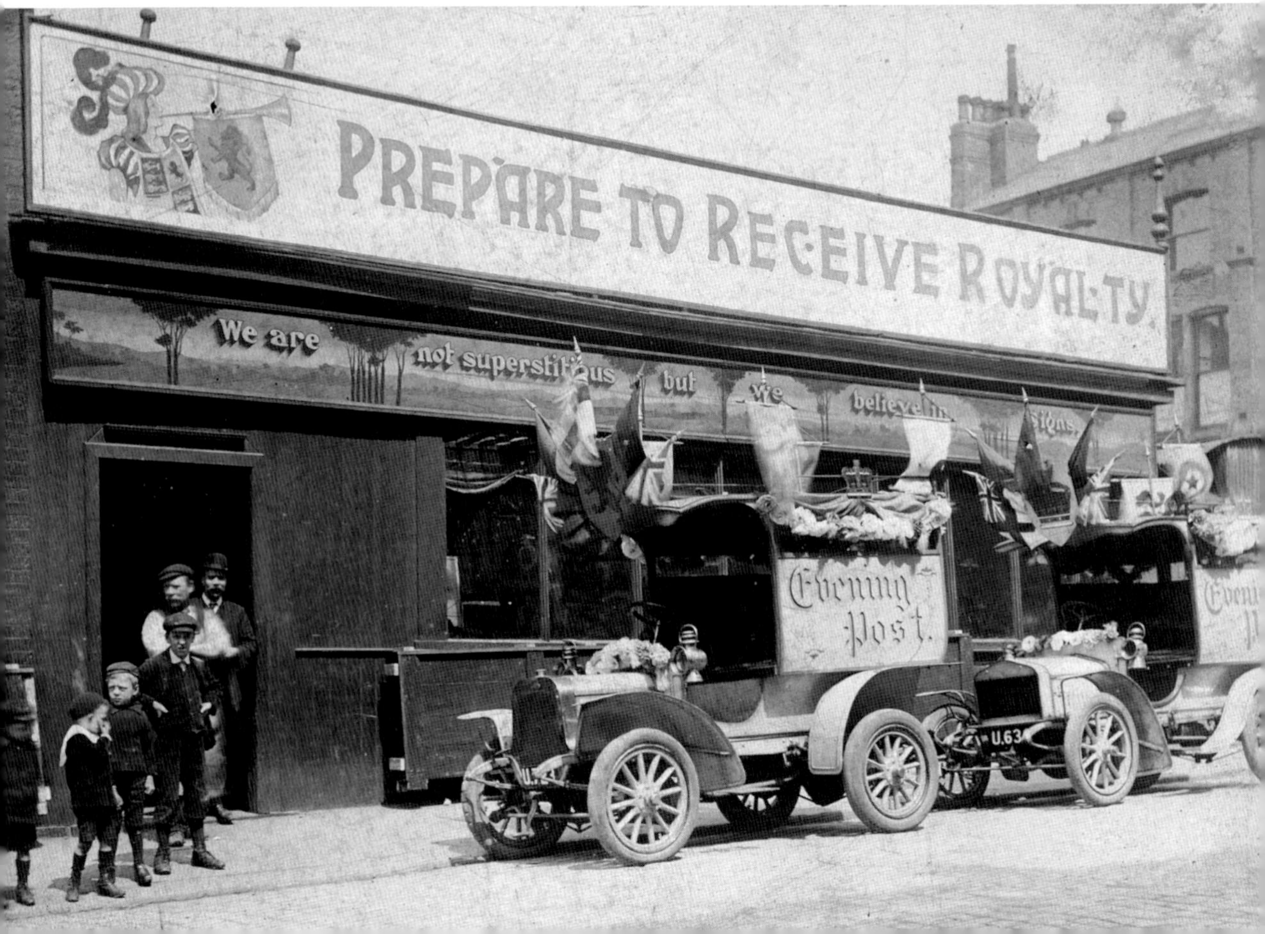
PREPARE TO RECEIVE ROYAL-TY.
We are
not superstitious
but
we
signs
Evening Post.
U.63

living tableaux", which involved the costumed actresses standing stock still as they struck carefully choreographed poses amid theatrical lighting. Music at the event was provided by the likes of the Farnley Brass Band, the Stanningley Old Band and the drums and fifes of the Leeds Rifles.

In sporting news there was the announcement of rabbit coursing at Cardigan Fields, and a report of an accident suffered by Albert Goldthorpe, the well-known Hunslet rugby player, who had broken an arm while jumping over a hedge at his home near Stourton. Quite why he was engaged in this activity wasn't fully explained.

Meanwhile, the first significant cricket match at the new Headingley cricket ground on St Michael's Lane was taking place between a side representing the North of England and the touring Australians, whose captain William Murdoch told a *Yorkshire Evening Post* reporter that he was suitably impressed.

Confirming that the ground was bigger than any in Australia, his only reservation was that it stood "some distance out of the town", although he added that "probably wouldn't matter as Englishmen did not object to walking and besides, a good tram service would show that to be no detriment".

Yorkshire, meanwhile, were still without a county cricket championship to their name, having tied with Kent for third place behind Lancashire and winners Surrey.

It would take the *YEP* three years and nine months before it made any profit, but circulation steadily grew and with it the size of the newspaper. Leeds became a city in 1893 and the *YEP*'s importance was underlined three years later when it increased in size to six pages.

In 1903 Alexander Paterson moved on, replaced by new editor Alfred Turner. But the hard work had been done and the *Yorkshire Evening Post* was well on its way to being a success. By 1935 it had reached 24 pages of news, sport and features and, at the outbreak of the Second World War, the *YEP* – nicknamed 'The Buff' on account of the colour of the paper it was printed on – was selling some 190,000 copies each night in a city with a population of around 480,000.

It was a paper that had delivered on the promise made by Alexander Paterson in that very first edition to report "news of all kinds" that would both interest and inform the residents of Leeds. Its reward was to have now won a place in their hearts and in their homes.

Opposite:

Top:
The first offices of the YEP on the corner of Albion Street and Bond Street, April 1948. If you look closely you can see the Evening Post sign on the left.

Bottom:
Early Yorkshire Evening Post delivery vans, 1908.

King George V arrives at Leeds Town Hall, August 23, 1933.

King George VI and Queen Elizabeth view wartime bomb damage in the city.

BY ROYAL APPOINTMENT

Royal visits to Leeds have provided golden memories for generations of Loiners, who have poured on to the streets in their thousands to welcome members of the monarchy to the city.

Amid a sea of fluttering Union Jacks these occasions have marked the opening of important new buildings, formed part of civic and national celebrations, and given public recognition to organisations working tirelessly on behalf of the city and its people.

The *YEP* wasn't around to record the visit of Queen Victoria on September 7, 1858 when she officially opened Leeds Town Hall. It did, however, have the solemn duty of reporting her death.

The Stop Press column has long since disappeared from regional newspapers, but it was put to good use on January 22, 1901, when that evening's paper informed readers of the monarch's passing at her holiday residence on the Isle of Wight.

"We deeply regret to announce that Her Majesty the Queen passed away at Osborne this evening," it recorded. "Details are given in the space reserved for Late News."

The Queen's death had been expected and the *YEP*'s journalists had already been busy preparing articles detailing her association with Leeds and retelling the story of her remarkable life, which were duly rushed into print as part of a special edition.

Three-quarters of a century after Victoria had unveiled the Town Hall, the *YEP*'s reporters were on the spot when her grandson King George V had the honour of cutting the ribbon on the Civic Hall.

The King had been something of a regular visitor to the city, particularly during the First World War. The *YEP* was there in September 1915 when he and his younger sister Princess Victoria presented officers and men with medals at Beckett's Park War Hospital in Headingley.

He then returned three years later with Queen Mary to tour clothing and munitions factories, including the works of John Barran & Sons, the ready-to-wear clothing pioneers who at the time employed more than 3,000 people.

Crowds are held back during the visit of King George V in 1933 to open the Civic Hall.

But George's most significant visit to Leeds came on August 23, 1933, when he opened the impressive new Civic Hall, work on which had begun two years earlier as part of a major redevelopment of a corner of the city previously dominated by slums.

Crowds numbering in the tens of thousands thronged the city centre as the King and Queen Mary made their way to the building, which he officially opened by using a golden key to unlock the wrought iron gate at the main entrance.

It was noted that the King was particularly pleased that the badge of the Pals' Battalion, which suffered such heavy losses in the First World War, was displayed in the Assembly Hall. Queen Mary, meanwhile, admired the colour schemes in the different rooms, and commented upon the various woods used.

Afterwards, the Civic Hall's architect, Emanuel Vincent Harris, told the *YEP* that he was happy with the 'dry run'. "That proved to me that the essentials of the building were fairly right," he said. "I feel satisfied that when little incidental things are put in order, and the wheels greased, so to speak, the building will satisfy Corporation and civic requirements, and fulfil the purposes for which it was designed."

The following day's editorial column in the paper spoke of a 'Mondayish' feel to the city after the previous day's rousing celebrations, but took heart from the fact that Leeds had done itself proud.

"No man is worth calling a man unless he recognises and is prepared to reverence something he feels to be greater than himself. That was the case with Leeds yesterday," it said. "It wanted to show its loyalty to the Crown and, at the same time, its affection for the King as a man; and there was no flunkeyism in that attitude. Sycophancy is for mean souls; and mean souls would not have behaved as the Leeds crowds behaved yesterday.

"Their self-imposed discipline was marvellous. They gave the police practically no trouble. In some cases, a few Boy Scouts, whom the crowd could have overwhelmed if it liked, were enough to maintain order, and keep an unbroken line."

The Leeds crowds had not been quite so orderly for the visit of King Edward VII and Queen Alexandra a quarter of a century before. On July 7, 1908, the royal car passed beneath a Triumphal Arch which had been specially erected on Wellington Street near City Square to welcome the couple. They were opening a new electrical engineering wing at Leeds University and to have lunch at the Town Hall, where the King bestowed a knighthood on Lord Mayor Wilfred Hepton.

The *YEP* reported that it was "a day of memorable scenes and incidents". The regular downpours didn't help (although the arrival of the royal train at the Central Station coincided with a reappearance of the sun) and members of the Territorial Army suffered the indignity of being heckled by the crowd as they paraded along the route.

"The Territorials had to run the gauntlet of the crowd's chaff, coming, as always, mainly from the working-class girls who think the volunteer fair game," ran the paper's account. "'Straighten thi'sen up lad,' said one of these critics as the 'Terriers' went by. 'There's some on 'em luke as if a good feed 'ud do 'em no 'arm,' said her companion, for the fat man was clearly her ideal."

There was also a near riot when the crowds felt the police were too heavy-handed in dealing with "an adventurous patriot determined to get a good view of their Majesties". He climbed up a lamp post "and from that risky eminence was inclined to survey the scene contentedly".

The police had other ideas, however, and when the man, "said to be a miner", refused to come down, an officer was dispatched up the pole to fetch him.

There was a huge turnout for the arrival of King Edward VII and Queen Alexandra at Leeds Town Hall, July 7, 1908. Decorations for the occasion line East Parade (below).

Children's Day Queen Joan Thompson presents a bouquet of flowers to Princess Elizabeth and Prince Philip at Roundhay Park, July 1949.

Opposite:
The Queen meets Duke Ellington at the Civic Hall, October 20, 1958.

"The result was something of a struggle, but eventually the man was brought down – though this scene was not completed until after the King and Queen had gone past," said the report.

"So little in harmony with the feelings of the crowd was this somewhat needless piece of officialism, that citizens of a standard of respectability that would qualify them for special jurors grew indignant in their criticism of the action of the police, and when an attempt was made to take the man to the lock-up his friends set about an effort to rescue him. Said a spectator: 'There was every appearance of a riot'."

The first Queens Hotel had been opened in 1863 at a cost of £50,000 to its owners The Midland Railway Company. When the firm was taken over by London, Midland and Scottish Railway the decision was taken to demolish the old building and erect a new one in its place.

So in 1935 the hotel was closed and razed to the ground. Two years later the Princess Royal and the 6th Earl of Harewood opened the new Queens, built by William Airey and Sons of Leeds.

The *YEP* related to no doubt envious readers that the guests at that night's gala dinner feasted on caviar, smoked salmon, Dover sole and fillet of beef, washed down with the finest champagne. Afterwards they danced to music provided by famous bandleader Joe Orlando and his Gleneagles Hotel Band.

Queen Elizabeth II has made many visits to the city during her record-breaking reign, but her first high-profile trip was made before she even came to the throne.

In July 1949, the 23-year-old Princess Elizabeth was guest of honour at Children's Day at Roundhay Park, where 'Queen of the Day' Joan Anne Thompson climbed the stage to present her with a bouquet of flowers.

More than half a century later, as the Queen prepared to visit the city on the final leg of her 2012 jubilee celebrations, Joan told the *YEP* of her brush with royalty.

"I remember being chosen as Queen of Children's Day but I was 14 and didn't give it much thought at the time," she said. "I was chosen from my school in Osmondthorpe and later we all went to the Civic Hall.

"I had to welcome the Queen, then I went up to present her with a bouquet and curtsied. She didn't actually say anything but she seemed lovely. In fact, I got a shock from the Duke of

Edinburgh because as I was about to leave he stood up and proceeded to bow to me!"

Two years earlier, in November 1947, *YEP* reporters had travelled to the capital to report first-hand on the Princess's wedding to Philip Mountbatten, noting that "as early as 6am a spiv could not have sold you an inch of kerb-stone in the Mall, where thousands of people had spent the night under the bare November trees waiting for the Royal Wedding procession".

The paper printed a four-page news and picture souvenir to mark the occasion and reported that the Princess's face had been "flushed with excitement" as she left Buckingham Palace en route to Westminster Abbey.

Later, the crowds who had gathered beneath the palace balcony chanted "We want the bride" before Elizabeth and Philip emerged and "remained for six minutes acknowledging the tumultuous cheers of thousands of wellwishers".

In October 1958 the royal couple came to the city for a two-day visit which took in the Leeds Centenary Musical Festival, marking 100 years since Victoria's opening of the Town Hall. On this occasion a thrilled Queen met American jazz great Duke Ellington, whose records she so enjoyed.

Prince Charles shares a joke at Thornbury Barracks in Pudsey, then examines the YEP's report of his visit to officially open the paper's new headquarters on Wellington Street, December 10, 1970.

The pair tied up the reception line at the Civic Hall for several minutes chatting about music and the meeting would inspire him to compose The Queen's Suite, which he recorded with his orchestra the following year. Only one copy was made and it was sent directly to Buckingham Palace. The suite, one of Ellington's most beautiful works, remained hidden from the public until after his death in 1974.

During that same visit the couple toured Burton's clothing factory on Hudson Road, before being taken on a 63-mile car journey around Leeds and the surrounding area – the route carefully chosen so that at no time would the royal car pass the same spot twice. In October 1965 the Queen and the Duke returned to open Seacroft Civic Centre.

Over the years she has mingled with the great and the good – often visiting her relations at Harewood House, the late Lord Harewood being her first cousin.

The Queen meets her public at Elland Road during her Silver Jubilee tour, July 12, 1977.

A decade-long rift between the pair caused by his remarrying after divorce from first wife Marion was healed by the time of the Silver Jubilee visit to Leeds in 1977 when the Harewoods were invited to a civic reception attended by the Queen.

In 1982, she met sculptor Henry Moore at Leeds Art Gallery, returning in 1990 to visit Chapeltown and Harehills. In March 1996 she opened the Royal Armouries at Clarence Dock, where she was presented with two maps made by local game manufacturers Waddington's during the war to aid British prisoners in their attempts to escape from German hands.

To Prince Charles has fallen the honour of officially opening two city landmarks. On December 10, 1970 he toured the new £5m home of the *Yorkshire Evening Post* on Wellington Street, where thankfully there was no reference to "monstrous carbuncles", the phrase he would later memorably use to denounce just that sort of clunky modern architecture. That evening he opened the new Leeds Playhouse, the predecessor to the West Yorkshire Playhouse, attending a Royal Gala performance of *Oh Glorious Jubilee* by Clifford Hanley.

Speaking of jubilees, the royal visit that remains the most memorable for so many in Leeds came in 1977, during the Queen's nationwide tour to commemorate the 25th year of her reign.

On June 7 that year dozens of the city's roads were closed to traffic to allow people to eat, drink, dance and sing to celebrate the Silver Jubilee together. A series of street parties were held, complete with Union Jack bunting and trestle tables that groaned under the weight of sausage rolls, sandwiches and jelly and ice cream.

Both preparations and celebrations went on for months, but the jubilant mood didn't stop officials from issuing spirit-sapping warnings about food hygiene and noise levels. One printed in the *YEP* noted that "many people will celebrate with dancing in the streets, but this should not be intolerable to others". Revellers were urged to limit amplifiers to 200 watts and to make sure they pointed music speakers away from houses.

When the Queen herself arrived in the city on July 12, 1977, accompanied by Prince Philip, a sea of people lined the streets. The roads were festooned with masses of red, white and blue bunting as the royal couple were driven from Leeds City Station to the Civic Hall and later on to a reception at the Town Hall.

The headline in the next day's *YEP* read: 'We love the Queen chant 40,000', with a report from Elland Road where tens of thousands of youngsters had packed the stadium and local children had entertained the couple with various sporting displays.

"When the Queen finally stepped into the ground a fanfare by the Junior Bugle Guard of the Light Infantry followed by the National Anthem was hardly audible for the cheers.

"The royal couple took up seats in the West Stand to watch the displays and children persistently broke into deafening chants of 'We want the Queen'. At one point the chanting reached such a pitch that both the Queen and the Duke could not help breaking into smiles. They seemed extremely impressed by the enthusiastic reception."

The Queen and Prince Philip were then driven around the stadium in an open-top Range Rover, before departing for the Great Yorkshire Show at Harrogate.

One of the most popular royals to visit the city was undoubtedly Diana, Princess of Wales. The 'People's Princess' first came to Leeds in March 1982, when she and Charles opened an extension at St Gemma's Hospice in Moortown.

Still only 20 at the time and six months pregnant, Diana appeared rather shy but made a point of meeting every patient. She was the grateful recipient of several gifts including a white newborn baby jacket, a matching maternity bed jacket and red and blue baby bottle covers.

Princess Diana receives bouquets during a walkabout in Leeds after visiting the city's Relate centre, May 19, 1993.

Opposite:
Diana enjoys a joke with day care visitors at St Gemma's Hospice in Moortown, September 18, 1991.

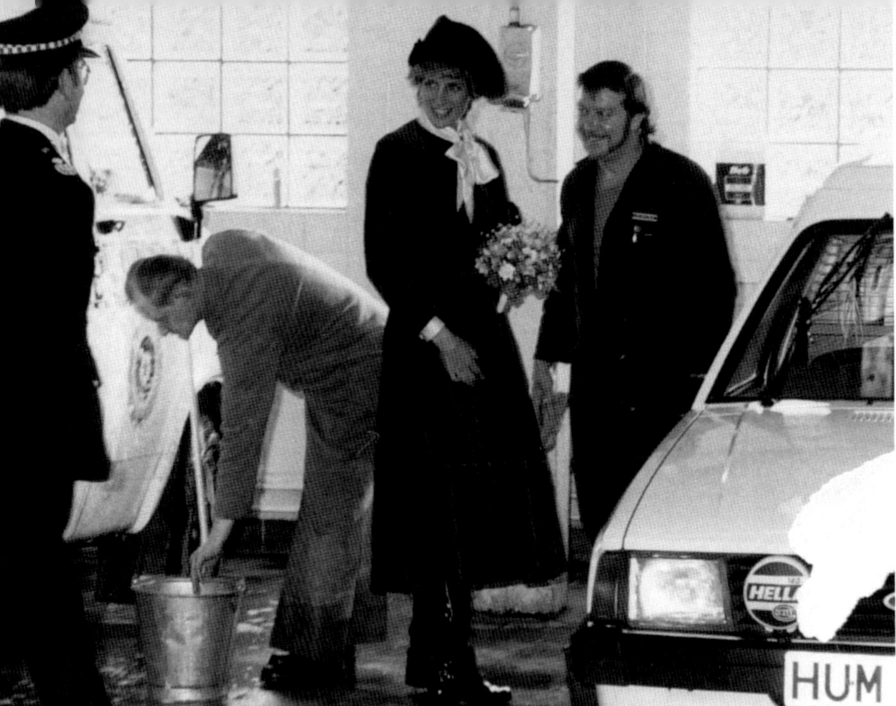

A cleaner carries on working during a visit by the Princess of Wales to West Yorkshire Ambulance Service.

The press pack had been desperate to find out when the new arrival could be expected, but one of the St Gemma's patients ended up beating them to the scoop.

Diana confided in 74-year-old Edwin Wilson that Prince William was due on July 1, her birthday. He told the *YEP* afterwards: "I didn't realise she was telling me anything special until one of the staff told me that no one knew the exact date." Edwin declared himself "pleased as punch" to hear the news.

That evening's edition carried the visit on its front page with the headline 'Princess of Hearts: Radiant Di makes it Royal tonic day for Leeds'. It told readers how "Princess Diana smiled her way through the wards of St Gemma's Hospice today, and captured the hearts of patients and staff alike.

"The Royal mum-to-be and Prince Charles were driven to the hospice through streets thronged with flag-waving, cheering crowds."

The only grumble was that schoolchildren who had waited patiently at Roundhay Park arena to see the couple were upset that they could only stay for five minutes rather than the planned seven. Charles was running late for his visit to Harrogate and Diana had to catch a train back to London. Overwhelmed with flowers as she had left the hospice, it was the same at Leeds station as the Princess was swamped with bouquets from well-wishers.

Diana returned to St Gemma's nine years later to open the newly built Prout Conference Centre. In the mid-1980s there were trips to Cookridge Hospital and West Yorkshire Metropolitan Ambulance Service. As president of children's charity Barnardo's she stopped off at their Horsforth offices in September 1988 and the following July visited the National Breakdown Recovery Club in Pudsey.

Diana clearly loved Leeds so much she even came twice in two months. On April 6, 1993 she

The Queen chats with the crowd during a walkabout outside the United Caribbean Association in Hall Lane, Chapeltown, 1990.

attended the Health of the Nation Conference on Mental Health at West Yorkshire Playhouse, meeting among others the actor Brian Blessed.

Then, on May 19, she staged a walkabout after visiting relationship counselling service Relate on Call Lane. Having recently separated from her husband it was a visit that seemed all too sadly appropriate. Still, she could always count on being met by hordes of smiling faces whenever she ventured to this part of West Yorkshire.

Leeds took Diana to their hearts – and it seemed that she felt the same way too. When she died in 1997 there was a special memorial service at Leeds Parish Church and countless bouquets of flowers were left in tribute.

In 2012, the *YEP* reported that a team of street cleaners had been hard at work for a fortnight making sure the city centre looked spick and span in readiness for the Queen's Diamond Jubilee visit on July 19.

Her Majesty was met by jubilant crowds as she staged a walkabout on a Briggate that was heaving with wellwishers. Taking time to stop and speak to local schoolchildren, the Queen and Prince Philip "were greeted at every step by a huge ovation and the frantic waving of a sea of miniature Union Jacks".

A few lucky youngsters were even hoisted out of the crowd to meet Her Majesty, with one, Junior Frood, so overwhelmed he burst into tears. His mum Kerry told the *YEP* that eight-year-old Junior, from Meanwood, was a huge fan of the Queen and had stayed up late writing a special letter to her, even researching her favourite colour so his yellow carnations would prove a hit.

"He was in floods of tears he was so happy," she said. "He asked Prince Philip to give the flowers to the Queen but he said, 'Wouldn't you rather give them to her yourself?'

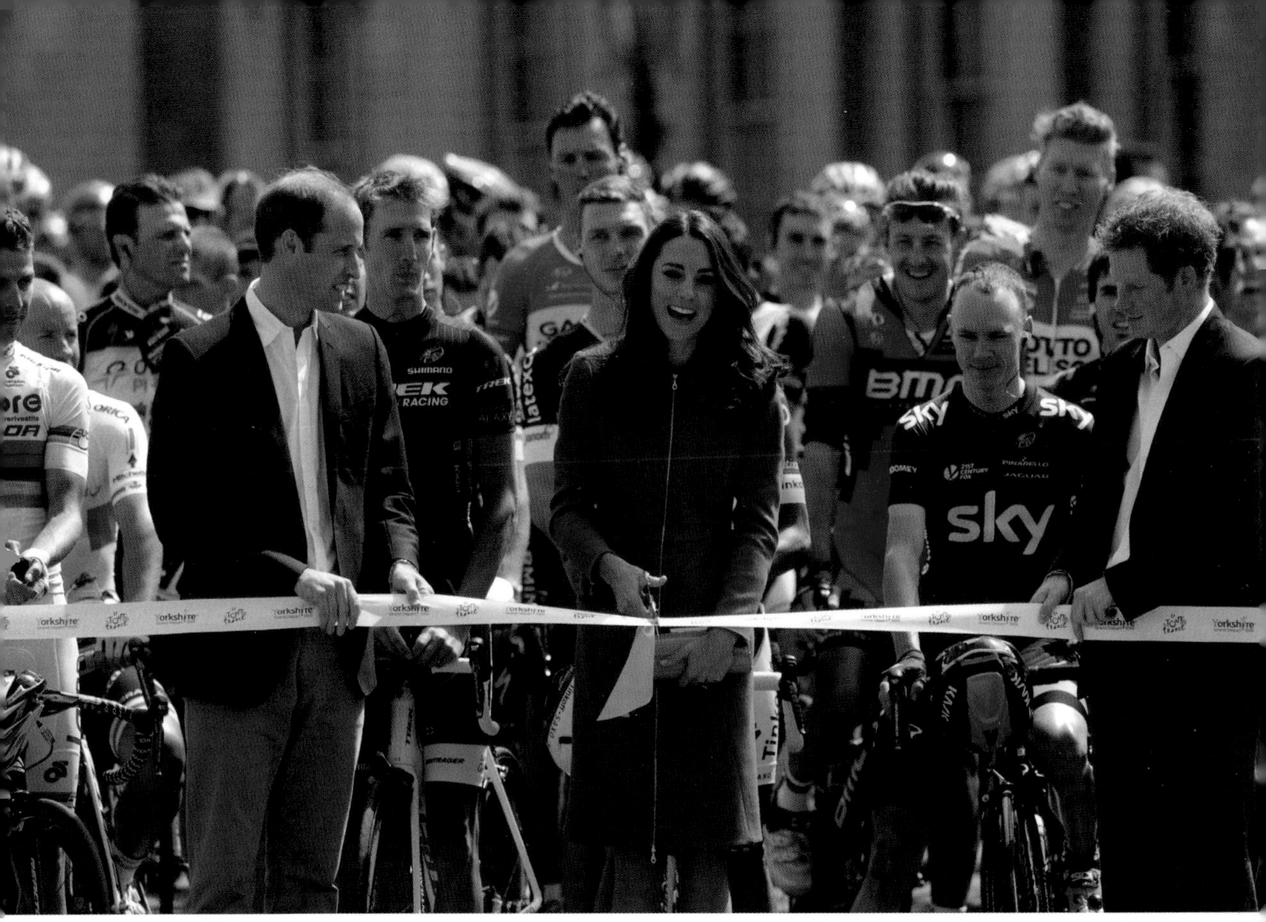
SHIMANO
RACING
sky
PINARELLO
JAGUAR
Yorkshire

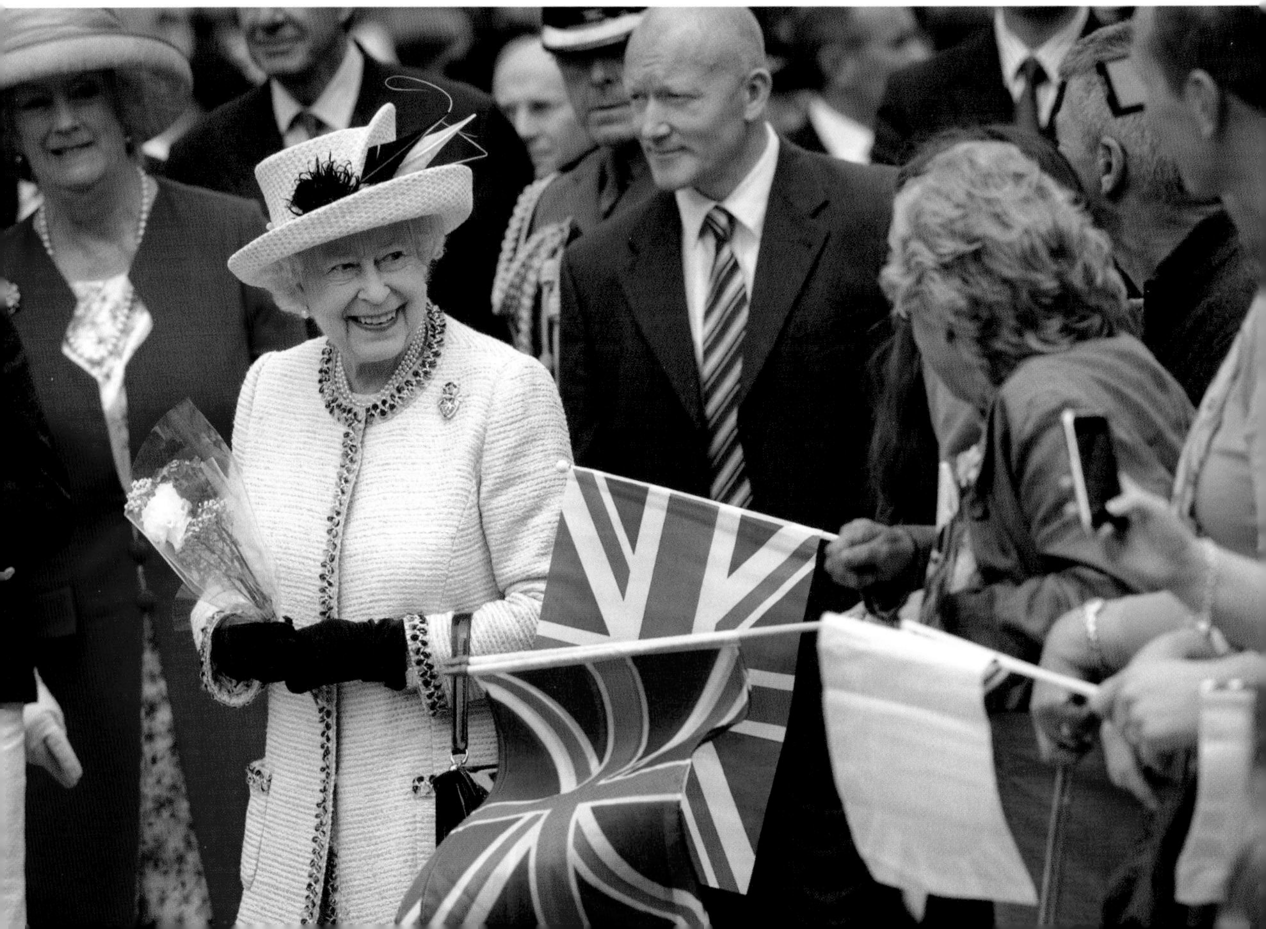

"The letter said, 'Thank you for looking after me and our country. You are amazing people'."

The royal party went on to tour the newly-refurbished City Varieties, where they enjoyed a performance of *The Good Old Days*, based on the long-running television show filmed at the theatre, by members of the City Varieties Youth Theatre Company.

There was also time for a visit to the Leeds Arena, then still under construction and a year away from its opening night. Youngsters from Little London Community Primary School treated Her Majesty to a Zulu tribal song, laying claim to being the first act to play the £60m venue – a full 12 months ahead of rock legend Bruce Springsteen.

The younger royals were on hand to perform the ribbon-cutting duties a couple of years later when the Duke and Duchess of Cambridge were joined by Prince Harry at Harewood House. It was their job to welcome the world's best cyclists to Leeds for the Grand Départ of the 101st Tour de France.

Cyclists gathered outside the 18th century stately home, taking off their helmets as they were greeted with renditions of *La Marseillaise* and *God Save The Queen*, performed by the Band of the Corps of the Royal Engineers.

The Duchess of Cambridge, wearing a bottle green coat and grey clutch purse, the Duke and Prince Harry chatted with the lead riders, including Britain's reigning Tour de France champion Chris Froome. Then Kate cut the ribbon to officially start the race and there was even a flypast by the Red Arrows who left a trail of red, white and blue in the skies over the city.

For Harry it was a case of being back on rather familiar territory. The Prince had come to Leeds to see his former girlfriend Chelsy Davy during her brief stint studying law at the university.

The trio certainly did themselves proud, succeeding in bringing a smile to the faces of the crowds who gathered to catch a glimpse of them – just as William and Harry's mum had done so many times before them.

Opposite:

***Top:* Prince William and brother Harry look on as the Duchess of Cambridge cuts the ribbon at the ceremonial start of the Tour de France at Harewood House, July 5, 2014.**

***Bottom:* The Queen meets crowds on Briggate, July 19, 2012.**

TITANIC COLLIDES WITH ICEBERG.

GEST LINER BADLY DAMAGED IN THE ATLANTIC.

HELP SUMMONED BY WIRELESS.

INIAN STEAMS 120 MILES TO THE RESCUE

WOMEN TAKEN OFF IN LIFEBOATS.

IER VESSELS SPEEDING TO THE SCENE OF THE DISASTER.

OWNERS ACCEPT REPORT WITH RESERVE.

he ancient Greeks made the aphorism, se who go to sea are only four inches death," and to-day it recurs to the world all the significance and freshness of the of its origin.

w York comes the report that when off banks of Newfoundland last night the e Star steamer Titanic, the largest l afloat, ran into an iceberg, and was amaged that at once she commenced to at the bow.

ut the news is unconfirmed. Circumstan- reports from New York state that other s, including two other White Star boats, Olympic and the Baltic, have received wireless telegraphy urgent calls for aid, that they are steaming to the Titanic's stance. Yet the White Star authorities Liverpool have not heard a word of the posed disaster, and the underwriters re- time goes by without definite news being received as to the safety of those on board.

The officials of the company, however, are confident that the lives of the Titanic's passengers are in no grave danger.

HELP ARRIVES.

LINERS AND SMALLER CRAFT STEAMING TO RESCUE.

TITANIC SAID TO BE UNSINKABLE.

(BY OUR PRIVATE WIRE.)

A wireless message, says the Exchange New York correspondent, has been received at Halifax at 4.30 this morning stating that most of the passengers from the Titanic had been put in the lifeboats, and that the sea was calm.

The White Star officials at New York state that the Virginian is standing by the Titanic, and that there is no danger of loss of life.

The Mauretania and Cincinnati are responding to the signal as well as the German liners Prinz Adalbert, Amerika, Prinz Fredrich Wilhelm, and other smaller ships.

Mr. A. S. Franklin, Vice-President of the International Mercantile Marine, in a statement this morning, says no message has been received reporting the accident, and if the collision has occurred the vessel is in no danger, since she is absolutely unsinkable. There is no cause for serious anxiety.

A wireless message, which was sent to the Virginian and other vessels in the vicinity of the disaster, has failed up to the present to bring any response. No news is expected for some hours.

A rate of 50 guineas per cent. is being quoted by underwriters this morning for business with reference to the Titanic.

THE LOSS TO THE COMPANY.

In an interview a prominent underwriter in the city said: Even if the vessel gets into port, her owners will have to calculate on a loss of at least £150,000, but if she becomes a total loss, it will be a very serious matter for the company. The ship cost £2,000,000 to build, and her hull is valued for insurance purposes at a million sterling.

"Then there are all sorts of miscellaneous matters which have to be taken into account—disbursements, passage money, freight (mostly paid in advance), stores, baggage, and other things. I don't suppose the owners are covered to the extent of more than a million and a quarter, or, at the utmost, a million and a half.

WHITE STAR STOCK UNAFFECTED.

The reported accident is not credited upon the Stock Exchange, and the White Star shipping stock has not been affected.

So far as can be ascertained there is no specie on board the Titanic, but it is understood that the vessel was carrying a large number of valuable postal packets.

REPORT RECEIVED WITH DOUBT.

NO INFORMATION AT WHITE STAR OFFICES.

GREAT ANXIETY IN LIVERPOOL.

Not the slightest confirmation has been received in Liverpool of the news that the Titanic is sinking, or has met even with accident.

The head offices of the company, which are situated in Liverpool, have received no news whatever on the subject, whilst the Underwriters' Association, one of the biggest concerns of its kind in the world, is similarly uninformed. This fact, coupled with one or two other circumstances, tends to throw considerable doubt on the authenticity of the report.

Shipping authorities, when interviewed this morning, stated to our representative that they would attach no credence to the reports until they were officially confirmed. At the same time, they pointed out that this is a dangerous time for captains whose ships are in that area because of the moving ice, which is just breaking up and is very troublesome. Even the most expert captain might be pardoned for running into an iceberg through the difficulty which so often exists in avoiding them.

e to believe the reports until they have re definite knowledge.

ation on what has taken place is very ited, but according to the cablegrams from w York the Virginian, which was then out 170 miles west of the Titanic, received first call shortly before midnight. The tement ascribed to the Virginian, received New York about 3.45 a.m., is:—

The Titanic reported she had struck an iceberg. The steamer said that immediate assistance was required.

the owners of the vessel and the under- iters are hoping, there has been no acci- nt, it is curious that such precise details of e vessel's whereabouts are wired from New ork. We are told, for example, that the erator on the Titanic told the Virginian at the weather at the time of the collision as calm and clear, the position of the liner en being 41.46 north, 50.14 west.

ll be seen from the rough map which we re- roduce, this would fix the Titanic's position out 1,000 miles from New York and 2,000 iles from Liverpool. The Virginian's officers, e are further told, expected to reach the ricken liner about ten o'clock this morning, hile both the Baltic, which was 200 miles way, and the Olympic, would be alongside ot much later.

TWO WELL-MARKED ROADS.

eports agree that the sea is calm, and that he lives of those aboard are not in danger. There are two well-defined tracks for the big tlantic liners. Custom decrees that the vessels hall take one route out and the other back, nd if a vessel diverges seriously from her ustomary route (possibly to make better ime) complaint is made. Thus the risk is essened of two big liners colliding.

observance of tracks ensures, moreover, that a disabled steamer, especially in these days of wireless telegraphy, has a reasonable chance of speedy succour. This fact, together with the important one that the modern liner's system of watertight compartments is so complete as to render her unsinkable, and the calmness of the weather, augurs well for the safety of the passengers. e news is confirmed that the Titanic's maiden voyage has thus ended in disaster, sympathy will go out to her commander. For Captain Smith has been singularly unlucky. He was in command of the liner's sister ship, the Olympic, when she collided with the Hawke in Southampton Water, and on that occasion he had the confidence of every man in the Atlantic service.

that occasion the Olympic had to exchange her passengers to another vessel, and return to the builders' yard, which she had only recently left. Thus, the world's largest liners, the Olympic and the Titanic, if to-day's report be true, have been disabled on their first voyages.

[illegible]test messages received this afternoon are [illegible]t by 4.30 this morning most of the pas[illegible]gers had been transferred to the lifeboats, and that the White Star officials at New York [illegible]re the Virginian is now standing by. These are probably only rumours; news that can be accepted without any reserve is still lacking.

NO NEWS AT ADMIRALTY.

Inquiries at the Admiralty, which is in wireless communication with warships, show that up to 12.30 p.m. no news had been received there of the Titanic. No warship reports having picked up a wireless message from the liner.

NEW YORK [illegible] OFFICES BESIEGED.

[illegible]ATIVES CAUSE DISTRESS[illegible]G SCENES.

[illegible] Line are, says the Cen[illegible]

TITANIC'S DEPARTURE.

UNPARALLELED SCENES AT SOUTHAMPTON.

A LUXURIOUS LEVIATHAN.

WAS THERE AN OMEN OF THE DISASTER?

The departure of the Titanic from Southampton on Wednesday was the occasion for scenes of unparalleled enthusiasm.

Viewed from Trafalgar Quay, in the brilliant setting of Southampton Water, under a blue sky flecked with fleecy clouds, and the ocean greyhounds of yesterday—the St. Louis, the Oceanic, and many others—dwarfed in the near distance, the scene was tremendously impressive.

Never before in the history of the mercantile marine had so great a triumph of naval architecture as the Titanic left a port. So (says a correspondent) there was a new sensation in the occasion of the leviathan's movement as she rounded the Test Quay, majestically displayed her lines, and bore down on the Solent.

An officer aboard on the day of departure said that he had been on the Titanic four and a-half days, and, apart from his own sphere, knew very little about her. In three hours, having walked some six miles, new wonders and improvements revealing themselves in all directions, one was only able to take "samples" of extraordinary interest in themselves and of great importance to the ocean traveller.

On the Titanic sunshine was taken out. The gloom and depression of November's fogs off the Banks had been annihilated. The first-class passenger sat down to dinner in the splendid saloon, with its windows of cathedral-grey glass, and the attendants switched on cunningly hidden electric lights on the outside. The effect was naturalness itself.

HONEYMOON SUITES.

One could engage for £870 the voyage a "private ocean trip." There were honeymoon suites, with honeymoon decks set apart for the millionaire brides and bridegrooms of the future; state-rooms decorated in every different style and period, with lovely, ample cot-beds in brass, mahogany, and oak; lounges decorated in Louis XV. style; verandahs with climbing plants and ramblers; real coal fires as well as hundreds of radiators; restaurants and cafes; reception-rooms upholstered in the daintiest silk, with gorgeous panels and richly carved cornices—the whole forming an impressive ensemble in perfect taste, satisfying to the eye.

Fully an hour before she sailed, the gymnasium, in charge of a professional gymnast, was in working.

On one side a lady was having a camel ride and recalling the delights of the Pyramids; in another corner there was a bicycle race; many passengers took their own weights on the automatic chairs, and some had a spin on the mechanical rowing machines.

In the squash racquets court two Americans were "fighting the battle of their lives"—it might have been at the Bath Club, so thoroughly at home did they look.

In the third-class, or steerage, departments the loveliest linen, glass, and cutlery were displayed ready for luncheon, while the easy-chairs, card tables, pianos, and settees reminded one of the first-class accommodation on many lines twenty years ago.

THE TOUR OF THE LEVIATHAN.

But the most fascinating feature, perhaps, of the Titanic, was the trips of "discovery." Men and women set out to explore. They were shot into the depths by splendidly equipped electric lifts. They called at the post-office for a chat with the postmaster on the sorting arrangements. They wandered to the swimming baths and the luxurious Turkish saloons.

They examined the kitchens, with their 21,000 dishes and plates, tons of silver and cutlery, and acres of glass and linen. They touched the pianos on every deck in every corner of advantage, or listened to the band; scanned the array of novels and more serious works in the libraries; and learned all sorts of wonderful things about the electric buttons which control this 47,000-ton vessel, command its engines, and its little army of services alike.

AN UNTOWARD INCIDENT.

The departure of the Titanic was marred, however, by one untoward event.

Among the crowds still waving handkerchiefs there was a sudden silence. The gigantic triple expansion engines had begun to work. Near by were the Oceanic and the New York—great vessels in their day—now dwarfed to comparative insignificance.

Directly the huge screws of the Titanic began to revolve, the suction caused the seven great stern ropes of the New York to part, and the American liner's stern swung round into mid-stream.

All eyes were fixed on the New York. The Titanic's screws were stopped almost instantaneously, and the New York was towed to safety. Then the Titanic slowly sped down Southampton Water, the faces of her passengers peering at every nook of the seven tiers along the whole length of the liner, until she melted away in the distance, and her maiden voyage had begun.

Nominally of the same size as her sister ship, the Olympic—45,000 tons—the Titanic proved upon final measurement to be about a thousand tons bigger, this being in consequence of some three inches extra in length.

DISTINGUISHED PASSENGERS.

After leaving Southampton, having on board 320 first-class passengers, 270 second-class, and 1,100 steerage, the liner called at Cherbourg, and then at Queenstown, before passing into the Atlantic Ocean. Capt. E. J. Smith (commander, R.N.R.) was the master of the vessel, and other leading officers were Surgeon W. F. N. O'Loughlin, Assistant-Surgeon J. E. Simpson, Pursers H. W. McElroy and R. L. Barker, and Chief Steward A. Latimer.

There were a number of distinguished first-class passengers, who included Lord Ashburton, his Excellency Manuel de Lizardi, the Hon. and Mrs. L. Graves Johnson, Mr. Gustave Fcholle (secretary of the United Legation), Col. and Mrs. J. J. Astor, Major Archibald W. Butt, Col. Archibald Gracie, Mr. and Mrs. N. Rothschild, Miss Ada L. Adams, Mr. O. G. Adams, Mr. and Mrs. Wm. T. Adams, Mr. and Mrs. Robert B. Adams, Mr. O. Agromonte, and Mr. and Mrs. Arthur Campbell Allan, Mr. W. T. Stead, Mr. Chas. M. Hayes (President of Grand Trunk Railway Co.), Countess of Rothes, Mr. J. B. Thayers, Mr. Geo. Widener, Mr. J. G. Rewchlin, Mr. Bruce Ismay (Chairman of the White Star Line), Mr. T. M. Carnegie, Mrs. F. M. Carnegie (jun.), Mr. Thomas Carnegie, the Hon. John Ridgeley Carter, Mr. Geo. Eastman, Mr. W. K. Vanderbilt (jun.), Mr. John Vanderbilt, and Mr. F. P. Younghusband.

LEVIATHAN'S DIMENSIONS.

SUPERIORITY OVER HER SISTER SHIP.

BUILT AT A COST OF £1,250,000.

Although the Titanic has the same dimensions—length 882ft., breadth 92ft.—as her sister ship the Olympic, her gross tonnage of 46,382 tons is 1,004 tons greater, and thus she is the largest vessel at present afloat.

This difference (says "The Times") is accounted for by the fact that the measurement spaces have been considerably increased in the later vessel. Thus on the top or boat deck several extra rooms have been provided forward of the gymnasium, and the same has been done on the upper promenade deck, which contains the lounge, the reading-room, and the smoking-room with its two verandahs commanding a view aft over the stern.

An innovation on the promenade deck consists of two elaborate suites, each with sitting-room, two bedrooms, bathroom, and servants' room, which in the height of the season cost £870 each. Reserved to each of them is a private promenade space on the deck, the whole in each case occupying as much room as four suites costing £400 each.

These private promenades are enclosed with steel screens pierced with large oblong windows, and the interior walls are half-timbered and rough-cast, the roof being formed with oak beams.

On the same deck the restaurant, which with its a la carte service has proved a most successful institution, has been considerably increased in size, and on one side it has been provided with a Cafe Parisien, decorated with trellis-work and creeping ivy, which, however, is not growing.

10,000 PIECES OF PLATE.

The service of plate comprises in all about 10,000 pieces. The accommodation on the upper, saloon, and main decks has been increased by the addition of a number of suites and of state-rooms with wardrobes, and more space has been thrown into the reception-room attached to the dining saloon, the seating accommodation of which has also been increased so that over 550 persons can dine simultaneously.

For the rest, although there are naturally numerous small improvements, which experience has suggested, the vessel is substantially the same as her sister. The propelling machinery consists of the same combination of reciprocating engines and turbines as is fitted in the Olympic.

SUPPLIES FOR A LARGE FAMILY.

Such was the requirements of the liner's large family that it was computed that in the busy season 75,000lb. of fresh meat would be consumed; also, 35,000 fresh eggs, 25,000 poultry, 40 tons of potatoes, 5 tons of sugar, 1,000lb. of tea, 1,000 bottles of wines, 15,000 bottles of ale and stout, and 12,000 bottles of minerals.

For just a year was the ill-fated vessel to reign supreme as the largest vessel in the world. Then her pride of place would have passed to the new ship, the Imperator, which the Hamburg-American line is building, and expects to put into service in April or May next year. Her tonnage in round figures will be 50,000—to the Titanic's 46,328.

THE TITANIC AND HER INTERIOR ECONOMY.

THE TITANIC'S POSITION.

BANGOR
BAY OF FUNDY
NOVA SCOTIA
HALIFAX
BOSTON
C. COD
NEW YORK
LONG I.
OLYMPIC
VIRGINIAN
TITANIC
TITANIC ABOUT 2,000 MILES FROM LIVERPOOL AND 1000 MILES FROM NEW YORK
ATLANTIC OCEAN

OCEAN GIANTS OF LAST DECADE.

GERMAN LINER OF RECORD TONNAGE BUILDING.

It is interesting to note the tonnage of liners built within the last ten years. In 1901 the White Star liner Celtic was launched, and she was the first vessel to exceed 20,000 tons. Since then the principal liners launched have been:—

1904.—Baltic (White Star) .... 23,000 tons

1907.—Lusitania and Mauretania (Cunard) .... 31,938 tons

1910.—Olympic (White Star) .... 45,000 tons

At the present time the Aquitania (Cunard), of 45,000 [illegible] the Imperator (Hamburg-[illegible]

SPORTING NOTES.

RACING.

The first of the Newmarket meetings opens to-morrow, and the Craven fixture generally enjoys a good attendance, large fields, and excellent sport.

For that fine sprint event, the Crawford Plate, Beethoven's running at Liverpool should give him a good chance, the more so as Nankeen's success has since enhanced the form.

Edward has won a fine trial, and is much fancied at headquarters, and one of the pair may win.

Badoora may be successful in the Visitors' Plate, and Polonium in the Fitzwilliam Stakes.

Cylgad may take the Fifty-third Biennial Stakes.

For the Newbury Spring Cup on Saturday Long Set looked remarkably well in the paddock, and Mercutio was much cooler than at Lincoln.

Eton Boy and Cyrena were much liked, but All Gold was sweating and Sunspot was palpably short of a few gallops.

The story of the race is soon told. Going to the front at the distance, Long Set quickly asserted his superiority and won by a length and a half from Mercutio, who beat Eton Boy two lengths for second place, the fourth berth being filled by Protestant Boy.

Long Set, as is well known, was originally bought out of a selling race by Mr. "Sol" Joel, who won the corresponding race three years ago with another ex-selling plater in Arranmore.

Long Set promises to become almost as great a favourite with the racing public as was Victor Wild.

St. Girons gave a good display in the race, and with ordinary luck should score soon.

Glinka, in the Royal colours, showed great speed, and on a fast course like Epsom or Brighton is sure to be heard of.

That popular little sheet, "The Mid-day Sporting Special," is going great guns just now. Both "Ranger" and "Field Glass" have been right "among 'em."

At Newbury, "Ranger" was particularly busy. On the opening day he sent Hall Cross (Nap), Jingling Geordie, and Mediator, the two first-named being his double.

On Saturday he sent five winners and two non-runners. His winning selections were as follow:—Bill Bang (7 to 4 agst), Long Set (11 to 10 agst), Martynia 7 to 4 agst), Himan (4 to 1 agst), St. Pat III. (nap, 6 to 4 agst).

In addition to these Ranger added one more to his long list of winning doubles with the following pair, Martynia and St. Pat III., the odds working out at a shade under 6 to 1 agst.

"Field Glass," whose selections scored 29 points at Warwick on Thursday, gave four winners and two non-runners on Saturday, his successful double being Long Set and Himan.

BOWLING IN THE PARKS.

At a meeting of the Executive Council of the Yorkshire County Parks' Association, the following draw for the Yorkshire Challenge Cup was made, and the fixtures for the coming season confirmed.

First Round (to be played on the ground of the first-named club):—

Division I.—A Ackroyd v. Birley; B Hanwells v. Hunslet; C New Wortley, bye; D Woodhouse, bye.

Division II.—A Stanningley, bye; B Dewsbury v. Armley; C Pudsey, bye; D Cross Flatts v. Bramley.

Division III.—A [illegible] v. Frith Park; B Meanbrook v. Tinsley; C [illegible], bye; D Normanton, bye.

Division IV.—A [illegible] v. Peel Park; B Horton v. Windhill; C [illegible] v. Bradford Moor; D Lister v. Bowling.

First round to be completed on or before June 15th.

Second round to be completed on or before July 20th.

Third round to be completed on or before August 17th.

Second round (in each division): Winner of A v. Winner of B; and Winner of C v. Winner of D.

Third round (in each division): Winner of A B v. Winner of C D.

Semi-finals: Winner of Division 1 v. Winner of 2; Winner of Division 3 v. Winner of 4.

Final: Winner of Divisions 1 and 2 v. Winners of 3 and 4.

YORKSHIRE COUNTY FIXTURES, 1912.

May 27.—(Whit Monday)—Sheffield District v. Halifax, Normanton, and Dewsbury, at Sheffield.

May 27.—(Whit Monday)—Bradford District v. Leeds District, at Stanningley.

May 28.—(Whit Tuesday)—Day match—First annual trial—Yorkshire v. Nottingham, at Nottingham.

June [illegible]—[illegible] Class for Yorkshire Merit.

June [illegible]—Yorkshire v. Lancashire, at Manchester.

July [illegible]—Cheshire v. Yorkshire, in Yorkshire.

July [illegible]—Yorkshire v. Cheshire, at Sale.

August [illegible]—Bank Holiday Monday—Yorkshire Merit finals on the Bramley Liberal Club Bowling Green.

August [illegible]—Day match—Nottingham v. Yorkshire, at Pudsey.

August [illegible]—Lancashire v. Yorkshire, at Sheffield.

September [illegible]—Semi-finals and final Yorkshire Cup.

In Paris this spring the white blouse in every form will be very much worn with all tailor gowns.

The sale of milk and mackerel on Sundays is legalised by Parliament. The former was legalised in the reign of Charles II., and the latter in the reign of William III.

Successful experiments in tobacco-growing, for the purpose of procuring a poison to destroy insects on plants, have been carried out at the Wye (Kent) Agricultural College.

Sir William Eden says that "there is only one beautiful angel in sculpture. . . . These modern angels with their laurels and their palms and their offensive, domineering, superior attitude are dreadful people."

BABY'S TERRIBLE ORDEAL.

LEFT STARVING FOR FOUR DAYS IN OUTHOUSE.

A BRADFORD MYSTERY.

MOTHER OVERJOYED AT THE RECOVERY OF HER CHILD.

Little Hetty Kenningham, the daughter of a Bradford tram-driver has just had a terrible experience and a narrow escape from death by starvation and exposure.

Her home is at 32, Lowfield Street, off Manchester Road, Bradford, and she is only a year and nine months old. All trace of her was lost from early last Wednesday evening to shortly before four o'clock yesterday morning, when Police-Sergeant Ross found her in the outbuilding of an unoccupied house, barely a hundred yards from her home.

The officer was on duty in the upper part of Ryan street early yesterday morning, when he heard a faint cry and, after searching among the back yards of the houses, finally tried the door of the convenience of the house 186 Ryan Street. It appeared to be locked, and he was just going away when he again heard the cry, apparently proceeding from inside. He struck a match and looked through an opening at the top of the door. He could see a piece of boarding jamming the door, and with some difficulty forced this away. The baby was then found lying in a corner suffering terribly from starvation and exposure.

The child's disappearance had been previously notified to the police, and the officer was able to immediately restore her to her parents. Dr. Sharp was soon in attendance and gave it as his opinion that the baby would recover from her four days' ordeal with careful attention.

THE MOTHER'S STORY.

Mrs. Kenningham, who was seen at her house by an "Evening Post" representative to-day, is naturally overjoyed at the return of her little one. She has been living in Lowfield Street about five months, and Hetty is her only child. She said that though greatly relieved when the news came early yesterday morning that her daughter had been found, she was much shocked by the terrible condition to which the child had been reduced. "She was," said Mrs. Kenningham, "in a shocking condition."

"It was," she added, "a mystery as to what had happened to her, because nobody had seen her. She was not out two minutes on Wednesday before I sent a little girl seeking her, and when I found she was missing I sent straight to the Town Hall. She has never gone out more than a yard or two before that I know of, except along to the shop to get sweets."

To get to where she was found, the child had only to cross Ryan Street, go up a passage similar to the one leading to her own home, and she would then find herself in the yard of two back-to-back houses off Ryan Street. One of these is occupied, but the other is empty, and somehow or other she got unobserved into the out-house of No. 186.

HAD JAMMED THE DOOR.

Mrs. Kenningham explained that Hetty had been accustomed to running across their own back yard to the out-house, and, apparently, after toddling across the road, she had gone up the passage from Ryan Street and made straight for the out-house. Once inside, it appears as though she must have pulled the boarding down, and in her struggles, jammed the door.

How she could have been there from Wednesday night to Sunday morning without being heard, is somewhat of a mystery, and the neighbours are a little sceptical about her having been there all the time, inclining to the view that she may have been left there. When she was first missed, everybody in the neighbourhood made search, and one neighbour actually tried the door of the out-house in which the child was found. As it appeared locked, and she heard no sound, she made no further investigation in that direction.

A NEIGHBOUR'S STATEMENT.

Mrs. Holden, who occupies the second house, sharing the yard in which the out-house is situated, said this morning: "When they came here yesterday morning and said they had found the bairn in there, I could scarcely credit it. It looks a mystery to me." She further explained that she had been in the yard many times, and had never heard any unusual noise. During Thursday she was putting washing out within a foot or so of the place, whilst every day little children had been playing about in the yard.

THE CHILD GETTING BETTER.

Little Hetty has survived her terrible experience in a remarkable manner, though she is obviously far from well. This morning she was looking happy enough sitting among wraps in a rocking-chair before a cheerful fire, and nursing a "teddy bear." She is a bright looking little child.

On Saturday night the father arranged for a large party of his fellow-workers in the tramways department to join in a search for his missing child, and they turned up yesterday for that purpose. They were then, of course, informed by the joyful parents that the baby had been found. It has been a terribly anxious time for Mrs. Kenningham, and she summarised her sufferings in the remark, "Oh, it has nearly killed me."

A CARAVAN IN FLAMES.

LITTLE GIRL FATALLY BURNED IN SURREY.

By the burning of a caravan at Horsell, Surrey, on Saturday night a little girl lost her life and another was seriously injured.

Caroline and Amy Carey, [illegible] respectively ten and six years, daughters of Mr. and Mrs. Albert Carey, van-dwellers, were left in charge [illegible] their elder sister Maggie while their parents went [illegible]ping.

After putting the children to bed the girl left the caravan to attend a younger child in an adjacent caravan.

A little later Caroline ran out of the van screaming for help, and in a few minutes the vehicle was enveloped in flames. With great courage Mr. W. F. Alexander, a neighbour entered the van and brought out the child Amy, whose nightgown had been burned from her body.

Both children were conveyed to the Woking Cottage Hospital, where Amy died a few hours later, and Caroline lies in a precarious condition.

TO-DAY'S MARKETS.

CORN.

LIVERPOOL.—Wheat on spot was steady to firm without change from Saturday, and in quiet request. Latest: May delivery, 7s. 11⅛d. per cental. Flour steady with a normal demand. Maize was only in quiet inquiry; prices of Saturday were repeated to ½d. per cental advance. Other cereals were steady. Weekly stocks: Liverpool, Fleetwood, and Manchester—Wheat, 11,098 tons increase; maize, 1,310 tons increase.

Futures.—Wheat: Futures opened quiet. Trading: May, 7s. [illegible] to 7s. 11⅛d.; July, 7s. 11⅛d. to 7s. 10⅞d.; October, 7s. [illegible] to 7s. [illegible]. Maize: Futures opened nominal. All per cental.

PROVISIONS.

GLASGOW SUGAR.—Official Report: The market opened with a fair business done at Saturday's prices. Private Report: Rather more business was done at Saturday's prices.

CORK BUTTER.—Firsts, 113s.; seconds, 100s.; fresh butter, from 10½s. to 101s.

FISH.

HULL.—A moderate supply and a good demand. [illegible]

GRIMSBY.—A moderate supply and a good demand. [illegible]

MANCHESTER TRADE.

MANCHESTER.—Business was very slow this morning, as all round the market buyers hesitated or refused to pay producers' rates. The engagements of manufacturers enabled them to maintain a very firm attitude, and consequently out of a fair export enquiry the workable part was only small. Home trade improvement was slow. Yarns, if anything, were easier in tone than on Friday, with a quiet trade in evidence.

WOOL.

BRADFORD.—The tone in this market was quieter to-day. Prices at the London sales have not been carried upward to the extent that many anticipated, and consequently buyers were more inclined to stand aloof before covering their further requirements in tops, whether combing or crossbred. It was not possible to buy any cheaper, but the advanced quotations put forward before the opening of the London sales were withdrawn. Home-grown wools were steady. There was a little more doing in raw mohairs and prices were unchanged.

METALS.

LONDON (Opening Report).—Copper steady: G.M.B., cash, £72 7s. 6d. to £72 [illegible]; do. three months, £71 [illegible] to £71 [illegible]. Tin quiet: fine brands, cash, £191 10s. to £192; do. three months, £194 [illegible] to £194 [illegible]. Lead: English, £16 10s.; foreign, £16 [illegible] to £16 [illegible]. Spelter: Foreign, £25 [illegible] to £26.

IRON.

GLASGOW (First Report).—Cleveland steady: large business done at 54s. [illegible] and 54s. [illegible] cash; [illegible] Turnover, about 35,000 tons. Cumberland idle; sellers, 70s.

ANSWERS TO CORRESPONDENTS.

"Constant Reader."—Shotley is in County Durham.

"Inquisitive."—[illegible] Prof. Barnes appeared at the Empire, Leeds, about two years ago.

It is seven-and-forty years to-day since Abraham Lincoln, President of the United States, was shot.

It is said that some of the convicts at Wormwood Scrubbs burst into tears when they heard the prison choir sing "Homeland."

It was explained at Wood Green Police Court that the word "butterflies" was a "technical term" for painters and decorators who worked upon Bank holidays.

PROGRAMME FOR TO-MORROW.

NEWMARKET CRAVEN MEETING.

THE CRAWFORD PLATE [illegible]

[illegible]

THE LONG COURSE SELLING PLATE [illegible]

[illegible]

THE FITZWILLIAM STAKES [illegible]

[illegible]

THE VISITORS' PLATE [illegible]

[illegible]

THE APPRENTICES' HANDICAP [illegible]

[illegible]

THE FIFTY-THIRD NEWMARKET BIENNIAL STAKES [illegible]

[illegible]

THE ASHLEY PLATE [illegible]

[illegible]

Mr. R. C. Thompson's Meath Valley

Mr. E. C. Price's To-Day

Captain Homfray's Hibernia

SELBY STATIONMASTER'S APPOINTM[ENT]

Mr. J. C. Waterhouse, who since June, 1[illegible] been stationmaster at Selby, has been appointed mineral traffic superintendent at Gascoigne Wood, a great distributing centre for the West Riding coalfields. Before going to Selby Mr. Waterhouse was for four years yard master at Normanton. He was formerly for over thirteen years at the head office of the North-Eastern Company in York, having entered their service as a boy in his native town of Darlington. For 25 years he served as chief clerk at Gascoigne Wood. Mr. Waterhouse is the eldest son of the late Mr. John Waterhouse, of D[illegible] who for over half a century was connected [with the] North-Eastern Company in that district.

MR. WATERHOUSE.

A golf ball driven from a course at [illegible] smashed through the window of a passing tr[ain and] struck a passenger a severe blow on the che[ek].

At the annual vestry at Great Baddow, ne[ar Chelms]ford, Mr. C. H. Finch, the people's warden, [produced] a quantity of bad, foreign, and defaced coins [from the] bag," which he described as "exceedin[gly poor] offerings for the service of God.

The Yorkshire Evening Post.

,110 | Registered for Transmission in the United Kingdom. | LEEDS. | TUESDAY, MAY 4, 1926. | DONCASTER. | DAILY ONE PENNY.

...ERS.

...er for a general strike has ... we ask our readers to ...quality of that to which ...earance of our advertisers. ...al means of publicity. We ...concentrated upon giving ...wspapers the wildest rum-...ors, is one of the essential ...

...istressing in the extreme. ...who believe in democratic ...supremacy of Parliament. ...second, is to exercise the ...tolls, so that the supplies ...f work laid on the Govern-...y increased. The third, and ...ord or act that may embit-...l violence or disorder. To ...art-breaking. Just when ...e whole fabric of industry ...er-reaching. The worst of ...ns who are innocent of any ...wever, "grin and bear it," ...come it without any back-...

...E DAY.

[illegible]

...HE OPTIMIST.

HULL RAILWAY CLERKS BREAKAWAY.

DISAPPROVE STRIKE ACTION—AND GO TO WORK.

Hundreds of railway clerks and supervisory grades resumed work at Hull after wiring their disapproval of strike action to their executive, but are only performing ordinary duties.

There was no stoppage of work in Belfast to-day, and the transport services throughout Ulster are being conducted as usual.

Shipyards are working at Sunderland.

BROADCASTING TO-NIGHT.

BAND MUSIC, SONGS, AND FLUTE SOLOS.

LEEDS-BRADFORD.

[illegible]

7.30.— BACH'S "48." Interpreted by Claude Biggs.

[illegible]

8.0.— POPULAR ORCHESTRAL CONCERT.

THE WIRELESS ORCHESTRA. Conducted by DAN GODFREY.

[illegible]

HOW THE BREACH CAME.

NO CONCESSIONS FROM THE SIDE OF LABOUR.

(From a Labour Correspondent.)

[illegible]

THE TROUBLED SEAS.

THE WORLD'S EYES ON BRITAIN.

WIDESPREAD EFFECTS.

"CAPACITY FOR EMERGING FROM DIFFICULTIES."

NEW YORK, Tuesday.

The general strike in Britain is featured by newspapers all over the country. Some of the leading newspapers are printing two or more pages of cables. Opinions are:-

"New York Times": The Labour Leaders' own statements imply that the threat of a general strike was partly bluff. When Mr. Baldwin squarely met the challenge he pushed the coal strike into a secondary position and raised the issue of constitutional and orderly Government. The Labour leaders were apparently as much dismayed as anybody.

The "Herald Tribune" says The British temperament makes a revolution impossible. Passive resistance, however, may shatter British traditions and eventually turn Europe topsy-turvy.

The "World": To talk of civil war is fatuous. The British are a people with a signal capacity for emerging safely from forbidding difficulties. British labour is hard-headed, and the section inspired from Moscow is small.—Exchange.

BEYOND OUR FRONTIERS.

Paris, Tuesday.

The newspapers are much occupied with the general strike and some comments are:-

The "Matin": The issue of the battle, that will be followed with lively interest throughout the world, extends beyond the frontiers of England and the political and social evolution of other countries may be seriously affected.

The "Quotidien": We hope the crisis will not be aggravated by disturbances and that an equitable settlement will soon be reached.

The "Echo de Paris":-The conflict concerns the very life of Britain. It is tragic to see the labouring classes risking their bread in the future.-Central News.

Berlin, Tuesday.

Business people in Germany are expecting to reap considerable advantage from the general strike in Britain. Should the stoppage continue the German coal industry, which has had to export coal at extremely low prices, looks forward to a profitable period.—Exchange.

New York, Tuesday.

The next fortnight is expected to be critical for the tourist traffic business, if the strike continues. Half-a-million Americans are preparing to go abroad, and ships are already at the rate of one a day on some lines. It is estimated that 8,000 British seamen are here, mostly on freight ships.—Exchange.

INDIAN TRADERS' POSITION.

Calcutta, Tuesday.

The far-reaching effects of the sudden cessation of all transport in England is seen in the position in India.

Importers fear that orders, particularly for machinery and textiles, will be non-fulfilled or delayed.

Already, the prices of all imports, including foodstuffs, are inclined to rise, and heavy international demands for Bengal coal are expected.—British United Press.

TO-DAY'S MARKETS.

BUSINESS AS USUAL IN LEEDS

STOCK MARKETS AND THE CRISIS.

A DAY OF CALMNESS.

LITTLE ATTEMPT TO ENGAGE IN BUSINESS.

From our City Editor
London, Tuesday.

Transport difficulties occasioned by the strike, resulted in a poor attendance at the Stock Exchange to-day, and little attempt was made to engage in actual business. Members were chiefly occupied with discussing the strike, and their varied experiences in getting to town under the difficult conditions.

Prices can be obtained for practically all the leading securities, but quotations are necessarily nominal, although "Middle Prices" reflect nothing in the nature of a slump.

The 5 per cent. War Loan, for instance, is still quoted around 100, and 3½ per cent. Conversion around 75½, the price which ruled overnight.

Prices are readily obtainable for most of the leading foreign securities, such as Rio Tinto, French Currency loans, Peru Corporation issues and the principal foreign railways.

The Home Railway market has scarcely opened, and in industrials, attempts are only made to make prices in shares like J. Lyons, and others allied to the supply of foodstuffs.

Leading Iron, Coal and Steel shares are nominally lower, but an interesting feature is that prices of these shares, and also of several other Industrials, are less wide in character.

The suggestion is that the feared selling pressure has not developed, and jobbers, therefore, can more easily keep an even book.

The movement of Sterling exchange on New York is being watched with considerable interest. Yesterday it declined from 4.86¼ to 4.85⅞, and to-day opened at 4.85¼.

The Stock Exchange is still occupied with its fortnightly settlement, and as account day is on Thursday, there is no reason to anticipate that any steps will be taken in the way of closing the House. The Stock Exchange, in fact, may be said to have accepted the situation with comparative calmness.

The Course of Prices.

1 p.m.

There is a fair demand for money on Lombard Street to-day, but short loans are again quoted around 4 per cent. discount rates remain steady, short bills and three months' fine bills being quoted at 1[illegible] per cent.

Stock Exchange markets are quiet, owing to strike influences and in a few instances, prices have again been marked down, although the selling pressure which was feared overnight has not developed. Gilt-edged stocks are comparatively steady at 5 per cent. War Loan being 10[illegible], consols 54[illegible], and 3½ per cent. Conversion 75[illegible].

Sterling Exchange on New York has moved a little further against us to 4.8[illegible].

French Francs are weaker at 148[illegible], and the Belgian rate has fallen to 1[illegible]. Foreign Bonds are quiet, but French Currency loans are firmer, 5 per cent. being 11[illegible]. Turkish Unified is better at 1[illegible].

The Home Railway market is idle, but quotations for Foreign Rails are readily obtainable. Leading Argentines are steady at the overnight quotations. United Havanas are 6[illegible].

In Industrials, Iron and Steel engineering shares have been nominally marked down, but dealings are a matter of negotiation. Vickers are quoted 6s. 6d. Armstrongs 7s., Siemens 29s. 6d. and Callender's Cable 7[illegible].

In Textiles, Courtaulds, after opening at 6[illegible], have receded to 6, and Dunlops have eased from 23s. 3d. to 23s.

SPORTING NOTES BY "RANGER."

TURF GOSSIP AND PROGRAMME FOR CHESTER.

To-morrow's "nap" selection: Hidennis. Double: Jennie Deans (Badminton Stakes) and Hidennis (Chester Cup), at Chester.

The Chester Cup comes up for decision to-morrow, and an interesting race looks like being provided, among those that will command a strong following being Spithead, Hidennis, Vermilion Pencil and Nalders.

Spithead won the corresponding race twelve months ago, but I prefer Hidennis and Vermilion Pencil, my vote going to Hidennis whose course of hurdling during the winter has benefited him considerably.

Jennie Deans ran well enough when fourth to Arete at Newmarket to be worthy of support for the Badminton Stakes, and Royal Hussar may complete a double for the same stable by taking the City Selling Plate.

I fancy Elspeth for the Dee Stand Selling Welter Handicap, and St. Marceaux for the Stewards' Maiden Stakes. Dusky Brave is fancied for the Prince of Wales' High-Weight Handicap, while Maritza filly should run forward for the Stamford Stakes.

Bookie will represent the Manton stable in the Dee Stakes on Thursday.

It is announced that Ystra has broken down, and that she has probably finished her racing career.

CHESTER MEETING.

PROGRAMME FOR TO-MORROW.

2. 0—BADMINTON STAKES [illegible]

THE ABOVE HAVE ARRIVED.

[illegible]

2.30—CITY SELLING PLATE [illegible]

THE ABOVE HAVE ARRIVED.

[illegible]

3.15—CHESTER CUP STAKES [illegible]

THE ABOVE HAVE ARRIVED.

[illegible]

3.50—DEE STAND SELLING WELTER HANDICAP [illegible]

THE ABOVE HAVE ARRIVED.

[illegible]

4.20—STEWARDS' MAIDEN STAKES [illegible]

THE ABOVE HAVE ARRIVED.

[illegible]

4.50—PRINCE OF WALES' HIGH-WEIGHT HANDICAP [illegible]

THE ABOVE HAVE ARRIVED.

[illegible]

5.20—STAMFORD TWO-YEAR-OLD STAKES [illegible]

YORKSHIRE "CARR...

MANY INCONVENIENCES OVERCOME.

VOLUNTEERS FOR SERVIC...

GOOD TEMPER AND TOLERANC... PREVAILS.

Leeds in common with the rest of ... country, showed a keen determination ... face the issue cheerfully and boldly.

When the work-a-day citizen set out ... business, it was to find no trains, fe... newspapers, few trams, and a gene... scarcity of transport vehicles.

Copies of "The Yorkshire Post" ... "Leeds Mercury" were passed from ha... to hand and soon the gravity of the si... tion was realised throughout the city.

Between eight and nine things live... up a little, the strings of early morn... workers walking down to the city be... supplemented by others quite needle... hurrying for the usual tramcar. A ... spirit prevailed among owners of pri... cars, and promptly the walkers were ... ed up and given "lifts."

With so many of the leading indust... of the city involved in the strike, gro... of workers gathered outside worksh... discussing the situation. In spite of ... seriousness of the situation, cheerful... and good temper prevailed, and there ... much good-humoured chaff.

As the morning wore on traffic in ... city became less congested, and the gr... of workers broke up. Some took to ... tering round the streets, others made ... of the open spaces in the suburbs for ... playing of football and other games ... [illegible]

CHEERS FOR FIRST TRAM.

[illegible]

SPECIALS "CALLED UP.

[illegible]

VOLUNTEERS FOR SERVICE

[illegible]

A NATIONAL APPEA...

ISSUED UNDER THE AUTHORIT... HIS MAJESTY'S GOVERNMEN...

VOLUNTEERS URGENTLY REQUIRED.

Men, women and children must be ... ESSENTIAL SERVICES MUST ... MAINTAINED.

VOLUNTEERS ARE URGE... NEEDED. ARE YOU PREPARE... SERVE?

[illegible]

LABOUR PARTY ACCEPTS LLOYD GEORGE'S OFFER.

BUCHAREST FALLS INTO THE ENEMY'S HANDS.

BLOCKADE OF GREECE BY ALLIES.

GERMANS DEMAND PARTIAL USE OF THE SCHELDT.

WOMEN KILLED IN A FACTORY EXPLOSION.

The enemy announce the occupation of Bucharest. Ploesti has also been taken, and this involves the loss of the rich oil-fields.

The left wing of Falkenhayn's army has taken Sinaia, at the foot of the Predeal Pass, on the Roumanian side. In anticipation of this, the Roumanians had abandoned their fortified positions in the Pass.

The remainder of the Orsova army, though cut off and surrounded, has again put up a fight, and has reached the enemy's rear on the Aluta river. In the latest encounter it lost 1,600 prisoners.

A Berlin telegram alleges that since the war began the enemy have captured 100,000 Roumanian prisoners of war.

With the capture of Bucharest, five capitals are now in the hands of the Huns, the others being Brussels, Belgrade, Warsaw, and Craiova, the ancient capital of Roumania.

The Allies are to blockade all Greek ports in enforcement of their demand for reparation for the outrage at Athens.

The news from Athens again causes alarm by what it omits, as well as by what it tells. The Foreign Office says the Press telegrams which are being received are not trustworthy, the Royalists having control of the cable, while correspondents are under threats of violence.

There have been further atrocities in the city. The Mayor and a Venezelist General were most brutally treated. Measures have been taken for the speedy removal of the British Legation staff, in case of need.

The Germans are reported to have demanded partial use of the Scheldt, the Dutch waterway to Antwerp.

Attacking west of the Meuse, the Germans penetrated some French trenches. From the British front only trench raids and artillery duels are reported.

Twenty-six women have been killed and about thirty injured in an explosion at a national shell factory in the North of England.

LATEST OFFICIAL NEWS FROM FRANCE.

ATTEMPTED RAIDS ON BRITISH LINES FAIL.

BRITISH HEADQUARTERS, Thursday, 11.20 a.m.

There is nothing to report during the night.

Wednesday, 9.55 p.m.

This morning we successfully raided the enemy trenches south-east of Neuville St. Vaast.

The enemy attempted raids west of Beauvains and north-east of Roclincourt, both of which failed. We took a few prisoners.

On the rest of the front, except for some heavy shelling by the enemy in the neighbourhood of Beaucourt l'Abbaye and Mouquet Farm, and on our front west of the Ancre there is no incident of importance.

THE FRENCH REPORT.

This afternoon's French official report says:—

We made a successful surprise attack on the enemy trenches to the east of Metzeral, and brought back some prisoners.

There is nothing important to report on the rest of the front.

MORE PAY FOR NURSES.

ASKED TO SIGN FOR GENERAL SERVICE FOR AS LONG AS REQUIRED.

The War Office announces that it has been decided to increase the pay of all members of Queen Alexandra's Imperial Military Nursing Service Reserve and the Territorial Force Nursing Service who, having completed twelve months' service, are willing to sign an undertaking for general Army service for as long as required.

The pay of V.A.D. and special probationers in military hospitals staffed by Queen Alexandra's Imperial Nursing Service or the Territorial Nursing Service will also, after they have completed six months' approved service, be raised from £20 to £22 10s. per annum, and provided they are willing to sign an undertaking for Army service for so long as necessary they will be eligible for further half-yearly increments of £2 10s. up to a maximum of £30 per annum.

In addition, the board and washing allowance of all the above classes has been raised by 1s. a week.

NEW EMPEROR WISHES THE ALLIES WOULD TIRE OF WAR.

Amsterdam, Thursday.

A telegram from Vienna states that the German Emperor and the Emperor Karl spent yesterday at the Austrian Main Headquarters, together with their military advisers, discussing the military and political situation created by the capture of Bucharest and Ploesti.

The Emperor Karl has sent a telegram to the King of Bulgaria, who was not present at the conference, expressing satisfaction over the military achievements of the Central Powers. The telegram concludes by expressing the German Emperor's confident hope that "We shall succeed, in the near future, in convincing the enemy of the futility of further bloodshed."

The Emperor has sent a similar telegram to the Sultan of Turkey, expressing a hope of speedy and final victory.—Press Association.

ALLEGED BRITISH REPULSE IN BALKANS.

Amsterdam, Thursday.

The following official report is issued in Sofia:—

On the Cerna and the Vardar there was violent artillery fire. An enemy attack near Grodenitza was repulsed.

Battalions which tried to advance on the northern bank of Lake Tahinos were repulsed.

—Central News.

The area round about Lake Tahinos is held by British troops.

GERMANY'S POTATO SUPPLY.

Amsterdam, Wednesday.

In the course of a lecture at Recklinghausen, Herr Stegerwald, one of the directors of the War Feeding Department, said according to the "Lokalanzeiger," that from January 1st, 1917, no more potatoes could be used in Germany for making bread.

The use of potatoes would be replaced by a more thorough grinding of corn to the extent of 93 instead of

56 KILLED AND INJURED IN MUNITIONS EXPLOSION.

TRIBUTE TO THE WOMEN EMPLOYED AT A NORTHERN FACTORY.

The explosion at a North of England shell factory on Tuesday night is referred to in the following official announcement published to-day:—

The Ministry of Munitions regret to announce that an explosion occurred last night at a National Factory in the North of England.

According to the report received, 26 women workers were killed and about 30 injured. Prompt and effective steps were taken to deal with the emergency, and the damage done to the factory was slight.

The great majority of the workers in the factory are women, and their behaviour is deserving of the highest praise. They displayed the greatest coolness and perfect discipline, both in helping to remove the injured and in continuing to carry on the work of the factory, in spite of the explosion.

The effect of the accident on the output of munitions will be negligible.

Fortunately the explosion was confined in its effect to the building in which it occurred. The killed and injured were included in the staff engaged in the immediate vicinity of the machinery, where the explosion is believed to have been caused.

The mishap served to demonstrate the smoothness of the arrangements formulated to meet such an infrequent emergency—indeed this is the first accident of moment that has happened since the works were erected—and the abundant assistance that was instantly forthcoming has been gratefully recognised.

PROPOSED NEW PENALTIES FOR ABSENTEE MINERS.

A COMMITTEE FOR EVERY COLLIERY.

Delegates from the various branches of the Miners' Federation of Great Britain, who have come to London to attend the National Labour Conference on Food Prices to-day, met at the Central Hall, Westminster, yesterday, to deal with several questions left in abeyance by the special conference of the Federation held at Southport a fortnight ago.

After considerable discussion, the delegates decided by a majority to endorse the resolution of the Southport conference in favour of the establishment of a local joint absenteeism committee to govern every colliery, with power to inflict fines or other penalties not only on miners who persistently absent themselves from work, but also on colliery officials, who, by negligence or maladministration, place hindrances in the way of securing a continuous maximum output of coal.

Rules for the guidance of these committees were also agreed to.

THE EX-KING MANUEL'S VISIT TO LEEDS.

Leeds is to have a distinguished visitor this week-end in the ex-King Manuel, of Portugal. His Majesty is deeply interested in the Red Cross movement, and he is to visit the city to inspect the orthopædic work which is being carried on by the Leeds surgeons.

He will arrive early to-morrow evening, and during his stay he will be the guest of Sir Berkeley Moynihan, at Carr Manor, Meanwood. On Saturday his Majesty will visit the General Infirmary and other institutions, and at mid-day he will be the principal guest at a private luncheon which Sir Berkeley Moynihan is giving at the Leeds Club, in Albion Place. About 35 invitations have been sent out, the five Members of Parliament for the city being among those invited.

Ex-King Manuel is to pay a similar visit to Liverpool.

NO BUNKER COAL FOR NEUTRALS AT BRITISH PORTS.

Washington, Thursday.

The Government has decided not to protest against the refusal of the British Government to supply bunker coal to neutral ships at British ports, considering the matter one of purely domestic control, even though it affects neutral shipping.—Reuter.

INCREASES IN BRITISH TRADE FOR NOVEMBER.

The Board of Trade returns for November show that imports amounted to £88,922,506, an increase of £17,300,232, and exports to £42,488,254, an increase of £6,849,088.

Imports for the eleven completed months of the year were £872,812,712, an increase of £90,913,338, and exports £486,532,440, an increase of £115,832,623.

Imports of food, etc., were up by over seven millions, of which grain and flour represented just under three millions, meat nearly two and a half millions, and other food and drink over £1,800,000. Tobacco im-

THE FIRST OBSTACLE GOT OVER.

MR. LLOYD GEORGE TACKLES LABOUR FIRST.

NEXT EFFORT TO PLACATE IRELAND.

NEW MINISTRY PRACTICALLY ASSURED.

(From Our Parliamentary Correspondent.)

London, Thursday.

After many alternations, the condition of affairs is less tangled. Mr. Lloyd George, as was announced late last night, is complying with the King's request to form a Cabinet. He has the cooperation of Mr. Bonar Law, and the two gentlemen have consulted this morning, and are reported to be making progress.

Nobody underestimates, and certainly Mr. Lloyd George does not underestimate, the difficulties confronting him. His well-known courage and vigour make one point in his favour; a second and still more important one is that the country now recognises the gravity of its position in the war, and that everywhere there is a sincere desire not to obstruct the new Ministry.

The stability of the new Government may depend on the Labour and the Irish votes. Mr. Lloyd George will have with him practically the whole of the Unionist party in the House of Commons. It is said that he looks for the adhesion of only 70 Liberals. If, in addition, he can command the support of the Labour party, he will be able to carry on. This morning he was in touch with the organised groups of this party, Mr. Henderson being his intermediary, and this afternoon it is announced that they will support the new Government.

If it is true, as reported, that he has offered the Labour Party two seats in the Cabinet and three Under-Secretaryships, he proposes to be liberal indeed with them. Anyway, the arrangement with the Labour people practically makes the Ministry assured. There are mutterings already from the Syndicalist side of the movement. This is because they will not be among the chosen. Keen observers will watch the currents in the Labour Party, and their influence on the new Coalition generally, with special interest; they will be important.

Of the Irish vote he is much less sure. Mr. Redmond has his price. He is out for Home Rule, and in the present temper of his supporters he dare not accept anything falling short of that. The difficulty is that if a compromise is effected on this, the relation of Ireland to compulsory military service remains. We may expect Mr. Lloyd George to seek a solution, and if he can get the support of the 84 Irish members his Ministry will be secure.

As to his fellow-Ministers, there is not much that is profitable to say. We know that Mr. Asquith, Viscount Grey of Fallodon, the Marquess of Crewe, Mr. McKenna, and Mr. Runciman refused to serve under Mr. Bonar Law's leadership. The supposition is that most of them will refuse to come in under Mr. Lloyd George. As to Mr. Runciman, there is a doubt. He has done excellent work, and has a thorough grip of his Department, and renewed pressure will be brought upon him. On the grounds of patriotism and of the inadvisability of a change of control at the present juncture, he may remain in office.

SMALL CABINET PROBABLE.

The names most freely canvassed this afternoon are:—

Mr. Bonar Law.	Sir Edward Carson.
Lord Derby.	Lord Curzon.
Lord Milner.	Sir F. E. Smith.
Mr. Runciman.	Mr. Winston Churchill.
Mr. Henderson.	Mr. Barnes.

The last Cabinet had 23 members. The probability is that the next will be much less. There is some talk of Mr. Lloyd George being in favour of a Cabinet not much larger than the War Council he recommended to Mr Asquith. If he decides on a maximum of six there will be no surprise; and if the number goes beyond that, then he will obviously revert to the proposal that brought about all the trouble, and elect a small War Council which shall have a free hand.

The deduction in your Latest Edition last night, that the conference at the Palace held out some hopes of a settlement, was correct in the light of events. My information is that the King proposed a continuance of the old Ministry on the lines to which Mr. Asquith had agreed last Saturday. This was found impossible. Then an effort was made to preserve the Coalition with Mr. Bonar Law as potential Prime Minister, Mr. Asquith and his principal Liberal colleagues to serve under him.

When the conference broke up there was no decision on this point. It is stated in one quarter that Mr. Asquith was offered the Lord Chancellorship. This also fell through after Mr. Asquith had conferred with Viscount Grey and others at Downing Street. Presumably Mr. Bonar Law then decided it would be hopeless to expect any support from the Liberal side of the House, and he thereupon advised the King of his inability to form a Ministry.

This was the occasion—at 7.30 p.m.—of the King requesting Mr. Lloyd George to form a Government, so it will be seen that until late in the afternoon there were still possibilities of Mr. Asquith remaining in office, either as Premier or as a Minister.

THE HISTORY OF THE CRISIS.

There is sure to be a great deal said and written on the origin of this crisis, and it is worth while to note what Sir William Robertson Nicoll has to say of it in to-day's "British Weekly." Sir William is on friendly terms with Mr. Lloyd George. He makes bold to say that Mr. Lloyd George did not want the office of War Secretary, thinking he could do greater service out of office; and that he has never desired to be Prime Minister. Having accepted the post of War Secretary:—

Though at once confronted by difficulties, he was able to effect something. But, under the present system, under which everything has to be referred to the Cabinet, he was continually thwarted.

Remonstrances and memoranda were ignored. The war went from bad to worse. Every day brought its story of humiliation, of indecision, and of disaster.

Mr. Lloyd George became convinced that we are not winning the war, and that with present methods we never should win it. Everything was stagnant, and the Government were apparently unable to do anything.

Even when verbal concessions were made to popular demand they were not carried into effect. The country in emergency was willing to follow any direction, and it had none.

Most people will prefer the milder and more authoritative presentation of the case by Lord Derby yesterday. Lord Derby, indeed, is a prop of very considerable support for Mr. Lloyd George at this juncture. His disavowal of intrigue and his transparent honesty of purpose will go far towards acquitting Mr. Lloyd George of any charge of self-seeking. The situation will not be cleared up without some bitterness remaining, but I conclude as I started—the portents, on the whole, are favourable, because everybody wants to concentrate the whole strength of the nation in winning the war.

Probably an official announcement as to the

2 CABINET SEATS AND 3 UNDER-SECRETARYSHIPS.

TO-DAY'S CONFERENCE.

ACCEPTANCE OF MR. LLOYD GEORGE'S CONDITIONS.

Last evening Mr. Lloyd George, after his return from seeing the King, when he undertook to form a Ministry, immediately opened up negotiations with the Labour party.

In anticipation of that event the Labour M.P.'s were summoned to a conference this morning. The feeling of the meeting was one of regret at Mr. Asquith's resignation. The view was expressed that the representatives of the Labour party would rather have served under Mr. Asquith, but at the same time the leaders of the party made it perfectly clear that they are prepared to serve under any Premier who is ready vigorously to prosecute the war.

From the views freely expressed at the meeting this morning, it appears that the Labour party are more determined than ever that the war, both on land and sea, shall be more strenuously waged.

"The Labour party," said one of their M.P.'s to-day, "will heartily co-operate with any Government which will pursue a more vigorous policy, because we believe that if the Government had taken a more decided stand at the beginning, the war would have been over by now."

While it is certain that Mr. Lloyd George's Cabinet will necessarily be a small one as recent Cabinets go, there is no doubt that Mr. George is anxious that Labour shall have more representation in his Government, and he is understood to be prepared to appoint representatives of the Labour party to subsidiary positions in his Government. In this connection the names of Mr. Wardle and Mr. John Hodge are mentioned, in addition to that of Mr. A. Henderson.

At this morning's conference Mr. Henderson officially informed his colleagues of Mr. Lloyd George's invitation. A general discussion took place, and the views of the party were expressed. Mr. Henderson was instructed to interview Mr. Lloyd George, and then further report to the Labour party, who arranged to meet later in the day.

After Mr. Henderson had placed before Mr. Lloyd George the views of the party, he returned to the Central Hall, Westminster, and informed the conference that Mr. Lloyd George would be pleased to meet representatives of the organised Labour groups. These immediately joined Mr. Henderson, and the party, which included Mr. Ramsay Macdonald, Mr. J. O'Grady, Mr. Philip Snowden, and Mr. Will Thorne, went to the War Office.

The meeting of the Labour party was at the same time adjourned until two o'clock, it being arranged to reassemble at the House of Commons. The Independent Labour Party is among those represented at the conference.

TWO PORTFOLIOS OFFERED.

The Central News learns that at this conference Mr. Lloyd George, who was accompanied by Lord Derby, made a very impressive speech, and invited the Labour members to give their views as to the re-construction of the Cabinet. The Labour representatives expressed their opinion that the party was clearly anxious to discuss the new Government's policy towards Labour.

It was intimated by Mr. Lloyd George that the interests of Labour would be well looked after, and the offer was made that Labour should be represented in the new Cabinet by two members, and represented on the War Council by one member, whilst three Under-Secretaryships would be at their disposal.

These proposals were discussed this afternoon on the resumption of the conference at the House of Commons, as well as the personnel of the new Cabinet as it would affect Labour.

It was officially announced late this afternoon that the Labour party has decided, by a majority, to take part in the new Government.

The party also passed a resolution expressing the earnest hope that an endeavour will be made by the new Government to settle the Irish question.

FRANCE SATISFIED IT IS FOR THE BEST.

French opinion to-day is favourable to Mr. Lloyd George.

The "Figaro" says: "Lloyd George will have with him all men of action of all parties, who recognise in him a real chief, because they have seen him at work and know they can count upon him. He will have with him the entire British people and all Allies, and the crisis will thus have its logical solution by placing at the head of the Government a man who is the best incarnation in the fight to the death against Germany, of the resolve to conquer, and the decision to spare nothing in order to arrive as rapidly as possible at a final result. The formation of a Lloyd George Ministry will be for Germany equivalent to a Vote of Credit by the House of Commons."

"Gaulois" says: "The crisis was useful, and nothing can come of it but an increase of the magnificent effort of which our Ally is offering a moving spectacle."

—Reuter.

GERMANY PROFESSES PLEASURE.

BETHMANN-HOLLWEG THE ONLY MINISTER REMAINING.

Amsterdam, Wednesday.

Discussing Mr. Asquith's resignation the "Koelnische Volkszeitung" says:—

"We can regard events in England with complete composure. Although before the war Mr. Asquith never incited feeling against Germany, he has fought against us in the course of the war in a manner which we cannot describe as chivalrous. If he now withdraws from the political stage this is a matter for satisfaction to us.

"The leading man in the most powerful of enemy countries confirms by his resignation the failure of the war policy hitherto followed by the Quadruple Entente."

After pointing out with satisfaction that of all belligerents Germany alone retains the same Minister who led her at the outbreak of war, the paper concludes, "This is a symptom of the situation. If strong men in England now come into power, this can only please us, for we hope that decision will come all the earlier."

The "Cologne Gazette" sees in Mr. Lloyd George the man of the hour, and says so long as England and Mr. Lloyd George is not conquered England herself will remain unconquered. Mr. Asquith's resignation clears the situation.

"Now the last forces of the enemy will be brought into the field, and when they too have hurled themselves in vain against the strength of Germany then we shall find an England that is ready for an honest peace."—Reuter.

SIR WILLIAM ROBERTSON'S SHORT "RESPITE."

"ALWAYS WEAR A HAPPY FACE."

General Sir William Robertson, this afternoon, speaking at a meeting of the Westminster branch of the Red Cross Society, at Westminster City Hall, humourously referred to the short respite which he was having owing to the political crisis.

"I am glad," he said, "that it has been possible for me to come here this afternoon, even though it must only be for a few minutes. It happens that I am a little less busy to-day than usual, because there is a great deal of other business doing, and with which I am not connected—(laughter)—and so I have an easy time just now. Still I can tell you that I have enough to fill up my time at the War Office."

Sir William then proceeded to refer to the work of the Red Cross, urged people to pay frequent visits to the wounded in hospitals, and always to wear a happy face.

MR. ASQUITH AS LORD CHIEF JUSTICE.

From "A Londoner's Diary" in the "Evening Standard," to-day:—"The gossips of the Inns of Court, knowing that Lord Reading is a warm favourite for the woolsack, cast about for his successor as Lord Chief Justice, and find him—again in Mr. Asquith."

SUCCESS OF BRITISH LOAN IN JAPAN.

Pekin, Thursday.

The British loan in Japan has met with extraordinary success, and there is every reason to expect that it has been over-subscribed.—Exchange.

LEEDS STOCK EXCHANGE.—Forenoon.

British Oxygen	50/-	Lister and Co. Ord.	18/10½
Gas Light and Coke Ord.	[illegible]	Yorkshire Iron and Coal Ord.	[illegible]
Wall Paper Def.	3/3		2/3
Leeds and Wakefield Brew. Pref.	[illegible]	Midland Deferred	55
		London and N.W. Ord.	93½

† Late business done previous day.

Afternoon.—Consols 2½ per cent. 54 1-16, War Loan 4½ per cent. [illegible] [illegible]

WELCO is the most popular Cocoa of the day. Save the coupons—6½d. per ¼lb. tin.—Advt.

RHEUMATISM, SCIATICA, GOUT, Kidney Disease, Cured by Dr. Skelton's Renal Pills ... from LANE'S HERBAL MEDICINE STORES ... [illegible]

PARLIAMENT MEETS FOR TWO MINUTES.

ADJOURNMENT UNTIL TUESDAY AGREED TO.

There was a big attendance of members when the House of Commons assembled this afternoon, both sides of the House being fully occupied, while a large number also stood at the Bar, in the expectation that the proceedings would be quite short and formal. A few peers occupied the Lords' Gallery, and there were only a few of the public in the Strangers' Gallery.

Mr. Whitley, who was in the Chair, at once rose and said that in view of the circumstances prevailing, he thought hon. members would not desire him to go through the list of questions in the usual manner. (Hear, hear.) If that was so, he should propose to give instructions that the questions appearing on the paper should be set down for the day on which the House met next week.

Mr. E. Harvey asked whether there would then be any extension of time for questions in order to clear up the arrears. (Cries of "No.")

Mr. Whitley replied that it did not lie within his power to alter the rule.

Mr. Ginnell asked whether unstarred questions for to-day would be answered in the usual manner; and Mr. Whitley replied that he presumed that depended on whether or not there was any one in a position to answer. (Laughter.)

Mr. Gulland then rose, and moved that the House adjourn until Tuesday next.

Mr. Whitley put the question. There was no opposition, and it was carried without dissent.

Members at once filed out of the Chamber, the sitting thus terminating inside two minutes. This is probably the shortest sitting of the House on record.

LIBERAL PARTY TO MEET.

It is officially stated that notices have been issued by the Liberal Whips for a meeting of members of the Liberal party in both Houses of Parliament, to be held at the Reform Club, at 12 o'clock to-morrow, Friday. Mr. Asquith will preside.

HEAVY DEFEAT FOR ITALIAN PACIFISTS.

THE PREMIER'S DECLARATION.

Rome, Wednesday (received to-day).

In the Chamber, to-day, a resolution of the official Socialists was read, requesting the Government to represent to the Allied Governments the urgent necessity of calling together, through the medium of the United States and other neutral States, a congress of plenipotentiary representatives of the belligerent countries, with the object, after a suspension of hostilities, of closely examining the admitted principles of agreement and the concrete objects and claims of the various parties in the war, to the end that a speedy solution of the points at issue and the salvation of Europe might be attained.

Signor Boselli, the Premier, said that the Chamber, in discussing the statements of the Government, had already entered into a full discussion of the question of peace, and the Government did not wish to limit in any way the full liberty of this discussion; but the resolution of the Socialists would be inopportune at the present moment, because the Chamber, as it could not vote in favour of a premature and uncertain peace, could also not vote generally against peace. (Cries of "Bravo.")

The principles enunciated in the resolution (he continued) are no doubt worthy of praise, but we do not know whether these principles are recognised and accepted by the Central Powers. Moreover, it is necessary to avoid even a shadow of suspicion that Italy, who does not desire a separate peace, is not heart and soul with her Allies. (Loud and prolonged cheers.)

The Chamber must not pass a resolution which could in any way diminish the ardour of our soldiers, or weaken the energy of the country. (Loud cheers.) Thus we can hasten victory which means hastening peace. (Renewed cheers.) It is only by this means that peace can be made durable.

The Premier's demand that the discussion be postponed for six months was accepted by 293 votes to 47.—Reuter.

MARCONI BLACKMAILER SENT INTO PENAL SERVITUDE.

CLOSE OF THE TRIAL IN LONDON.

The trial concluded at the Central Criminal Court this afternoon, before Mr. Justice Darling, of Thomas Absalom Jackson (38), who was charged with demanding money with menaces from the Marconi Wireless Telegraph Company (Limited), and from Mr. Godfrey Charles Isaacs, and with offering to prevent the publication of certain matters with intent to extort money.

Prisoner was found guilty, and sentenced to three years' penal servitude.

Mr. Muir, addressing the Jury, said that if evidence could have been got against others, they would have been by the prisoner's side in the dock.

Mr. Cecil Hayes submitted that throughout Jackson was innocent, and that the only object in Mr. Isaacs' prosecution was to get at the "Financial News."

Signalmen Tinsley and Meakin, who were imprisoned in connection with the Gretna railway accident, are to be released on Friday, the 15th inst.

LATE NEWS.

BERLIN CLAIMS A SUCCESS ON THE FRENCH FRONT.

To-day's Berlin official communication announces the capture of Hill 304 south-east of Malancourt, on the left of the Meuse, capturing five officers and 190 men.

LABOUR PARTY'S CONFERENCE ON FOOD PRICES.

EXTREMISTS AIR THEIR BITTER POLITICAL OPINIONS.

A crowded national conference of representatives of trade unions, co-operative societies, trade councils, local Labour parties, Socialist societies, and women's industrial and co-operative organisations, was held in London, to-day, to consider the question of food prices.

Mr. G. J. Wardle, M.P., who presided, said it was unfortunate that the present crisis had coincided with a political crisis of the first magnitude, so that at the outset they found themselves without a Government with any authority to make their representations to at the moment.

The problem they had to consider was of vital interest to the nation, and inseparably associated with the question of bringing the war to a successful conclusion.

Mr. J. R. Clynes, M.P., moved a resolution advising Government purchase of all imported essential foodstuffs, the commandeering or control of home produce and ships, and the marketing of supplies at prices which would secure the full benefit of these measures to the consumer.

Mr. Ammon, the Fawcett Society extremist, alleged that the belatedness of Government action was due absolutely to the apathy and the "betrayal" of the Parliamentary Labour party. He went on to protest against any alliance with "a man who had sold his political friends, and betrayed every sense of honour, dignity, and honesty which was held to be common among English public men."

A REBUKE FROM THE CHAIR.

"I wonder if this is a step to a representative of Labour in the Cabinet of such a man?" he said. "We have been betrayed and misled . . . Soldiers used to break strikes everywhere. We have been . . . and we are told that there is no possibility of expression in the House of Commons. Let the expression go from here." (Applause.)

They had been too trusting, he said, and must be cautious in regard to a man in supreme command who was "a charlatan and a proved liar to Labour."

These strong remarks moved the chairman to call the speaker to order.

At this stage also Mr. Wardle and the other members of the Parliamentary Labour party left to resume their conference on the Cabinet situation. Derisive shouts were levelled at them by a small section as they were leaving.

Replying to these, Mr. Wardle declared: "They do their duty, and we strongly resent—and we have a right to resent—suggestions that we have either sold ourselves body and soul or that we intend to do so. Of whatever action we may take or may have to take I only desire to say this: Whether we stand or fall it will be in our opinion in the interests of the Labour movement and of the country." (Applause.)

A FOUR MILLION ACRE SCHEME.

The Miners' Federation put forward a resolution which was adopted, urging the Government to take over at least four million acres of land now laid down to grass or lying fallow, including suitable private parks, and provide sufficient labour and machinery to cultivate it and gather the harvest.

Another resolution was adopted urging that the Government should purchase wheat and ensure for the duration of the war and six months after a sixpenny quartern loaf.

CLOSING PRICES.

BRITISH FUNDS, ETC.—Local Loans 54½, Water Board [illegible] RAILWAYS.—Brighton Def. 61½, Gt. Northern Pref. [illegible] Ord. [illegible] Def. Con. Ord. [illegible] Great Western [illegible] and North-West. 94½, Metropolitan Consolidated [illegible] [illegible] Pref. 44½, Midland Def. 55½, North British Pref. [illegible] North-Eastern Ord. 99½.

AMERICAN SECURITIES.—Denver Ordinary [illegible] [illegible]

COLONIAL AND FOREIGN RAILWAYS.—Canadian Pacific 175, Grand Trunk Ord. [illegible]

FOREIGN BONDS.—Argentine 1886 5 per cent. 94½, [illegible]

MISCELLANEOUS.—Armstrong Whitworth [illegible]

SOUTH AFRICAN SECURITIES.—[illegible]

DEEP LEVELS.—City Deep [illegible]

RHODESIANS.—[illegible]

WEST AFRICAN SECURITIES.—Ashanti Goldfields [illegible]

NIGERIAN TIN SHARES.—Bayfield [illegible]

COPPER SHARES.—Rio Tinto Def. 63½.

MISCELLANEOUS.—Broken Hill Proprietary [illegible]

RUBBER SHARES.—Anglo-Ceylon [illegible]

OIL SHARES.—Anglo-Persian Pref. [illegible]

War Loan 4½ per cent. 94⅛.

CORN.

MANCHESTER.—Market strong. Wheat: Foreign, [illegible]

CATTLE.

DUBLIN.—Spirited demand; 5,465 beasts in market; [illegible]

PRODUCE.

LIVERPOOL.—Sugar firm; [illegible]

LONDON.—Sugar remains unchanged. Coffee futures [illegible]

COTTON.

LIVERPOOL.—American futures opened 7 to 8 down, [illegible] Probable sales 8,000.

Later.—American 3 up to 4 down: December, [illegible] January-February, 12.01d.; March-April, 12.11d.; May-[illegible] 12.23d.; July-August, 12.30d. Egyptian nil.

LEEDS LEADS

1890 – 1939

Throughout the course of its life, the *Yorkshire Evening Post* has been a witness to history. For one and a quarter centuries it has told the story of Leeds and its people, reporting on the events that have helped shape their lives and that of the city they call home.

But when it came to one of the biggest – and most tragic – events to ever strike Leeds, the *YEP* wasn't allowed to say very much at all.

On December 7, 1916, with the First World War raging on the battlefields of Europe, the paper told of disaster on the home front.

'Fifty-six killed and injured in munitions explosion' ran the headline above an official government statement that gave sketchy details of an explosion "at a National Factory in the North of England".

"Twenty-six women workers were killed and about 30 injured," it went on. "Prompt and effective steps were taken to deal with the emergency, and the damage done to the factory was slight.

"The great majority of the workers in the factory are women, and their behaviour is deserving of the highest praise. They displayed the greatest coolness and perfect discipline, both in helping remove the injured and in continuing to carry on the work the factory, in spite of the explosion. The effect of the accident on the output of munitions will be negligible."

Strict wartime censorship meant there was a ban on reporting precise details of the incident. Only later could the *YEP* reveal that the explosion had occurred at Barnbow, the munitions factory near Cross Gates that had been busily feeding the Allied war effort.

Officially known as National Filling Factory No. 1, it was Britain's biggest shell factory, employing 16,000 mostly female workers from Leeds and the surrounding towns. They became known as the Barnbow Canaries because the explosive chemicals they worked with turned their skin yellow.

But even though the sprawling site was hard to miss, the press were prevented from making any reference to it. This meant little was publicly known of the incident, the worst tragedy in the history of the city in terms of fatalities, until six years after the war had ended.

The explosion had occurred in Room 42 of the factory, where around 170 women worked in the dangerous job of filling shells. The death toll would rise to 35, with Field Marshal Sir Douglas Haig paying tribute to the devotion and sacrifice of those who lost their lives.

But in the days and weeks that followed the tragedy, the only clue to their fate was the line "killed by accident" in the many death notices that began to appear in the pages of the paper.

The *Yorkshire Evening Post* had come into being some 26 years earlier, at a time of enormous change in Leeds. At the dawn of the 19th century its population stood at a little over 53,000. By the close it was eight times that size as Leeds flourished in an industrialised Britain that had become the 'workshop of the world'.

Two years before the paper's very first edition, Frenchman Louis Le Prince had filmed the first

The women who worked at the Leeds munitions factory were dubbed the 'Barnbow Canaries' because the explosives turned their skin yellow.

moving pictures in a Roundhay garden and then of trams and the horse-drawn and pedestrian traffic crossing Leeds Bridge. His was an invention that would change the world.

Leeds was busy being transformed too. The tramway opened in October 1891, providing a much-needed modern transport system – once it had turned fully electric, that is. Then on January 4, 1893, the *YEP* reported that at a meeting of the borough council, the first of the new year, it was agreed that a petition should be sent to Queen Victoria asking for her to grant city status.

"The Town Clerk then read a petition to the Queen from the Mayor, Aldermen, and burgesses of Leeds, in which it was pointed out that Leeds was an ancient borough, that it was now populous, that it embraced an area of 21,572 acres, that its rateable value was £1,305,492," ran the report.

"Its population was now 400,000, having showed a steady increase. It was the fourth largest municipality in the kingdom, and although larger than Bristol or Newcastle was yet a town, while these were cities.

"The petition also pointed out the importance of Leeds as the centre of the woollen trade, as a railway centre, and as an Assize centre, and in conclusion asked that the title and dignity of a city should be conferred upon the borough."

Victoria duly agreed and the newly minted city of Leeds decided to create City Square by way of celebration, though it would be a decade before it was completed. Vast crowds gathered to witness its eventual unveiling on September 16, 1903.

In those early days of its existence the *YEP* seemed to have a taste for the darker side of life, perhaps reflecting where it felt its market lay. It carried endless stories in tiny typeface of murder cases, court hearings, industrial accidents and assorted unhappy endings of unfortunate folk both at home and abroad.

Anything with the whiff of scandal, such as the case of a businessman who claimed to have been robbed by a lady with whom he shared a cab but was adamant that he didn't want his name to be made known in court, was catnip to the newspaper's editors. But there was still room for some levity here and there. In 1893, the same year that Leeds became a city, the *YEP* told of an "interesting ceremony" that had taken place between a Mr and Mrs Howcroft of Skinner Lane. It was the couple's 50th wedding anniversary, a considerable feat at a time when the average life expectancy hovered around the mid to late forties.

It was reported that the couple had 15 children, "thirteen of whom are still living" and were present at the celebration. The article was accompanied by an illustration of the couple. In fact, all in all, it was not so very different from the countless golden wedding stories that have appeared in the *YEP* in the 100 and more years since.

A visit from the great Harry Houdini also brought tremendous excitement – not least because the escapologist almost died during a rare failure at the Empire Theatre. Always the master self-publicist, Houdini declared that he planned to escape on stage from a padlocked water can full of beer supplied by local brewer Joshua Tetley & Son in his performance on February 9, 1911.

But the teetotal American hadn't counted on the effects of the alcohol fumes and lost consciousness, his vigilant assistant Franz Kukol having to haul him out.

History doesn't record whether he was impressed by the Leeds sense of humour when, after what was nearly his final performance, a wisecracking stage-hand asked him: "Why run away from the beer Mr Houdini? It's what most of us run after."

There was a first for the *Yorkshire Evening Post* in 1913, when a special one-off Aeroplane Post was printed by the paper and flown from Leeds to the Great Yorkshire Show by aircraft pioneer Harold Blackburn.

Harry Houdini had a narrow escape at the Empire Theatre in Leeds in February 1911.

Members of the Leeds branch of the Women's Social and Political Union, otherwise known as the suffragettes, rally at Woodhouse Moor, May 4, 1913. *(Below)* Leeds suffragette Leonora Cohen in her later years.

In these early years of the 20th century many of the events that unfolded in Leeds mirrored those across Britain as a whole. The suffragettes, for instance, who campaigned passionately for women to be given the right to vote, were heavily active in the city.

Home Secretary Herbert Gladstone was "howled down" by them on two occasions in Leeds in November 1908, while 100,000 were in attendance at a suffragette meeting on Woodhouse Moor in July of the same year.

One of the movement's prominent campaigners was Woodhouse-born schoolteacher Mary Gawthorpe. In 2015, Leeds Civic Trust unveiled a commemorative blue plaque at her former home in Bramley.

Then there were the headline-grabbing exploits of Leonora Cohen, who joined the Leeds branch of Pankhurst's Women's Social and Political Union in 1911. She was jailed after taking part in a series of protests, the most famous being in 1913 when she smashed a jewel display case in the Tower of London with an iron bar. A note attached to the bar read: 'My Protest to the Government for its refusal to Enfranchise Women. Deeds Not Words'.

The incident saw her dubbed the 'Tower Suffragette' – but Cohen was swiftly released from prison after going on hunger strike.

In December that year the *YEP* reported how she seemed to be revelling in a game of cat and mouse with the detectives who were tasked with following her every move after she had won her freedom.

"Mrs Leonora Cohen, the well-known Leeds suffragette, who since her release has been staying at the WSPU offices on St George's Road, Leeds, left there this afternoon," it said. "Just before three o'clock an open carriage, drawn by one horse, drew up at the door, and a few minutes later Mrs Cohen, wearing a big coat and a green motor scarf, left the house.

"Mrs Cohen entered the carriage and at once drove off. The detectives who were watching the house at once jumped on their bicycles and followed. We understand that Mrs Cohen merely left for a drive through the Headingley district. It was expected she would return to her rooms again this afternoon."

Mrs Cohen later became the first woman president of the Yorkshire Federation of Trade Councils. She was even appointed a magistrate, a post she held for 25 years, and was awarded an OBE.

But not everyone was a supporter of the cause. The newspaper reported that a Mrs Florence Travers was among those women who seemed quite appalled by the suffragettes' methods.

"Women would show more true citizenship in qualifying themselves as guardians and members of borough and county councils," she declared, "than in spending money like water in organising processions and embroidering banners, to spread sex antagonism and gather noisy crowds to jeer at their platform oratory."

At the outbreak of the First World War, the *Yorkshire Evening Post* was caught up in the same giddy excitement that spread through the general public but which would quickly evaporate as the enormity of the conflict hit home.

In a bid to boost numbers of volunteers, the Army established 'pals' battalions of men from the same areas and workplaces. It meant that friends could enlist knowing they would serve alongside one another.

The downside, which soon became all too apparent, was that when a particular battalion was called into action it could result in entire streets and communities losing husbands, fathers and sons.

The Leeds Pals, officially known as the 15th (Service) Battalion West Yorkshire Regiment, were formed within a month of Britain declaring war on Germany.

On September 2, 1914, the *YEP* declared that "names for enrolment in the new battalion will be received at the Leeds Town Hall tomorrow from 9 o'clock in the morning until 9 o'clock in the evening.

"The hall will also be open on subsequent days until the full number of men is obtained. Already well over 200 men have signified their intention of joining. To assist in the recruiting an illuminated tramcar is to tour the city."

A decorated tram toured the city's streets to encourage men to join the Leeds Pals Battalion.

Opposite: **The YEP followed the Pals' progress, and their mounting casualties.**

The battalion, the idea of the Lord Mayor of Leeds, Edward Brotherton, would eventually number some 2,000 men and find itself thrust into the biggest battle in British military history.

The Battle of the Somme, the Allied offensive designed to break the deadlock of trench warfare in Northern France, began on July 1, 1916. It would prove immensely costly for the city of Leeds, as evidenced by the lists of killed and wounded that appeared in each day's paper.

"The price which has been, and is still being paid, for the great offensive on the Western front is once more reflected in the list of casualties to be published today," declared the *YEP* some three weeks into the battle.

"A not very encouraging message respecting the fate of the missing men of the Leeds Pals is contained in a letter from the battalion chaplain. 'We hear,' he writes, 'that you think in Leeds that many have been taken prisoner, but we don't think here that this is to be relied on. They

CASUALTIES OF YORKSHIRE REGIMENTS.

THE CASE OF THE MISSING.

LEEDS PALS' CHAPLAIN HOLDS OUT VERY LITTLE HOPE.

The price which has been, and is still being paid, for the great offensive on the Western front is once more reflected in the list of casualties to be published to-day.

Again Yorkshire and other North-Country regiments figure prominently in the lists. A not very encouraging message respecting the fate of the missing men of the Leeds Pals is contained in a letter from the battalion chaplain. "We hear," he writes, "that you think in Leeds that many have been taken prisoners, but we don't think here that this is to be relied on. They may have taken in five or six wounded men." From this one must regretfully conclude that the majority of those men posted as missing lost their lives in the great leap forward on July 1st.

That the older Leeds regiments, the two battalions of Rifles, have been equally in the thick of the fighting

Lieut. H. N. TURNER. West Yorks. (killed). Capt. R. H. MURRAY. Yorks. Regt. (killed). Photo: Wood, Darlington.

is shown by a letter from one of their officers. It appears that both battalions have been concerned in continuous fighting for over a fortnight. "Fortunately," he writes, "most of our casualties have been slightly wounded. We are still pushing all the time, and are going strong."

A Leeds officer in one of the West Yorkshire battalions, writing home, says: "No doubt you will have heard something about the wonderful German dug-outs, but I wish you could see some of them about here. One we have been in is a most colossal affair, and without the slightest exaggeration I can say that it would be possible to put nearly a whole battalion in it. It is dug very deep, and is quite shell proof, containing dining rooms, kitchens, and bedrooms. In fact, everything that one can want is there, including handsome mirrors and electric bells. One of the passages is at least 30 yards long, and every portion of this underground mansion is boarded up."

CASUALTIES TO OFFICERS.

Lieutenant H. Norman Turner, West Yorkshire Regiment, eldest son of Mr. Arthur Turner, Dunollie, Halton, near Leeds, was killed in action on July 14th, while leading his men. He was educated at the Leeds Grammar School, where he became a members of the O.T.C. After matriculating with first-class honours, he was articled with Messrs. H. W. and J. Blackburn, chartered accountants, East Parade, Leeds. Shortly after the outbreak of war, he joined the Leeds pals as a private, and after a few months was given a commission. He was 22 years of age. His brother, Corporal

Pte. C. R. RYAL. Leeds Rifles (died of wounds). Sgt. H. HILL. Somerset L.I. (died of wounds). Pte. Trevor MASON. Lincolns (killed).

Pte. FRANKLIN. York and Lancaster (killed). Pte. Jas. LAZENBY. North'd Fusiliers (died of wounds). Pte. F. WHITTY. Green Howards (killed).

Reginald Turner, is with the Cameron Highlanders in France.

Captain R. H. Murray, Yorkshire Regiment (attached Royal Munster Fusiliers) was killed while attending to a wounded man on the firing step of a trench. Captain Murray, the only son of Mr. and Mrs. R. Murray, of West House, Richmond, Yorkshire, was a Cambridge University man, and rowed in the Selwyn College boat at Henley Regatta just before the war.

Second-Lieutenant Richard Pearce Brown, Durham Light Infantry, killed on the 17th inst., was cashier at the Doncaster branch of the London Joint Stock Bank when the war broke out. His parents live at Whitebrook, Monmouth. Before receiving his commission he served in the ranks of the Coldstream Guards.

Captain Richard E. C. Ranson, East Yorkshire Regiment, who met his death on the 21st inst., was the nephew of Miss Ranson, Spring Bank, Hull.

Mr. C. E. Plackett, of Glenmore, Gledhow, Leeds, has received news from the colonel of his son's battalion that there is good ground for believing that Captain C. H. Plackett, officially reported as missing, is a prisoner.

Captain Bernard Louis Wilcher, of the West Yorkshire Regiment, wounded in the leg by shrapnel, was, before the war, in the insurance business in Leeds, and is well known in the Headingley district. A keen Rugby football enthusiast, he has assisted his battalion in several matches.

A fellow officer of Captain Wilcher, and also a keen sportsman and athlete, Lieutenant William Henry Colbeck, has been wounded in the arm. A solicitor by profession, he was formerly with Messrs. Brook, Wade, Farr, and Louns-Walker, of Leeds, and he lives at Ben Rhydding.

Second-Lieutenant A. E. Mander, West Riding Regiment, who has been wounded, was an assistant master at the Crossley and Porter Orphanage, Halifax.

Second-Lieutenant J. H. Armistead, West Yorkshire Regiment, wounded, is one of several officer sons of Mr. Richard Armistead, surveyor and valuer, of Bradford. When war broke out he was reading for the Bar.

Another Bradford officer wounded (for the second time) is Second-Lieutenant H. C. Speight, West Yorkshire Regiment, the second son of Major Speight, the officer commanding at Belle Vue Barracks. He is going on all right.

Lieutenant Arthur Dickinson, Royal Field Artillery, who has returned to his duties since being wounded by shrapnel, is the husband of Mrs. Dickinson, of 97, Folkestone Street, Bradford Moor. He was in the retreat from Mons, and received a commission on the field.

THE LEEDS PALS.

A prominent member of the Leeds Pals who has been killed is Sergeant A. R. Greasley. He was 22 years of age, and was the son of the late Mr. T. H. Greasley, valuer and arbitrator, of Hull and Leeds, and Mrs. George Hendley, of 26, Stratford Terrace, Leeds. Educated at the Yorkshire Society's School in London,

Sgt. A. R. GREASLEY. Leeds Pals (killed). Photo: Scrimshaw. Sergt. CLAYTON. Leeds Pals (killed). Pte. R. WOOD. Leeds Pals (missing).

Lce.-Cpl. A. WINCH. Leeds Pals (killed). Pte. Horace ILES. Leeds Pals (killed). Pte. W. C. SHAW. Leeds Pals (missing).

he was an all-round athlete, winning the boxing championship of his company at Colsterdale and coming in second in the walking Marathon race at the Boulevard, Hull.

Sergeant Norman Jackson, youngest son of Mr. and Mrs. William Jackson, Chapel House, Tadcaster, was killed in action on July 1st. Before joining the Pals in September, 1914, he was in the offices of Messrs. John Smith's Brewery, Tadcaster.

Sergeant Frank Clayton, who was in partnership with his brother, Mr. William Clayton, incorporated accountant, Albion Street, Leeds, is reported missing. Sergeant Clayton, who is 40 years of age, enlisted in the battalion on its formation, and had served in Egypt and France. A Fellow of the Society of Accountants and Auditors, and a member of the Headingley Lodge of Freemasons, he is well known in business circles, and for some time was connected—in its early days—with the Leeds City Football Club.

In a letter received by his brother from the chaplain to the Battalion, little hope of Sergeant Clayton's safety is entertained. The letter states that careful inquiries have been made, "and though I cannot find anyone here ... who saw him, I can say with little doubt that your brother is amongst the killed. I am sorry to deprive you of hope, but it is better to know the truth than to bear the pain of uncertainty. We hear that you think in Leeds that many have been taken prisoners, but we don't think here that this is to be relied on. They may have taken in five or six wounded men."

The relatives of Pte. J. H. Hunter, of C Co., have received official intimation of his death in action on July 1. Formerly he was employed by the Leeds Sand and Gravel Co., and resided at 80, Seaforth Road, Harehills.

Miss L. Scawbord, 14, Wellington Terrace, Bramley, asks for news of her brother, Private Tom Scawbord, D Company.

Private H. Wilson, C Co., was wounded on July 1st, by bullet and shrapnel, in the right leg, right arm, and back, and is in Netley Hospital, Southampton. His wife lives at Quarry Lane, Brookroyd, Batley.

THE LEEDS RIFLES' LOSSES.

Private C. R. Ryall, aged 20, Leeds Rifles, was wounded in the shoulder at Ypres in November, 1915, and returned to England. He went back to France in May of this year, was wounded in the arm and chest on July 1st, and died from wounds on July 14. His mother lives at 16, Haymount Terrace, Newtown, Leeds.

L.-Corporal L. H. Kirk (31), who has died of wounds in Rouen Hospital, was for 11 years an employee of the Leeds City tramways. His widow lives at 5, Beech Grove, Armley, Leeds. He had been in the Rifles for nearly two years. He was the third son of Mr. and Mrs. Samuel Kirk, of Greenthorpe, Henconner Lane, Bramley.

Rifleman T. W. Nichols, Leeds Rifles, the eldest son of Mr. T. Nichols, Hunslet, Leeds, has succumbed to wounds received in action.

Pte. J. Whiteley, late of Pudsey, has been wounded in the left forearm, right hand, and right shoulder. He is in Bethnal Green Military Hospital, Cambridge Road, London, E.

Rfm. Frank Hallas is in hospital in France with shrapnel and bullet wounds in the left arm and shoulder. He is 29 years of age, was employed by Messrs. Nicholson, contractors, and resided at 35, Woodsley Road, Leeds. He is married, and has three children.

Sgt. A. Ewing, a well-known conductor on the Leeds trams, and goal-keeper for the tramways' football team, is recovering his sight in a hospital in France, after having lost it as the result of shell fire. He is 26 years of age, and has been in the Rifles five years, including fifteen months in France. His wife lives at 37, Compton Road, Harehills.

CASUALTIES TO YORKSHIREMEN OF VARIOUS UNITS.

Pte. Fred Whitty, Green Howards, has been killed in action at the age of 33. He fought through the South African campaign, and worked at Charlesworth's Robin Hood Colliery. His widow lives at 1, Midland Grove, Hunslet Carr.

Pte. J. F. Dillon (23), who has died of wounds in France, formerly worked at the Grand Central, Leeds,

Pte. J. H. HUNTER. Leeds Pals (killed). Photo: Fox. Cpl. Joseph GEE. K.O.Y.L.I. (killed). Pte. J. F. DILLON. R'l Fus. (died of wounds).

Lce.-Cpl. L. KIRK. Leeds Rifles (died of wounds). Pte. Jas. WADDINGTON. R'l. Munster Fus. (died of wounds). Pte. Jas. LEE. Leeds Rifles (killed).

and later in a London cafe. He joined the Royal Fusiliers eighteen months ago, and leaves a widow, who lives at 33, Jermyn Street, Kirkstall Road, Leeds.

Pte. J. Lazenby, Northumberland Fusiliers, killed in action on the 7th inst., had been in the Army six years. He was 25 years of age, and his relatives live at 3, Marian Mount, Woodhouse Street, Leeds.

Sgt. Harold Hill (24), Somerset L.I., has died of wounds at the age of 24. Soon after the outbreak of war he left the employ of Messrs. John Fowler and Co. (Limited) to enlist. He was the second son of Mr. and Mrs. George Hill.

Pte. Ernest Longley, West Yorkshire Regiment, the youngest son of Mr. Walter Longley, Park View, Newton Road, Leeds, was killed in action on July 1. He was 26 years of age.

Pte. Fred Walton, West Yorkshire Regiment, whose wife lives at 40, Burley Road, Leeds, fell in action on July 4.

Pte. J. G. Brook, West Yorkshire Regiment, eldest son of Mr. James Brook, 48, Lower Oxford Street, Castleford, was killed on July 1. He was 23 years of age.

Pte. Alfred Cecil Arnold, West Yorkshire Regiment, the fourth son of the late Mr. Alfred Arnold and Mrs. Esther Arnold, 10, Newton Grove, Leeds, died on July 18, from wounds received in action. He was 24 years of age.

L.-Cpl. Norman Lumby, King's Own Scottish Borderers, son of Mr. and Mrs. George Lumby, Benton Terrace, Yeadon, was killed in action in France on July 1. Pte Lumby, who was only 20 years of age, had previously fought in the Dardanelles.

Pte. Trevor Mason, whose wife lives at Carleton, Pontefract, is reported killed. He was in the Lincolnshire Regiment, and nothing had previously been heard of him since the last day of June. Mason was a printer, and was well known in Pontefract.

Pte. Clifford Parker, R.A.M.C., late of Pontefract Road, Purston, is reported killed on July 9. He enlisted in November, 1914, and prior to that he was a clerk in the costs department of the Acton Hall Colliery offices.

Mr. Ernest Wigglesworth, of Moor Top, Ackworth, has received official intimation that his brother, Pte. Fred Wigglesworth, aged 27, of the West Yorkshire Regiment, has died of wounds.

Mrs. McLaughlin, 8, Alma Place, Beckett Street, Leeds, asks after her son, Pte. J. McLaughlin, K.O.Y.L.I., who has been missing since July 1. Mrs. Foules, 28, Bentley Grove, Meanwood, Leeds, also asks for news of her son, Pte. A. Foules, A Co., Yorkshire Regiment, who is said, by a comrade, to have been wounded in the "big push."

Pte. J. T. Simpson, York and Lancaster, is in hospital at [illegible], suffering from wounds and shell shock. He is the eldest son of Mr. and Mrs. W. Simpson, gardener to the [illegible] Hall Estate, [illegible], near Wakefield, and was employed as manager of a branch shop at Rotherham, for Messrs. Freeman, Hardy, and Willis. He has a brother in the A.S.C.

Pte. Michael Moore, West Yorkshire Regt., whose wife and seven children live at 4, St. Saviour's Row, The Bank, Leeds, is in hospital suffering from wounds in the forehead.

Pte. John Manley, West Yorkshire Regt., whose home is at 16, St. Saviour's Row, The Bank, Leeds, is also in hospital, having been wounded in the legs.

Sergt. Thomas [illegible], aged [illegible], of the K.O.Y.L.I., who was awarded the D.C.M. in October, and resided with Mrs. Cooke, of Northgate, Pontefract, has written home to say that he has had his left arm blown off, and is at Southend-on-Sea. He jokingly says that the only pain he can feel is in his fingers.

Mr. Thomas Bossock, of Brackenhill, Ackworth, has received news that his son Pte. Joseph Bossock, who was buried in an upheaval with 10 others, has come out with only a wounded shoulder, and is now in hospital at Rochdale.

Gunner H. E. Hornby, West Riding Howitzers (younger son of Mr. John Hornby, Ilkley, headmaster of St. Jude's Schools, Leeds), was wounded in both legs last week, and is now in the Victoria Hospital, Keighley. Gunner Hornby was formerly in a Leeds insurance office.

Private Fred King, Manchester Pals, son of Mr. and Mrs. King, Bilston, Wetherby, has been wounded in the left knee by a bullet. Prior to the war he was a gardener for Lord Lonsdale at Lowther Castle, and later for Lady Frances Cecil, [illegible] Hall, Burton-on-Trent. He is in hospital at Whalley, Lancashire.

Sergeant E. Atkinson, of Chapel Street, Tadcaster, is wounded. He is one of four soldier brothers, one of whom has been killed.

Pte. Norman Pate, K.O.S.B., who before the war lived in Woodhouse Lane, Leeds, is in hospital at Woolwich with five wounds, one of them severe, received in action on July 1. Pte. Pate served through the Gallipoli campaign without [illegible] adventure.

THE TRAGIC DEATH OF A YORKSHIRE SCHOOLBOY.

At the inquest held at Broadstairs, Kent, on Gerald Meyrick, 13, only son of Mr. and Mrs. R. F. Meyrick, of Hall Orchards, Wetherby, it was stated that the lad was bathing with some school-fellows, when he got into difficulties. His plight was observed by Seaman George Hammond who swam out to rescue him.

Unfortunately, a powerful current swept both into deeper water, and in a few minutes, both were drowned before the eyes of the horrified lads on the beach.

A boating party went out, and were able to recover the sailor's body. The lad's body was washed ashore.

Returning a verdict to the effect that both were accidentally drowned, the jury paid a warm tribute to the sailor's bravery, and expressed sympathy with the relatives of the schoolboy.

A LEEDS MAN'S MILITARY MEDAL.

There are non-combatant as well as combatant branches of the military organisation, in which courage is a necessary quality, and in none more so than the Royal Army Medical Corps, whose first-aid men, during recent operations, have carried out some wonderful rescues of wounded men, often in circumstances of great danger. A Leeds man, Corpl. R. A. Filer, serving with the 3rd Northumbrian Field Ambulance, R.A.M.C., has been awarded the Military Medal for gallantry in attending on and removing the wounded, under very heavy shell fire. He is married, and lives at 19, Hardy Terrace, Beeston Hill.

CORPL. R. A. FILER.

At the next meeting of Manchester City Council the question will be raised of asking the Admiralty to allow the captured German minelaying submarine UC5 to be exhibited in the Manchester Ship Canal.

* Answers to Correspondents will be found to-day on Page 5.

A group of Leeds Pals pictured during the recruitment campaign. Yorkshire cricketers Roy Kilner and Major Booth are on the left of the front row.

may have taken in five or six wounded men.'

"From this one must regretfully conclude," intoned the paper, "that the majority of those men posted as missing lost their lives in the great leap forward on July 1."

The battalion casualties, sustained in the first few minutes after the Pals attacked towards the village of Serre on the first day of the battle, were 24 officers and 504 other ranks, of which 15 officers and 233 other ranks were killed.

Among them was Captain Evelyn Lintott, the former Leeds City footballer, and Second Lieutenant Major Booth – Major being his first name rather than rank – a cricketer for Yorkshire and England from Pudsey. It was said that there was not a street in Leeds that didn't have at least one house with curtains drawn in mourning.

The tragic fate of the Pals is embodied in the story of Horace Iles, whose death was reported in the *Yorkshire Evening Post* on July 24. A blacksmith's apprentice and painter and decorator

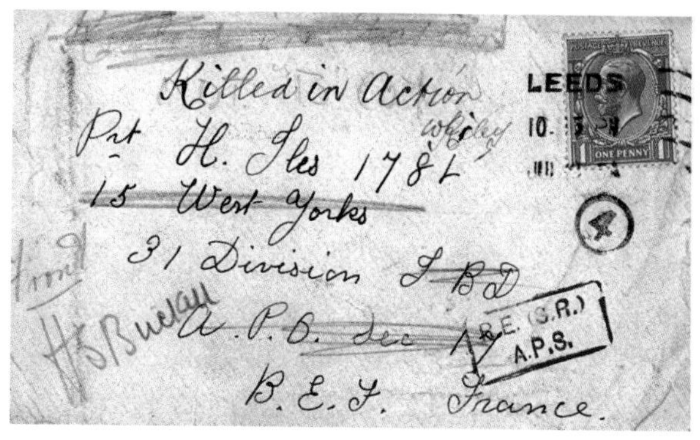

Left: **Horace Iles was just 14 when he enlisted to fight in the First World War.**

Above: **The letter returned to his sister Florrie after Horace was killed in action in France.**

from Woodhouse, he had joined up after being handed a white feather – an accusation of cowardice – on a city tram.

At the time he was just 14, yet such was the need for troops that army recruiters frequently turned a blind eye to those who were under age. Within two years Horace found himself alongside the rest of the Leeds Pals in Northern France, awaiting the Big Push.

On July 9, 1916, no doubt fearful of the enormous casualties being sustained at the Somme, his sister Florrie wrote a letter begging him to reveal his true age and come home.

"For goodness sake Horace, tell them how old you are," she chided. "I am sure they will send you back if they know you are only 16. You have seen quite enough now. Just chuck it up and try to get back, you won't fare no worse for it. If you don't do it now, you will come back in bits and we want the whole of you."

But even before she put pen to paper, her brother was already dead, the family informed of their loss by the words 'Killed in action' marked on the front of Florrie's unopened letter.

"The name of Serre and the date of 1st July is engraved deep in our hearts, along with the faces of our 'Pals', a grand crowd of chaps," said one of their number, Private Arthur Pearson, whose life was saved by two tins of bully beef in his pack which deflected a bullet. "We were two years in the making and 10 minutes in the destroying."

And the Pals were not alone. The Leeds Rifles, the city's more established volunteer corps, also suffered catastrophic losses, which were again detailed in the pages of the *YEP*.

"That the older Leeds regiments, the two battalions of Rifles, have been equally in the thick of the fighting is shown by a letter from one of their officers," one article reported. "It appears that both battalions have been concerned in continuous fighting for over a fortnight. 'Fortunately,' he writes, 'most of our casualties have been slightly wounded. We are still pushing all the time, and are going strong'."

The grim reading provided by the daily lists of wounded and killed, however, told a different story and many more men would die before the war was out.

The last British soldier to be killed in action, just 90 minutes before the armistice came into effect on November 11, 1918, was Leeds man George Edwin Ellison.

A 40-year-old regular, he had fought in the first gas attack and seen action on the Somme in 1916, yet somehow emerged unscathed.

Serving with the 5th Royal Irish Lancers, on November 11 he was scouting on the outskirts of the Belgian town of Mons where German soldiers had been reported in a wood.

In just over an hour the ceasefire would come into force, yet he wouldn't live to see it. The former coal miner was shot and killed, never to return to Leeds and his wife Hannah and son James, whose fifth birthday fell just five days later.

A number of men from the city were awarded the Victoria Cross, the country's highest military honour, for their courage under fire during the war. Among them was Leeds policeman John Crawshaw Raynes, who served as a Sergeant Major. He went out under heavy shellfire to save a wounded comrade at Bethune in France in October 1915. Moments later, a gas shell burst and, despite being badly gassed, he staggered to find his smoke helmet and gave it to the colleague he had rescued.

The very next day he himself had to be rescued when a house was knocked down by a German shell, burying eight men.

A young boy studies a poster publicising the YEP's Boots for Bairns campaign, December 1930.

The first to be pulled out, he insisted on staying at the scene to help free others trapped in the rubble, despite being wounded in the head and leg. Then, after having his wounds dressed, he immediately reported for duty with his Battery, which was again being heavily shelled.

After the war, the *YEP* ran appeals for the Sergeant Raynes Fund, set up to provide him with a more suitable home given his life-limiting injuries. He died at his home in Chapeltown in 1929 and was buried at Harehills Cemetery in a funeral attended by an estimated 25,000 people, including local dignitaries.

The end of the war at least saw Leeds manage to ride out the decline of the traditional textile industry, with tailoring, distributive trades and engineering chief among the 80 or so other industries thriving in the city.

By 1926, Montague Burton's bespoke tailoring factory on Hudson Road in Burmantofts was the largest and most popular clothing company in Europe, employing some 16,000.

That same year saw Marks and Spencer, formed at Kirkgate Market in 1884 with the slogan 'don't ask the price, it's a penny', become a public company as its astonishing success story

An aerial shot of Montague Burton's sprawling factory which employed some 16,000 workers, November 1937.

continued. Soon it would be opening its flagship store in London's Marble Arch. However, the General Strike also led to serious rioting in Vicar Lane and Duncan Street.

The postwar years saw the *YEP* launch one of its earliest campaigns in the shape of Boots For Bairns. Running from 1921 until 1940, it aimed to provide boots and clothing for poor youngsters in a city where rickets was so widespread that the condition acquired the unhappy nickname of 'Leeds Legs'.

Even in the 1980s, readers still regularly wrote into the paper to share their childhood memories of receiving new pairs of boots, shrewdly stamped in a way that discouraged parents from pawning them even in times of desperate need.

In 1931 Montague Burton was awarded a knighthood in the King's Birthday Honours, alongside Dr James Baillie, Vice Chancellor of Leeds University, which had been established in 1904. The news brought great excitement to both institutions.

"At the hour when Dr Baillie was expected to arrive at the university, close on 200 students gathered at the bottom of University Road," reported the *YEP*. "The Vice Chancellor's car was held up by a cordon of students drawn across the road, and two ropes were attached to the car.

"Amid rousing cheers, students then hauled the car and its

Burton, pictured in May 1949, became the largest employer in Leeds.

smiling occupant along the road to the main entrance of the university and when the Vice Chancellor alighted he passed between a double row of students – men on one side and women on the other. An enthusiast who had found a bugle made a valiant but not quite successful attempt to reproduce the atmosphere of a heraldic welcome.

"There was so much excitement at the factory of Montague Burton Ltd that to close down the works for the afternoon and give everyone a half-holiday was the only way to cope with the situation.

"The news spread rapidly throughout the factory and serious work soon became out of the question. Rooms in which were 2,000 girls were bubbling over with merriment and the congratulatory spirit, and there were loud demands that Mr Burton should make a triumphal tour, and visit all departments. Mr Burton was early at the office, but would not face that ordeal."

A Lithuanian Jew who had come to Britain at the turn of the century, Burton's secret was to offer high-quality made-to-measure suits at low prices. "A five guinea suit for 55 shillings", was his famous promise.

Burton's became the biggest employer in Leeds, with the Hudson Road factory containing vast workrooms of machinists, with whole families working on the same production line.

It also boasted the largest works canteen in the world, along with a health and pension scheme that pre-dated the welfare state. Free dental care, chiropodists and even sun-ray treatment were all provided for the factory staff.

A symbol of Leeds' growing status was the creation of The Headrow, the grand new avenue of the city, designed by Sir Reginald Blomfield in 1925. The major attraction was Lewis's new department store, opened in September 1932 at a cost of £1m. Its lavish marble floors, bronze decorated staircases, lifts and escalators brought ultra-modern shopping to Leeds, while its Christmas grotto and intricate window displays created memories for generations of youngsters.

The city was also forging ahead on transport. By 1901 the electrification of the city's tram system had been completed and there were several lines running between the city centre and Cross Gates, Chapel Allerton, Moortown, Roundhay, Middleton, Beeston, Armley, Hunslet and Kirkstall.

In fact, the network was far more extensive than that of the proposed Supertram, that much-vaunted but ultimately unsuccessful bid to clear congestion which hit the buffers more than a century later on the back of the Labour government's refusal to grant funding.

The *YEP* also reported on what was the first fully automated traffic light system to be permanently installed on a British street.

'The All-Electric Policeman', declared the paper's headline on the momentous day in March 1928 when the lights went live, informing readers that "the occupation of the traffic policeman is threatened by an electrical automatic traffic signal installation, which began operation on the corner of Park Row and Bond Street today. This is the first installation of its kind in Great Britain. Leeds therefore leads again".

The report told how "up to the time of its beginning, the usual burly figure of the policeman stood in the centre of the four roads. At the appointed minute the policeman stopped all four streams of traffic and retreated to the footpath. The electrical device came into instant operation".

The traffic lights at Bond Street and Park Row were the first of their kind in the country when they were installed in 1928.

The *YEP* assured sceptical motorists that the scheme was "simplicity itself". "The trial was an eminently successful one. Drivers quickly appreciated the objects of the device and there was no confusion."

More lights – dubbed 'Robot PCs' – swiftly followed at the junctions of Albion Street and Commercial Street and Commercial Street and Briggate.

"The first installation is working very well indeed," Mr Fred Bentley, Chairman of the Watch Committee, told the newspaper.

"Mr Bentley said he thought that when the public had got used to the signals the system would work splendidly. It would relieve the police of part of the heavy burden of point duty, and enable them to attend more fully to their ordinary duties."

In the 1930s, Leeds City Council seriously considered the possibility of beginning work on an underground system, with the main station beneath City Square. The plans were even published in the Railway Gazette in 1939.

The initial idea was to have terminuses running out toward Roundhay, Cross Gates, Bramley and Hunslet. The estimated cost at the time was £500,000 per mile.

In 1944, William Moorland, general manager of Leeds City Transport, submitted a further proposal to build an underground railway system in order to ease growing traffic congestion. His east-west line was to run from the Woodpecker Junction to Wellington Street, his north-south line from North Street to Lower Briggate and from Woodhouse Lane to Neville Street via City Square.

The cost of the scheme was estimated to be about £750,000 per mile but the idea was shelved on cost grounds in October 1945 when the Labour group took over. The reason given at the time was that, due to the cost of the war, the council wanted to wait until more favourable economic times. However, the plans have never been officially rejected.

A sign of Leeds's desire to move with the times was its demolition of slum housing to make way for what was then the largest social housing complex in the UK and one of the biggest in Europe. By 1914, Leeds had 78,000 back-to-back houses, which had actually been banned by national legislation five years before. The fact that plans for further back-to-back housing were already in place allowed even more to be built in the city into the 1930s.

After winning the 1933 council elections, Labour pledged to demolish 3,000 such homes annually for the next five years. They would be replaced by the Quarry Hill flats, a huge housing project based on the Karl Marx-Hof apartments in Vienna. Devised by Reverend Charlie Jenkinson, chairman of the council's housing committee, and city architect Richard Livett, the aim was to create simple, modern housing that dignified working class lives.

Quarry Hill flats aimed to create simple, modern housing that dignified working class lives but only survived for four decades.

Built in seven and eight-storey blocks, Quarry Hill was set in 36 acres of inner city land. There were 938 flats, occupied by about 3,000 people. Work began in 1934 and the first tenants moved in during 1938. Some elements, such as a concert hall, swimming pool, tennis courts and the full range of shops were never built.

One of their main features was the Garchey system of waste disposal, which the *Yorkshire Evening Post* got very excited about at its unveiling in November 1939 in an article entitled 'Quarry Hill Flat Marvels'.

"When the refuse disposal stations and laundry for Leeds Quarry Hill flats were formally opened this afternoon, guests of the Housing Committee were shown some of the marvels of the new estate – for instance, how a bucketful of household refuse tossed down a sink helps to provide steam and heat for the laundry.

"A vacuum system draws the refuse to the disposal station, and in a room with tiled floors and walls, so immaculate as to suggest the inside of a power station, it is sent through the tanks to an extractor which takes the water from the solids. The water goes to the sewers; the solids pass to incinerators which heat the laundry. This is the Garchey system and the plant at Quarry Hill is the first of its kind in this country."

But Quarry Hill was later plagued by problems: corrosion in the steelwork, concrete slabs working loose and the waste disposal system constantly blocked or leaking. All of these required costly repairs and the entire area was demolished in the late 1970s, after featuring as the setting for Keith Waterhouse and Willis Hall's Leeds-based sitcom *Queenie's Castle*, starring Diana Dors.

Throughout the 1930s there was a growing sense that a second war with Germany was looming large on the horizon, with incidents in Leeds lending credence to this gloomy forecast.

In August 1931, the German-built Graf Zeppelin hovered over City Square, with pedestrians wondering if it was just a passing display or whether the airship was engaged in something more sinister such as a spying mission. The *YEP* told how its appearance caused Loiners to "irrevocably lose their reputation for calmness in the stampede that followed news the Graf was over the city".

If some felt a pang of concern then there was good reason. A Zeppelin had attacked Leeds in September 1916, the crew seeking out the industrial targets of Barnbow and Kirkstall Forge. It had ended up aborting its mission when it came under fire, ditching its incendiary bombs over the Harewood estate.

In 1936, as Nazism swept all before it in Germany, British fascist leader Sir Oswald Mosley brought his Blackshirts to Leeds. Prevented from passing through the city's predominantly Jewish area, Mosley paraded more than 1,000 of his uniformed followers in Calverley Street before marching to Holbeck Moor.

The Communist Party led the organised opposition to the event, and the crowd of 30,000 who gathered on the moor contained a significant hostile element. As Mosley spoke, The Red Flag was sung in an attempt to drown him out, and stones were hurled at the fascists. Many of these found their targets, with Mosley himself being struck.

A pair of undercover detectives were among the crowd and three men were arrested and charged over the incident. However, the punishments handed down by the city's magistrates were relatively light, perhaps reflecting their own opinion of Sir Oswald and his brand of politics.

John Hodgson, a 19-year-old warehouseman, of Black Bull Street, and 28-year-old Herbert Broxup, a cloth finisher of Paradise Place, were fined for disorderly conduct. John William Crooke, 27, of Leopold Terrace, was sentenced to a six-week stay at Armley jail for assault.

Three years later, on September 3, 1939, came the news the country had been dreading. The front page of the *Yorkshire Evening Post* declared that the Second World War was under way

Oswald Mosley at the demonstration on Holbeck Moor which saw him pelted with stones, September 28, 1936.

Opposite: The Graf Zeppelin passes over City Square, August 1931.

following Germany's rejection of Prime Minister Neville Chamberlain's ultimatum to withdraw its troops from Poland.

"This is a sad day for all of us, and to none is it sadder than for me," the paper reported the premier telling the House of Commons. "Everything that I worked for, everything that I hoped for, everything that I believed in through my public life has crashed in ruins.

"There is but one thing left for me, and that is, I hope, with what strength and power I have, to forward the cause for which we have all sacrificed so much.

"I cannot tell what part I may be allowed to play myself. I trust I may live to see the day when Hitlerism has been destroyed – so as to restore the liberty of Europe."

Showing the gift for oratory that would go on to define his inspirational leadership, Winston Churchill, the then First Lord of the Admiralty, added: "There is no question of fighting for Danzig or fighting for Poland. We are fighting to save the whole world from the pestilence of Nazi Germany, and in defence of all that is most sacred to man."

On the same day the *YEP* reported that there had been a less than surprising spike in the price of sandbags, with thousands already in position to protect public buildings against air raids. "There is evidence of a substantial rise in prices, especially in the case of bags, which are reported to be costing double the amount charged recently," it warned.

"One of the firms supplying hundreds of tons of sand to Leeds people reported that they were inundated with orders. They have taken steps to keep lorries running throughout the weekend."

Leeds City Engineer Mr J E Acfield, meanwhile, was worried that some householders were erecting their Anderson shelters "in such a way as to make them actually dangerous" and urged them to adhere to the guidelines that had been issued by Whitehall.

For several weeks the *Yorkshire Evening Post* had been publishing extracts from a diary sent home by Leeds man Charles F Smith as he journeyed through Europe while the war clouds gathered.

His message to the people of his home city was: "If we fight, we must fight without hatred", as he blamed economic factors for Germany's aggression rather than the "inflamed nationalism" which he insisted was a "red herring".

Whatever the cause of the conflict, one fact was certain: Britain – and Leeds – were once again at war.

A Yorkshire Evening Post vendor announces the abdication of King Edward VIII, and right, how the paper reported the shock news, December 1936.

22 TELEPHONES 20401 and 2803

PARLIAM

BROADCAST TO AT 10 TO-NIGHT

"Mr. Windsor" Leavi Country

LABOUR APPEAL FO NEW START

The reign of King Edward VIII ceased this a noon when the Royal Assent was given in the H of Lords to the Abdication Bill, which had pa through both Houses.

An official announcement will be made to-mo regarding the title to be borne by King Edwar future.

KING EDWARD, after signing the Act of Abdication, is to b cast at 10 o'clock to-night. He will do so as "Mr. Winds subject of the new King, his brother.

The Second Reading of the Abdication Bill was carried in the of Commons by 403 to 5. It passed through Committee w amendment, and was sent to the House of Lords, which pas in six minutes.

Speaking in support of the Bill Mr. Attlee, Le of the Opposition, said: "I hope we shall see a start made. I believe that this is necessary if co tutional monarchy is to survive in the present age.

The accession of the new King will be proclaimed to-morrow. Windsor" will then leave the country for an unk destination.

The Attorney-General, in the House of Commons, to-day, said was no compulsion on King Edward to leave the country.

THE NEW KING

Reign Which Began This Afternoon

The Duke of York is now King (writes a lobby correspondent). It is not necessary for him to wait until the proclamation to-morrow before assuming the title.

Some people thought that when at 1.52 this afternoon Royal assent was given to the Abdication Bill it meant that King Edward was no longer on the Throne but that they would have to wait until to-morrow before another King reigned and that, in fact, Britain for 24 hours would be a Kingdom without a King.

This, it is learned on good authority, is an erroneous belief. Constitutionally England is never without a King. Immediately a Monarch dies his successor technically is reigning. Hence the phrase, "The King is dead—Long Live the King."

In the same way, as soon as the Abdication Act received Royal assent, the Duke of York became King of England. His reign began therefore at 1.52 p.m. to-day.

In House of Lords

When the House of Lords received from the Commons the Abdication Bill, the first reading was formally agreed to at once.

Viscount Halifax, leader of the House, then moved the second reading of the Bill.

Viscount Halifax, Lord Privy Seal, said in the gracious message they had before them yesterday the wish was expressed by His Majesty that the matter should be dealt with by both Houses with all practical expedition.

Lord Halifax said the Bill made it plain that after the Act of Abdication the Royal Marriages Act of 1772 should not apply in this case.

Lord Snell, leader of the Opposition, said it was necessary that the measure must be passed with all convenient speed, and in view of that necessity he gave his assent to the passing.

Lord Mottistone, on behalf of the Liberal party, said they desired to associate themselves with the statement made by the leader of the House.

The second and third readings were then carried, and the Bill was formally passed.

Royal Commission

A Royal Commission consisted of Lord Onslow, Earl Stanhope and Lord Denham, then, in the usual form signified the Royal Assent to the Act.

From that moment King Edward VIII, ceased to be the King of Great Britain and Ireland and the Dominions beyond the Seas and Emperor of India.

The ancient ceremony of giving the Royal Assent was observed.

Sir Claude Schuster, clerk of the Crown, stood at the side of the table. He bowed to the Royal Commissioners and read the title of the Act.

Sir Henry Badeley, the Clerk of the Parliaments, who stood at the other side of the table, also bowed to the Commissioners, turned round and announced the Commons at the Bar in Norman French, "Le roi veult."

The formalities concluded at 1.50 p.m.

Mr. Stanley Baldwin, Mr. Ramsay MacDonald and other members of the Cabinet, accompanied the Speaker to the Bar of the House to hear the commission read.

Speaking in a low voice the Clerk pronounced the words which ended King Edward's reign. The Speaker and members of the House of Commons ...

SECRET DESTINATI

King Edward Leaving Broadcast

When King Edward leaves to-night after his final broad will not go out of Europe. P his departure are being kept ab secret.

His destination will be revea after he has left England.

Only the final preparations in c with the King's departure remain t pleted. The bulk of his luggage ha left Fort Belvedere.

During the last few days many and trunks have been taken by shooting brake into London. No baggage was labelled.

Late last night a lorry, covered w paulin, left by a side entrance tradesmen's vans. This lorry wa on the London road by a motor cyc patrol.

King Edward is apparently tak of his most treasured personal b with him from Fort Belvedere. the packages in the shooting br bulky.

No Forced Exile

Suggestions that King Edward bound to leave the country, and effect, have to live in perma after his abdication, were finally cially disposed of by the Attorney announcement in the House of to-day that there is no compul King Edward to leave the cou

A number of countries have been as King Edward's destination—Sw France, Denmark and Italy.

The position of King Edward abdication, it was pointed out in tive quarters to-day, is not affecte fact that he is a Knight of the G of other orders of chivalry. King as a peer, was never dubbed a kn will therefore be plain Mr. Windsor abdication.

MRS. ERNEST SIMPS

Cannes,

Mrs. Simpson rose late to-day a fasting in bed. She is still repor sleeping badly and resting late sequence.

There are reports she is engage ing extensively. "She is working thing, whatever it is," said her Herman Rogers, when questioned reports. He confirmed that she wa lot of writing.

Rumours about the King's de after he leaves England continue Cannes. The latest is that he wil to Switzerland and then to Austria. United Press.

AT FORT BELVEDE

Police Patrol Priva Flying Field

Fog shrouded Fort Belvede to-day. Lights were not extin until after three a.m.

Throughout the night there was police guard both inside and out Belvedere. In addition the police ...

[illegible]T PASSES ACT ENDING KING'S REIGN

[illegible]TION

[illegible]LAMATION OF THE NEW KING

[illegible]O-MORROW'S CEREMONY

[illegible]mp and Pageantry in London

[illegible] new King will be proclaimed [illegible] James's Palace at 3 p.m. to-[illegible]w. The Accession Council [illegible]eet at 11 a.m.

[illegible] anticipated that the Pro[illegible]tion will be read in London, [illegible]en 3.15 and 3.30, at Temple [illegible]nd 3.45 to 4.0 at the Royal [illegible]nge.

[illegible]nbers of the Royal Family [illegible]ll members of the Privy [illegible]il are entitled to attend the [illegible]g of the Accession Council, [illegible]l as the Speaker of the House [illegible]mmons, the Lord Mayor and [illegible] officials of the City of [illegible]n.

[illegible] pageantry, and centuries-old [illegible]ial will be observed when the [illegible]g is proclaimed. The King's [illegible] of arms will appear in their [illegible]s gold uniforms, "habited in [illegible]bards."

[illegible]oclamation will be read from the [illegible]t Friary Court, St. James's Palace, [illegible]rald Wollaston K.C. Garter, King-of-[illegible]o only a few short months ago pro-[illegible]he accession of King Edward VIII. [illegible] be accompanied by the Earl [illegible] the Duke of Norfolk and officers [illegible]ld titles—Clarenceux King-of-Arms, [illegible]ng-of-Arms, the Heralds, and the [illegible]ts.

[illegible]d of honour from the Brigade of [illegible]and a detachment of household [illegible]ill be drawn up in the courtyard.

Quaint Ceremonial

[illegible]oclamation read, Sir Gerald will [illegible] "God Save the King." There will [illegible]fare of trumpets. A salute of [illegible] will break the silence, and there [illegible]w the National Anthem.

[illegible]St. James's Palace will proceed a[illegible]n in Royal carriages, carrying the [illegible] Arms Heralds, Pursuivants, and [illegible]al-Arms. It will be preceded by an [illegible] the Royal Horse Guards.

[illegible]oclamation will be read again at [illegible] Square, and then the procession [illegible]n to Temple Bar, where a quaint [illegible]eting procedure will be carried out [illegible] can proceed into the city.

[illegible]One Voice and Consent"

[illegible]ord Mayor (Sir George Broadbridge) [illegible] Sheriffs and Aldermen, will await [illegible]ession, a red silken rope barring [illegible] to the city until the ancient ritual [illegible]s completed. A triple fanfare of [illegible]s will announce the approach of the [illegible]e.

[illegible]vant Bluemantle, riding forward [illegible]ill be challenged by the City [illegible] and the procession will halt until [illegible]suivant has handed to the Lord [illegible]he order in Council directing the [illegible] of the Proclamation which the Lord [illegible]ill then do aloud.

[illegible]ceremonial ended, Norroy King-of-[illegible]ll read the Proclamation at the foot [illegible]cery Lane. The final ceremony will [illegible]ce on the steps of the Royal [illegible]e.

[illegible] wording of the Proclamation follows [illegible]t it will declare that the new [illegible]n is "with one voice and consent [illegible]ue and heart" proclaimed "our [illegible]ful and rightful liege Lord.

The King's Declaration

[illegible]ew King's declaration to the Privy [illegible] will afterwards be published as a [illegible]supplement to the London Gazette. [illegible]e Coronation declaration the King [illegible]lemnly and sincerely, in the presence [illegible] profess, testify, and declare that I [illegible]aithful Protestant, and that I will, [illegible]g to the true intent of the enact-[illegible]which secure the Protestant succes-[illegible] the throne of my realm, uphold and [illegible]n the said enactment to the best of [illegible]er, according to law."

[illegible]YORK'S CEREMONIAL

[illegible]proclamation of the new King will [illegible]ce at York on Monday at the Man-[illegible]use steps, the Minster, the Law [illegible] and Parliament Street, in the same [illegible] the proclamation of King Edward [illegible]ary.

[illegible]SH FOR SOUVENIRS

[illegible]ver Articles May Have Great Value

[illegible]National Jewellers' Association states [illegible]hereas indications yesterday were [illegible]e jewellery industry might be faced [illegible]ses amounting to hundreds of thou-[illegible] pounds, many jewellers to-day from [illegible] parts of the country report an [illegible]al demand for King Edward VIII [illegible]s.

[illegible]eason for this is that the hallmark [illegible]e mark on silver articles reflect the [illegible] which they were made, and Edward [illegible]uvenirs are being bought, as they [illegible]y to have exceptional value in the [illegible]

[illegible] London store had a run on Edward [illegible]oons and was sold out by noon. [illegible] reports are confirmed by the [illegible] Association of Goldsmiths.

[illegible]OWNING ST. QUIET

[illegible]ll After Excitement of Last Few Days

[illegible]e hurrying to work along Piccadilly [illegible]rning paused to glance at No. 145, the [illegible] the Duke of York, who to-morrow [illegible]proclaimed King. A police-sergeant [illegible] constables were on duty outside the

FACE THAT THOUSANDS CHEERED

The Duke of York in his car, listening to the cheers of thousands of people who had waited to see him, on his arrival at his home in Piccadilly late last night. *(Another picture on Page 16.)*

THE NEW KING AND QUEEN

ORIGINAL CHRISTMAS PLANS UNCHANGED

No Immediate Move to Buckingham Palace

The future plans of the new King and Queen were the subject of much speculation to-day. It is very unlikely that they will move into Buckingham Palace before the New Year.

Original plans for Christmas were that the Duke and Duchess of York, with their children, and Duke and Duchess of Gloucester should spend the festival with Queen Mary at Sandringham. It is most likely that this programme will be carried out.

The Duke of York will probably follow the example of his brother during the next few weeks, and will go to Buckingham Palace daily to carry out State business.

A number of changes are anticipated in the Royal household. In the new reign the post of Mistress of the Robes held by the Duchess of Devonshire during the reign of King George and Queen Mary, and lapsed in the last reign in the absence of a Queen, will be revived.

In this case the office of Master of the Robes, revived by King Edward VIII and given to Lord Colebrooke, will presumably cease.

All members of King Edward's household cease their duties automatically when the King abdicates.

The new King will have to appoint a new household, and the domestic staff at Buckingham Palace, Windsor Castle, and other Royal residences, will again receive six months' formal notice, as they did on the death of King George.

King 41 on Monday

On Monday, two days after his proclamation, the new King will be 41. His birthday will be observed in the usual way by the Services. In the various naval ports Royal salutes of 21 guns will be fired by saluting ships. In the Army similar salutes will be fired at all saluting stations, and there will be special parades.

The new King is expected to fly the Royal Standard at 145, Piccadilly, for some time, and to use the secretarial offices recently acquired at York House as well as the Palace for his official tasks.

Among visitors at 145, Piccadilly to-day were Lord Cromer (the Lord Chamberlain), Sir Claud Schuster (Clerk of the Crown), Rear-Admiral Sir Basil Brooke (Comptroller to the Duke of York), Sir Edward Peacock (Receiver-General of the Duchy of Cornwall), Lord Mount Edgcumbe and Major-General B. N. Sergison Brooke, General Officer Commanding, London District.

The Countess of Strathmore, mother of the Duchess of York, entered 145, Piccadilly, by the garden entrance and spent some time with her daughter. Princess Elizabeth accompanied her grandmother to the garden gate, and a nurse saw the Countess into her car.

About noon a crowd outside the house greatly increased, and police reinforcements were brought up to keep the throng, most of whom were women, on the move.

Several despatches were left by Royal Air Force men and by a Guards' despatch rider on a bicycle.

Among the first acts of the new reign will be the inspection of the Guards and of the Navy and Air Force establishments by the King. He will assume the supreme leadership of the fighting forces, just as King Edward did upon his accession.

TRIBUTE TO PRESS

Magistrate on "Discretion" During Crisis

A tribute to the Press for its "discretion

EX-FIANCE CHARGED

Waitress Says He Shot Her at Hotel

A young Brighton waitress gave a dramatic account at Lewes Assizes to-day of a shooting incident in her bedroom in which, she alleged, the man to whom she had previously been engaged was involved.

Reuin Frederick Kettley (28), fruiterer, pleaded not guilty to shooting Beatrice Rose West with intent to murder her, and not guilty to wounding her with intent to injure.

Miss West said Kettley borrowed £55 from her. They quarrelled and she gave him up. On September 6 she told him he had been lying to her, smacked his face and asked him when she was going to have the first instalment of her money returned. He said he would meet her that night.

They went to her room at the hotel where she was working. Witness told him she had decided to finish with him.

Witness said Kettley produced a gun.

"He pressed the gun against me. There was a report and I felt a piercing pain," said witness.

"I screamed, and he put the pillow over my face. I struggled and he said 'Well, be quiet then.' He said he was going to shoot his brains out."

He refused to get a doctor, and asked her to say it was an accident.

Miss West said that in October, 1935, Kettley put some money in a gas meter, turned on the gas and held her head down on a pillow by the gas fire. She struggled and got away. In August this year he had threatened her with a gun.

Kettley's mother, Mrs. Agnes Kettley, called as a witness for the prosecution, said Kettley told her, "I must have touched the trigger as I was putting it in my pocket, and it went off."

Kettley, giving evidence, denied that on the occasion Miss West had spoken of he had turned on the gas to commit suicide or so that the girl should die. He denied that he had threatened to shoot her in August.

When they were in the room at the hotel they were talking, kissing and smoking. When he was going he picked up the revolver and was putting it into his pocket when it went off. He had no intention of shooting the girl.

APOLOGY FROM DOCK

Solicitor who "Let His Profession Down"

Edgar Yates Harrison (42), solicitor, sentenced at Manchester Assizes to-day to 18 months in the second division for fraudulent conversion, expressed "humble contrition to the members of his profession for having let it down."

He pleaded guilty to having fraudulentyl converted to his own use £325, part of the proceeds of a sum received following the settlement of an action at Manchester Assizes a year ago.

Mr. H. Rhodes, prosecuting, said that one firm did not receive £225 from Harrison after the settlement of the case, and another party did not get £100.

Detective-inspector Airey said that Harrison was married in 1929, and had two children. He served in the Army as a lieutenant from 1914 until 1919, and was discharged as medically unfit.

In 1920 he was admitted a solicitor, and on the death of his father four years later, he too kover a practice, which at that time was successful. In 1931 he got into financial difficulties, and he was adjudicated bankrupt in July last.

Mr Kenneth Chambers, for Harrison, said that he had been a victim of his own foolish, unpractical nature.

The Judge said that Harrison had lost his position, his honour and his future.

FALL FROM WINDOW

Suicide of Leeds Man who Had Been Ill in Bed

A verdict of "Suicide while temporarily insane" was recorded at the Leeds inquest to-day on Arthur Partington (57), unemployed cart driver, of Chelmsford Street, who was found yesterday morning lying on the pavement outside his home.

His sister, Harriet Ann Nelson, said he [illegible]

THE NEW KING, FRIEND OF BOYS

YORKSHIRE CAMPERS' MEMORIES

"A GRAND FELLOW," SAYS MILLHAND

Holidays Under Canvas at Southwold and Romney

The new King has made contact with youth of all classes at his camps for public schoolboys and boys from working class homes at Southwold and Romney.

Many Yorkshire young men have happy memories of the Duke of York as a fellow camper, and one Bradford millhand who attended the camp summed up his impressions of the new King to-day in the words, "He is a grand fellow and an active sportsman." He added, "I wish him all the luck in the world."

THE Proclamation of the new King will have a special significance for old boys of Leeds Grammar School who attended his camp at Southwold.

Since the camp was started some years ago with the object of getting public schoolboys to make the acquaintance of boys from working class homes, the Grammar School has sent at least two boys every year. The brightest feature of the week's holiday is a visit by the Duke of York.

Boys who were entering on their last term at the school went to the camp. Many are now at universities, or have started careers.

Young men who have attended the camps and who are still living in Leeds told a "Yorkshire Evening Post" reporter some interesting stories of life at the camp whenever a Royal visit was paid.

Swimming with Duke

Mr. Robert Thornton, son of Mr. Thomas Thornton, Town Clerk for Leeds, stayed at Southwold in 1932 and was one of the campers who went for a swim with the duke in the sea.

"His visit was quite informal," said Mr. Thornton. "The day's routine was adhered to, and the Duke spent the greater part of the day going round the place, chatting with the boys. We organised sports, had a sing-song, and in the evening he was the chief guest at our concert."

Mr. Ronald Naylor, of Headingley Avenue, stayed at the camp in 1933, when the Duke paid his customary visit and stayed the night.

"He went for an evening swim in the sea soon after his arrival," he said. "He breakfasted with the party in the dining-tent, and took part in the sports in the afternoon.

At Camp Concert

"When the news reel vans arrived he brought out his own cine camera and took many yards of action pictures. He enjoyed the concert, and joined in the singing. Our favourite chorus that year was 'Under the Spreading Chestnut Tree,' accompanied by gesticulations. We had been rehearsing, and the Duke of York had to watch the party very closely to keep in unison with the arm waving part of the performance.

"When he joined the bathing party in the evening, an old fisherman appeared on the scene, attired in a uniform of blue and white stripes. At the time we thought the sailor had brought out an old treasure worn by one of his ancestors. Later in the

James Moran

evening the camp entertainment officer told the Duke and the campers that he made it himself.

"Before he left the Duke presented medals—large biscuits—to the chief crockery breakers and the star performers at the concert."

Boys from Mills

Ten boys employed by Messrs. George Garnett and Sons, Ltd., worsted manufacturers, of Valley Mills, Apperley Bridge, Bradford, have attended the camps.

Ronnie Cawood, a clerk at the mills, and Joe Hartley, another employee, were at Southwold in 1933. In conversation to-day Mr. Cawood said that although he had not met the Duke personally, he had had plenty of opportunity of noticing the manner in which he threw aside all formality and joined in the ordinary camp life.

"He took part in everything that was going on," said Mr. Cawood, to-day, "and went swimming with us twice a day. He slept in a tent just as we did; had the same meals, and dined with us in a big marquee. Everybody agreed that he was a jolly good fellow and an ideal camper."

Other boys from the firm who have been at camp with the Duke are Sydney Carlisle and Harry Holdsworth (last year); Norman Cawood and Ira Hullas; Frank Waddington and Jack Driver, and Roy Grimshaw and Stanley Webb (both of whom are now dead).

When the Duke and Duchess visited Valley Mills in 1928 the Duke recognised Roy Grimshaw and said, "I think I have seen you at camp." When he was informed that that was so he had a short conversation with Grimshaw.

The interest of Messrs. Garnett's staff in the Duke was deepened on the occasion of his marriage to the Duchess, for among those attending the ceremony in London was Frank Waddington, who was one of the first of the boys from industry to have the advantage of a holiday in the Duke's camp.

A Sociable Man

James Moran, aged 17, of Arcadia Street, Bradford, a millhand, with whom the Duke of York chatted at the Southwold camp, just over a year ago, also gave some side-lights on the character of the Duke.

"He is a fine fellow, and one of the most sociable men I have ever met," said James.

When the Duke visited the camp, he stopped James and asked him if it was true that he was the smallest boy in the camp. This was the prelude to an informal chat lasting 15 minutes.

The Duke asked the lad what was his work, if he liked his job, and what he thought of the camp.

One day, said James, the Duke was rudely awakened by the strains of a bagpipe played by a Scots boy who had just begun to learn to play. He took the joke in good part and immediately went swimming with the boys.

"He is a strong and excellent swimmer, and easily outstripped the best of us," said James.

A Broken Rule

During a meal the Duke unwittingly broke a strict rule. He gave the boys permission to smoke in the big marquee. Smoking was against the regulations, but the boys immediately accepted the Duke's invitation, and regulations were waived that day.

The boys at the camp were much impressed by the Duke's sporting abilities. James says he beat all comers at carrying weights.

"He is a grand fellow and an active sportsman, and I wish him all the luck in the world," concluded James.

STOP PRESS

(SEE ALSO PAGE ONE)

Broadcasting: Page 8

DAIL AND KING.

Mr. de Valera said in Dail to-day new Bills would not sever Commonwealth connection.

Mr. de Valera said legal and constitutional position remained unchanged. He was simply bringing constitution into line with actual facts of situation.

He had already informed Great Britain of what he proposed to do. What was now being done was matter of purely internal concern and had no connection whatever with other States of Commonwealth.

Connection with Britain would be maintained by co-operation and regularised by law so long as they continued in association at all.

KING EDWARD'S 'PLANE.

King Edward's 'plane has left Hendon aerodrome.

FOREIGN EXCHANGES.

Close N. York 4.90 5-8, Geneva 21.34¼, Brussels 28.99¼ (others same).

LEEDS UNITED CHANGE.

Thomson ill; J. Kelly will play inside-right to-morrow.

NEWMARKET SALES

Miss Paget Disposes of a Few Disappointing Horses

Miss Dorothy Paget sent a batch of horses in training to the Newmarket December Sales to-day. They were sold to make room for yearlings. They did not fetch big prices.

Melting Point, a three-years-old colt by Solario—Flux, who cost 2,000 guineas as a yearling, went to the British Bloodstock Agency for only 180 guineas. Ulvaro, a three-years-old gelding by Beresford—Ulva Ferry, for whom Miss Paget paid 1,500 guineas, was bought by Mr. Bird for 73 guineas.

There was some competition for the speedy four-year-old colt, Radamedes, by Diomedes—Radia. Mr. Ryan may have got a bargain in buying him for 470 guineas.

The two-year-old colt, Movieman, who has shown good form both in Ireland and England, did not seem dear to Mr. Arnold at 710 guineas. He was sent up by the Bedford House stables.

CARLISLE PROSPECTS

The Clerk of the Course at Carlisle states that the going there is good. Only a very heavy fall of snow can prevent racing from taking place there to-morrow.

OFFICIAL SCRATCHINGS

Milburn Hurdle, Sandown Park—Fairland. Mapperley 'Chase, Nottingham, and Pond 'Chase, Sandown Park—Dark Ravine. Carlisle engagement—Bayless. All engagements under the Rules of Racing in Mr. H. Blundell's name—Star of Light. All engagements—Golden Martlet.

BRADFORD SNOOKER

DAVIS v. LINDRUM

RANK OUTSIDERS SUCCESSFUL

ZAG AND BLUE BANNER[illegible]

Punch Also Springs a Surprise

From our own correspondent

SANDOWN PARK, Frid[illegible]

It was gratifying after so many dull [illegible] to find the weather in pleasant mood [illegible] Sandown Park to-day.

The going was in excellent condition.

Punch finished with a lot of dash to [illegible] the Three-Year-Old Hurdle Race. [illegible] matter of fact he had a little in hand [illegible] dispose of Lost Scent from the last obst[illegible]. There could be no excuse for the failure [illegible] Incendiaire and Tuscus, both of whom [illegible] well "there" two hurdles from home, [illegible] failed to stay.

Major Prior-Palmer did well to win [illegible] Effingham Handicap Steeple Chase on [illegible] own horse, Zag. The race was a tale of [illegible]. Only Zag finished, and as he went by [illegible] post his bridle was hanging under his [illegible]. The rider had to hold his reins high [illegible] order to keep the bit in Zag's m[illegible]. Major Prior-Palmer was cheered for his [illegible] horsemanship.

M. Redmond could not ride Pretty C[illegible] in the Long Ditton Selling Hurdle bec[illegible] of his fall with Great Bear in the pre[illegible] race. Ingham was substituted. And [illegible] victory pleased his many supporters, ju[illegible] by the cheering which greeted his win. [illegible] was joint favourite with Repondant. [illegible] had threatened in the words of an onlo[illegible] "to walk it" two hurdles from home, bu[illegible] had little speed from the last jump.

Silver Linnet was dashed at the last [illegible] in the Ewell Handicap Steeple Chase, [illegible] he was so tired that he fell and lay [illegible] five minutes completely winded. He [illegible] staggered to his feet, and walked off [illegible] lit. Blue Banner II brought off an [illegible]pected success. He was the outsider of [illegible] six runners, and his victory enabled [illegible] layers to "scoop the pool."

Santa Klaus fell after going half a [illegible] and the other five runners came to the [illegible] fence with no more than a length bet[illegible] them. Delaneige jumped finely, but ha[illegible] finishing speed.

1. 0—THREE-YEAR-OLD HURDLE (2m. and [illegible]) of 150 sovs.

10 7 PUNCH (Mr. Bowcher) ......Mr. O. B[illegible]
10 7 LOST SCENT (Mr. S. Wootton) ...[illegible]
11 3 INCENDIAIRE (Lady M. Herbert) [illegible]
[illegible]

Off at 1.1. Winner trained by Taber. [illegible]

1.30—EFFINGHAM SELLING HANDICAP STEEPLE CHASE (2m. and about 25yds.) of 150 sovs.

11 2 ZAG, 11 (Major O. Prior-Palmer) [illegible]
[illegible]

Off at 1.31. Winner trained Privately. [illegible]

There was no bid for the winner.

2. 0—LONG DITTON SELLING HURDLE (2m[illegible]) 150 sovs.

12 1 AND HOW, 7 (Major Evans) T. F. [illegible]
[illegible]

Off at 2.2. Winner trained by Taber. [illegible]

The winner was bought in for 200 guineas.

2.30—EWELL HANDICAP STEEPLE CHASE (2m. and about 125yds.) of 250 sovs.

11 2 BLUE BANNER II, 6 (Mr. L. [illegible])
10 8 DEMINKOFF, 7 (Lord Portal) [illegible]
[illegible]

3. 0—ANNUAL HANDICAP HURDLE [illegible]

12 7 VICTOR NORMAN, [illegible]
11 7 LE PETIT PIERROT, 4 (Mr. [illegible])
10 6 SILVER POINT, 6 (Mr. [illegible])
[illegible]

3.30—AMATEUR RIDERS' HANDICAP STEEPLE CHASE [illegible]

12 7 TIMBER, 7 (Mr. M. [illegible])
12 11 FLYING MINUTES, [illegible]
10 5 PIXTON, [illegible]
[illegible]

EYES OF THE WORLD

The stride was a little slower than on his famous walk to freedom, but there was still a familiar twinkling smile and warm handshake at the ready for those who lined up to greet him.

At Leeds Civic Hall the city's dignitaries – including those who had opposed the naming of Mandela Gardens after him in 1983 – now welcomed Nelson Mandela as one of the world's great statesmen.

The man who more than any other had ensured there was no bloodbath when apartheid was abolished and power changed hands in South Africa was in Leeds for a number of reasons. He was to receive the Freedom of the City. He was to formally open Millennium Square. He was to re-dedicate Mandela Gardens, named after him as a gesture of support as he spent his sixteenth year in prison on Robben Island.

He was also here in recognition of the hundreds of ordinary people of the city who had taken action to isolate apartheid South Africa, bring about the downfall of its government and hasten the introduction of democracy.

The Leeds Anti-Apartheid group was one of the many across Britain and around the world that used collective power to help destroy the system of racial segregation. Members operated in trades unions, schools and universities. They marched and demonstrated, lobbied politicians, raised funds. They organised boycotts of banks and other businesses with trade links that had helped prop up the apartheid regime.

And many of them were there in the 5,000-strong crowd that April day in 2001 when Mr Mandela took to the stage in Millennium Square alongside his fellow countryman Lucas Radebe, the captain of Leeds United. Even his momentary confusion of Liverpool for Leeds was forgiven as he thanked the city for its backing.

"Apartheid was seen to diminish the dignity of all humankind," the *YEP* reported him saying. "The people of the city of Leeds were no exception. We remember them for their outstanding and unstinting support."

As he danced to one of the performances from South African singing group Ladysmith Black

Right: The crowds in front of the Civic Hall welcome Nelson Mandela to Leeds.

Opposite: The great statesman takes to the stage in Millennium Square, April 30, 2001.

Thousands gather for the formal unveiling of City Square, with the Black Prince statue at its centre, 1903.

Mambazo, his beaming smile was mirrored in the faces of the thousands of Loiners looking on.

When it comes to staging big events, Leeds comes into its own. And the *Yorkshire Evening Post*'s journalists and photographers have been on the spot through the years to record every moment for posterity.

One of the grandest came in 1903 with the official opening of City Square and the unveiling of the statue of the Black Prince at its centre.

At the time, major cities were displaying their wealth, power and civic pride through sculptures, of which the equestrian statue was considered the most potent.

A statue of Edward Woodstock, who had been dubbed the Black Prince, was duly commissioned by industrialist and Lord Mayor Colonel Thomas Walter Harding.

Although the royal – famous for his battles with the French in the 14th century – had no obvious association with Leeds, it was felt that no local figure in history was quite heroic enough for the site. The Black Prince was chosen as a symbol of chivalry, good government, patronage of the arts and education, encouragement of industry, and democratic values.

Cast in bronze in Antwerp in Belgium, as it was too large for a foundry in Britain, the statue was brought to the city via barge. Legend has it that when Harding learned the monument was being transported facing backwards he ordered the boat to be turned around, so that the Black

Winston Churchill addresses crowds outside Leeds Town Hall, watched by Lord Mayor Hyman Morris, May 16, 1942.

Prince would enter his new home facing the right way.

Some six decades before Nelson Mandela's visit, Winston Churchill had stood in front of the town hall to deliver a trademark rousing speech which galvanised the war effort.

A crowd of 25,000 were there in May 1942 to get a glimpse of the Prime Minister in the flesh, despite the city being given just two hours' notice of his visit. Audrey Brechner was one of them, later telling the *YEP* her memories of the occasion. Her grandfather was Hyman Morris, the Lord Mayor at the time who was pictured alongside the premier.

"I was only 11 at the time but I have very clear memories of it," she recalled. "Churchill gave my grandfather a cigar. I don't know what he did with it but he never smoked it. I do remember it and how excited we were, and how thrilled my grandfather was because it was a great honour.

"I have got Churchill's autograph somewhere. When he went to the Civic Hall there was an official book all the dignitaries signed. My autograph book was put next to it so I got a lot of signatures as well."

Her grandfather, the first Jewish Lord Mayor of Leeds, also welcomed French leader Charles de Gaulle and the Princess Royal to the city during his term in office.

Sir Winston and Lady Churchill leave Leeds Civic Hall, June 17, 1945. Churchill's huge popularity in the immediate post-war period can be seen in the size of the crowds that have turned out to greet them.

Crowds of well over 100,000 gathered each summer for Children's Day at Roundhay Park.

In a typically stirring speech, Churchill told the city that day: "In the height of the second great war, it is a great pleasure to come to Leeds and bring to the citizens a word of thanks and encouragement in all the work they are doing to promote the common cause of many nations and in many lands.

"We have reached a period in the war when it would be premature to say that we have topped the ridge, but now we see the ridge ahead.

"We shall go forward together. The road upwards is stony. There are upon our journey dark and dangerous valleys through which we have to make and fight our way. But it is sure and certain that if we persevere – and we shall persevere – we shall come through these dark and dangerous valleys into a sunlight broader and more genial and more lasting than mankind has ever known."

Months after the war ended, Winston was back. This time it was as part of a whistle-stop election tour and tens of thousands waited up to three hours to see him. The *YEP* reported that he spoke for just 10 minutes but the crowd hung on his every word. And, as Churchill descended the Civic Hall steps, he turned to give his special Victory salute to patients who had been moved to vantage points in the Infirmary's Brotherton Wing so they could have a bird's-eye view of the scene below.

After Winston and his wife, Clementine, got in to their car the crowd streamed across the grass to the Portland Crescent side of the Civic Hall to wave farewell but police were unable to hold the people back and mounted officers had to clear a way for the limousine.

Children's Day Queen Diane Newton waves to the crowds at Roundhay Park, July 1960.

However, the crowd still wanted to be close to the Churchills and it was left to officials on the car's running board to push people out of danger as the vehicle turned in to Great George Street on its way out of the city. In October 1953, having been returned to 10 Downing Street, the Prime Minister was granted the freedom of the City of Leeds.

Seven years before that, the *YEP* had celebrated the return of another old favourite. The outbreak of war had called a halt to Children's Day, the annual celebration of the city's youngest citizens. Its resumption on July 6, 1946 was something of a special occasion for the city and the paper devoted several pages to the event, including a full page of pictures.

An accompanying editorial said: "The revival of Children's Day can be reckoned among the more cheering efforts of recovery after the war. An event which engages the eager interest of 70,000 to 80,000 children and their parents over a period of years cannot fail to have a progressive effect on the public attitude toward all forms of service to the young."

Children's Day came about after members of the Leeds Poor Children's Holiday Camp Association suggested it as a novel way of raising funds to send some of the city's neediest youngsters on short breaks.

It was the brainchild of Archie Gordon, the headteacher of Lower Wortley Council School. He proposed a mass carnival, followed by sporting events, fancy dress and gymnastics. It was hoped such an event would also encourage more children to take part in sports and other outdoor activities. Beginning in 1922, Children's Day was typically held on the first Saturday of July.

At its height, the event attracted up to 150,000 people who packed into Roundhay Park. Huge crowds gathered on Hill 60 to watch the mass displays of everything from physical fitness to country dancing and then made their way down to the arena for the main event of the afternoon: the entrance of the royal procession and the crowning of the Children's Day Queen.

Typical events included a Bonny Baby competition, a fancy dress parade on specially decorated floats and a Healthy Children's section, with winners receiving a silver spoon.

"Once we had all been selected – Queen, attendants, Crown bearer and page boys – we attended Schofield's store for dress and costume fitting," said Diane Parker, then Diane Newton, who was Queen for a day in 1960.

"Each year the dresses were different but the crown and cloak were kept in the Civic Hall and brought out each year. Shortly before the day itself we attended the *Yorkshire Evening Post* for studio photographs which were later presented to us in an album. On the day we were collected from our homes by car. We were taken to the Town Hall where we met a lady oil baron who had travelled from America just to see Children's Day as she had heard so much about it.

"From the Town Hall we travelled along the streets which were lined with people all the way to the Mansion House in Roundhay Park. Activities went on in the park all day long but we arrived just before lunch which we took in the Mansion House and then came the crowning ceremony.

"Along with my attendants, Crown bearer and ushers we entered the arena to the music of Queen for a Day. We walked around the arena to a dais in the middle where the ceremony took place. I don't recall being nervous but I did have my speech – which I had written myself with the help of my English teacher – pinned to the back of my bouquet."

In 1949 the city staged two Children's Days, the second on July 27 marking the visit of Princess Elizabeth to Leeds. Sheila Stone, then Sheila Hughes, was a 15-year-old pupil at Cross Flatts School in Beeston and later recalled the excitement of being a maid of honour.

"It was such a fabulous day, not just for the children but for everyone involved. Crowds used to be in their thousands. All of Hill 60 at Roundhay Park was just packed with people watching all the events."

In spite of its success, Children's Day came to an end in 1963 following a series of wet summers which saw numbers drop dramatically.

"Children's Day had such a good atmosphere, it was a real shame when it ended because it just made everyone so happy," said Sheila. "Children looked forward to it every year and the teachers from all the schools used to put so much effort in to make it all work."

One annual event that's still going strong today is the Leeds West Indian Carnival. It was the brainchild of Arthur France, who arrived in the city from the Caribbean island of St Kitts in 1957.

As a cure for homesickness, he decided to gather some friends together to plan a Caribbean-style carnival and the first took place in 1967 – three years before the Notting Hill version in London. Mr France, who was closely aided by Ian Charles, a Trinidadian who has also remained heavily involved down the years, even bought and plucked a dozen chickens to help make costumes. Nearly half a century later, the event attracts up to 150,000 and is estimated to bring in as much as £10m to the local economy.

In 1988 the Carnival celebrated its 21st birthday in style, with the *YEP* marking the occasion with a full page of coverage under the headline "Carnival's happy 21st, birthday fun all the way for 40,000 revellers".

Police Superintendent Gerry Ingham stated: "Everyone had a good day and I thank the

Above: Eye-catching costumes such as this one worn by Verona Brown in 2013 are a feature of the Leeds West Indian Carnival.

Left: Arthur France came up with the idea for the carnival as a cure for his homesickness.

Opposite: Crowds line the Headrow at the start at the first stage of the Tour de France, as Mark Cavendish leads the cyclists down the Headrow, July 6, 2014.

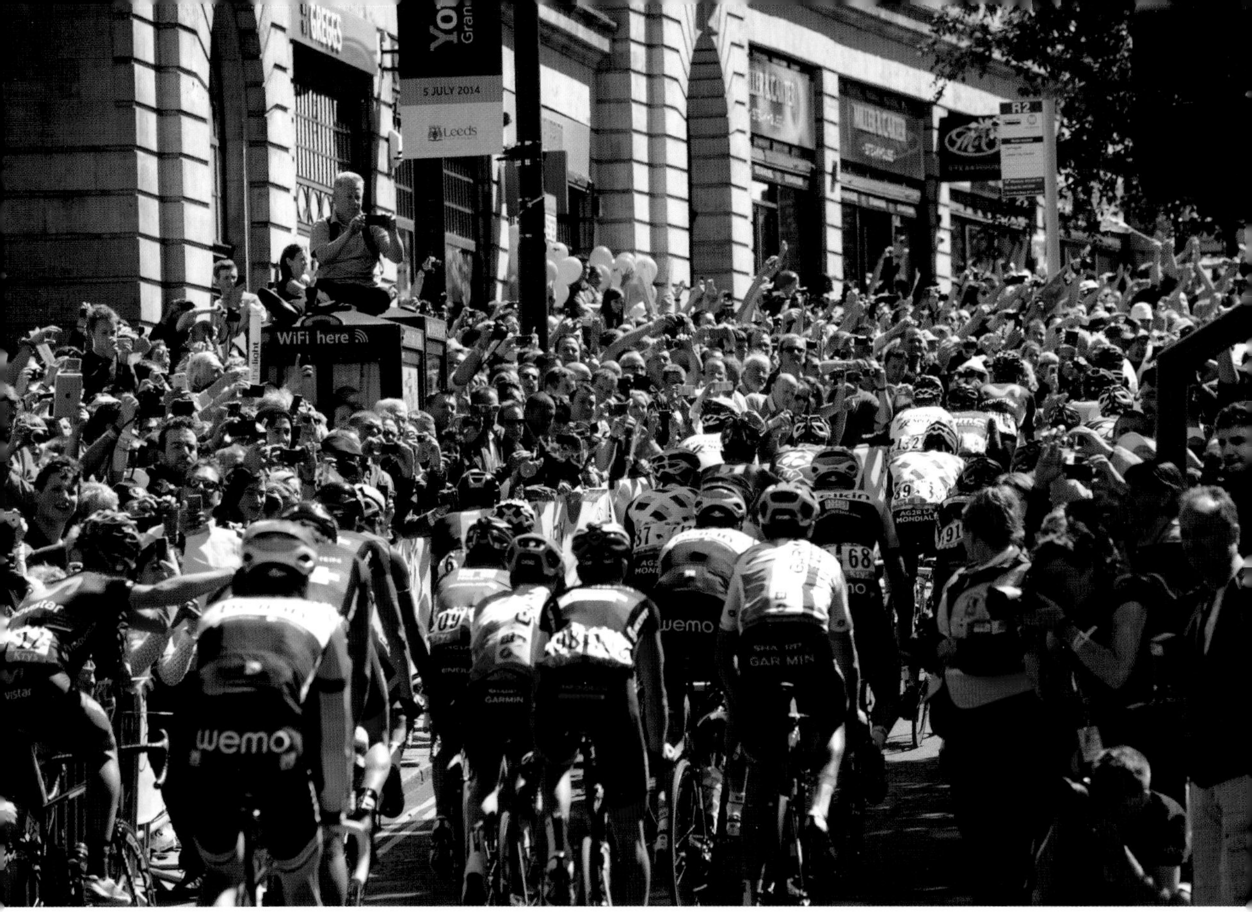
5 JULY 2014
Leeds
WiFi here
wemo
GARMIN

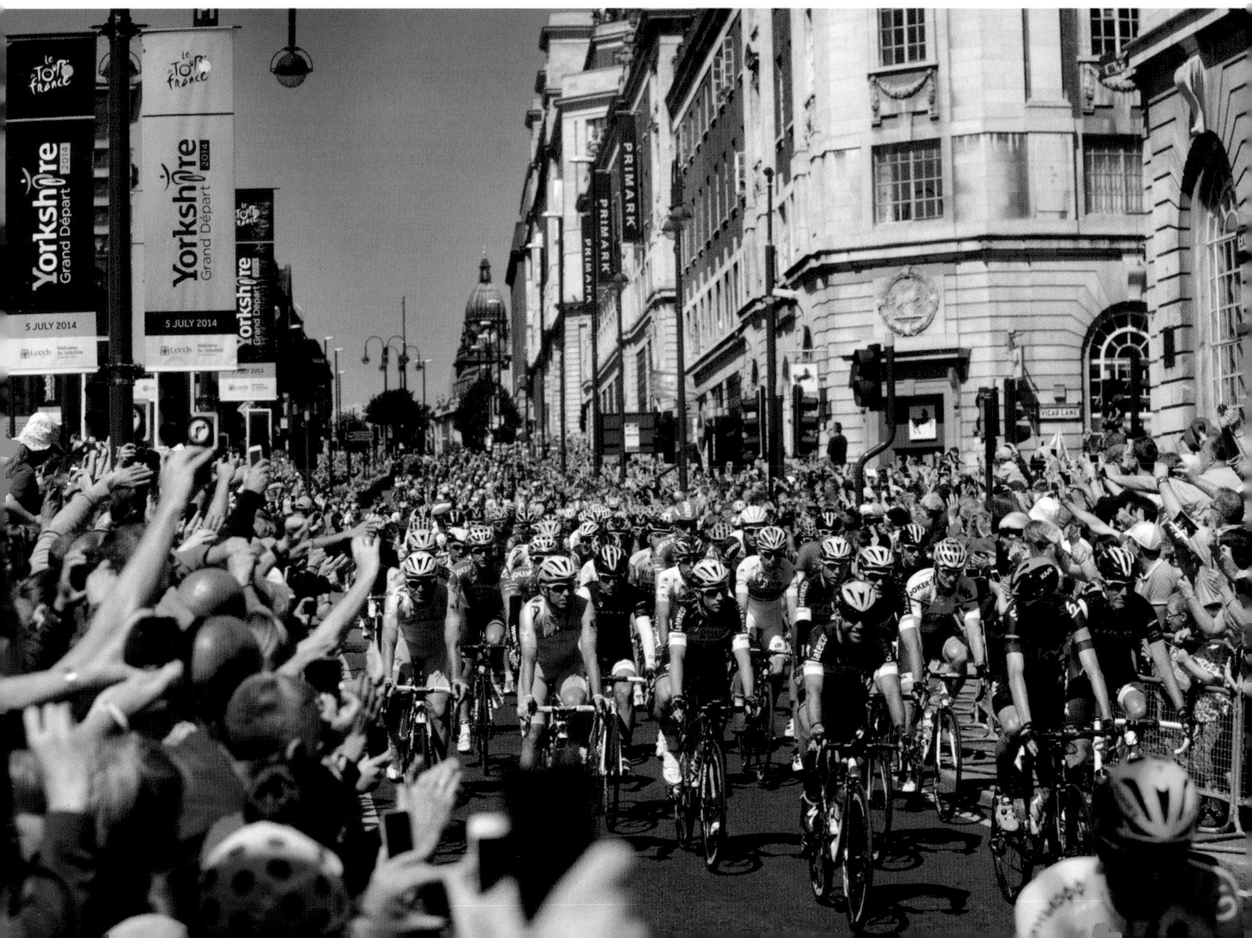
le Tour de France
Yorkshire
Grand Départ 2014
5 JULY 2014
Leeds
PRIMARK

Leeds West Indian Carnival in full swing, August 25, 1980.

organisers and the people as a whole for making it a happy and successful event with no incidents, no arrests and no trouble."

Gloria Pemberton, who took part in the first Carnival and dressed for the anniversary as a Red Indian, leading a troupe of about 150 in similar costume, was quoted as saying: "I think the atmosphere of carnival itself is very much the same as it was all those years ago but I think more people are at this one. It is always a very happy occasion."

Photographs included the obligatory friendly policeman and a shot featuring a costume made by the Palace Youth Centre, which picked out the faces of Winnie and Nelson Mandela in sequins on butterfly wings.

Two years later, the event was rocked by violence with one man being fatally stabbed and two others dying from gunshot wounds, one accidentally from a ricochet and the other in what was believed to be cold blooded murder.

Chapel Allerton councillor Garth Frankland told the *YEP* the deaths "were not directly linked to the carnival" as the parade was over by the time they occurred.

However, they cast a dark shadow over that year's Carnival, one which was thankfully lifted over subsequent years.

For its 30th anniversary in 1997, the *YEP* produced a celebratory 24-page supplement which included an interview with Arthur France, whose dedication to the Leeds Caribbean community had been recognised earlier that year in the shape of an MBE.

The three-day event traditionally climaxes in a carnival procession on Bank Holiday Monday through the streets of Chapeltown and Harehills. There is a Carnival Queen and, since 2008, a Carnival King.

That year, the report in the *YEP* read: "As the delicious smells of sizzling jerk chicken and spicy goat curry wafted through the air – and as the rum flowed – an array of reggae-blasting floats prepared the eager crowd for a procession to remember. And memorable it was.

"A magical menagerie of fantastic feathered creations, saucy, sequin-encrusted costumes, booty-shaking dancers, giant purple butterfly-like creatures and soaring magenta and orange birds, it was a feast for the eyes and the soul."

The eyes of the world were once again on Leeds in 2014 when the city secured the staging of the Grand Départ – the traditional start of one of the planet's biggest annual sporting events.

The 101st Tour de France came to Yorkshire for three magical days that July. But preparations at the *YEP* had begun the previous year, with a journalist specially appointed to cover the build-up.

The main event began on Thursday, July 3 when the cyclists made their way from Millennium Square to the First Direct Arena, where they were given a warm Leeds welcome as they were presented to the packed venue. That Saturday morning, tens of thousands of people abandoned their weekend lie-in to pack the city centre for the departure of the riders from outside Leeds Town Hall.

There was then an official royal send-off as the Duke and Duchess of Cambridge were joined by Prince William to start the race proper at Harewood House. And for every one of the next 118 miles of the first stage, the Tour was royally supported.

All in all, more than two million people lined the route between Leeds and Harrogate or crowded into fan parks, with 230,000 on the streets in Leeds alone. Tour director Christian Prudhomme later hailed a weekend which was "beyond his wildest imagination".

"I can see the Tour in their hearts, and in their eyes," he said. "For that, I say thank you to everyone in Yorkshire who has made this Grand Départ so very, very special.

"When you said you would deliver the grandest Grand Départ it was the truth, you have raised the bar for all future hosts of the Tour de France."

As well as being a grand day out for Leeds, the start of the Tour de France was found to have generated millions of pounds for the local economy, inspired an estimated 5,000 people in Yorkshire to take up cycling and spawned a cycle race for the region, the Tour de Yorkshire. With a global television audience of some three billion, it was expected to provide a significant boost to the city's tourist trade too.

There was one major event, however, that Leeds missed out on. In May 1972 the *YEP* reported that two delegations from Leeds Corporation were to fly out to visit 10 countries in Africa and 13 in the Caribbean to gather support for a Leeds bid to host the 1978 Commonwealth Games.

The paper reported that the cost of the trips had stirred considerable controversy within the council, and Labour leader Albert King was forced to defend them.

"In no sense could the visits be termed a safari," he said. "They would each last about two weeks, involve thousands of miles of travel and between 10 and 12 presentations. There will certainly be no time for beanfeasts."

In the end it was all for nought. The first round of voting for the right to host the Games ended in just 10 votes for Leeds and 36 in favour of Edmonton in Canada, where they duly took place.

NORMAN HUNTER
FRANKIE GRAY
TERRY YORATH
DAVID STEWART
ALLAN
MICK JONES
BILLY BREMNE
EDDIE GRAY

MARCHING ON TOGETHER

"I would like to read a letter which I've written to the *Yorkshire Evening Post* today so that we have a clear statement for all the supporters." So began one of the most dramatic press conferences ever to take place at Elland Road.

Chairman Peter Ridsdale announced that Leeds United's failure to qualify for the Champions League for a second successive season meant the club had no option but to sell star defender Jonathan Woodgate. Alongside him before the cameras on that dark day in January 2003 was manager Terry Venables, who sat stony faced as Ridsdale spelled out the situation. The club's debts had spiralled to almost £80m and, despite the words of reassurance, there was little doubt that Leeds were in crisis.

Woodgate's departure, coming just a day after the sale of striker Robbie Fowler, was the latest in a list of high-profile exits that had begun the previous summer with skipper Rio Ferdinand joining Manchester United. He was swiftly followed out of the door by Robbie Keane, Lee Bowyer and Olivier Dacourt. The team that two years earlier had been one game away from the Champions League final, having brushed aside Roma, Lazio and Deportivo La Coruna on the way, was quickly being dismantled.

"Should we have spent so heavily in the past?" Peter Ridsdale now mused. "Probably not. But we lived the dream. We enjoyed the dream. Only by making the right decisions today can we rekindle the dream once again in the future." But just two months later Ridsdale himself would exit stage left and the following season United slipped through the Premier League trapdoor. 'Doing a Leeds' promptly entered the English footballing vernacular, a shorthand warning to any club of the dangers of extravagant spending.

Peter Ridsdale and Terry Venables announce the sale of Jonathan Woodgate at an extraordinary press conference on January 31, 2003.

Opposite: **Super Leeds show the League trophy to the Kop before Billy Bremner's testimonial game against Sunderland, May 6, 1974.**

But then it's fair to say few football clubs have experienced such dramatic highs and lows as Leeds United – and the *YEP* has been there to cover every twist and turn in the story. From the club's humble beginnings through the title triumphs of Don Revie and Howard Wilkinson and on to the present day rollercoaster, just about the only thing that has stayed constant has been United's knack for making headlines on both the front and back pages.

Fans have become used to expecting the unexpected and it's perhaps little wonder, given that United owe their very existence to controversy. The club emerged from the ashes of Leeds City, who were expelled from the Football League amid allegations over illegal payments to guest players during the First World War.

'Leeds City revelations: The full story' screamed the front page of the *Yorkshire Evening Post* on October 14, 1919, with the scandal sparking a slanging match in the paper between former directors J Connor and GH Cripps, each blaming the other for the club's demise.

The Lord Mayor of Leeds, Joseph Henry, then waded in, telling supporters not to bear any hard feelings against the pair and insisting they had "only broken the commandment that said 'Thou shalt not be found out'".

"It was nothing less than a scandal," the *YEP* reported him saying, "that the feelings of the city should have been so entirely ignored by a body of men (the league officials) who acted as autocrats, scarcely hearkening to reason, and swayed by passion, as some of them were, because they were probably interested in some other club which aspired to get into Leeds City's place."

A few days later the Metropole Hotel was the scene of a remarkable auction as everything from City's players to their nets and physiotherapy equipment was sold off to representatives of more than 30 rival clubs. On October 25 of the same year there was some better news. The *YEP* revealed that "negotiations were completed this afternoon between the committee of the new Leeds United Association Club and the Yorkshire Amateurs FC, by which the two clubs will share the tenancy of the Elland Road ground and will have use of the enclosure on alternate Saturdays".

The report added: "The rapid progress made in the organisation of Leeds United will be very pleasing to all followers of Association (football) in the Leeds district, for a continuation of the game is now assured."

A ground having been secured, the newly-formed Leeds United were duly

John Charles shakes hands with Sunderland captain Don Revie in his final game for Leeds before his transfer to Juventus, April 1957.

Leeds United, 1956-57.
Back row, left to right: Kerfoot, Overfield, Ripley, Wood, Forrest, Hair.
Front row: Meek, Charlton, Charles, Dunn, Brook.

elected to the Football League in 1920, starting life in Division Two. Eventually promoted to the top flight, they had three successive seasons there before ending the decade with relegation.

In the 1930s, having bounced back into the top tier, they boasted the celebrated half-back line of Willis Edwards, Ernie Hart and Wilf Copping, the original hard man of English football. Then the famous football name of Milburn became synonymous with Leeds as Jack and George partnered each other at full-back.

At the outbreak of war, the league was put on ice. The boardroom, tea rooms and dressing rooms at Elland Road were requisitioned for the purposes of military administration. For a couple of hours each Saturday afternoon, however, the War Office allowed the ground to revert back to its original purpose, with guest players and local youngsters keeping football alive and kicking.

After the war, Leeds were managed by Major Frank Buckley, a well-known footballing figure who can take credit for developing one of the most iconic players to ever sport a United shirt. John Charles had signed for Leeds at the age of 17 after being spotted turning out for Gendros, a local club in his native Swansea.

"I remember the day when the Leeds scout asked my parents if I could go for a trial," he later recalled to the *YEP*. "My mum told him I couldn't because I didn't have a passport!"

Years later the Welshman told how he almost quit Leeds before his career at the club had even properly started. He had been home for a week after sitting on the bench for a United match at Cardiff and decided he was going to give up and head back to Wales. But on the tram to his Leeds digs to collect his belongings, Charles read the paper. It told him he had been picked for United's reserve team against Preston North End. It was at this point the teenager decided that if the club were prepared to show faith in him, the least he could do was stick it out at Elland Road and give it a proper go.

After being given three games at the end of the season by Buckley, Charles then played in every game in the 1949-50 campaign. But it was Buckley's successor, former England international Raich Carter, who made the inspired decision to turn him from a centre-half into a centre-forward. The man dubbed 'The Gentle Giant' on account of his incredible strength but good-natured humility proceeded to score a club record 42 league goals in 39 appearances.

United finished Second Division runners up in the 1955-56 season, securing a ticket back to the top tier after an absence of nine seasons. Having made a promising start to life back at the top which saw them lying second in the table, disaster struck. Fire gutted the main West Stand on September 18, 1956 with the damage estimated at £100,000. Jerseys, footballs, boots and the club's records all went up in flames.

The Lord Mayor of Leeds promptly launched a public appeal to raise £60,000, which was the difference between the insurance payment the club stood to receive and the cost of a new stand. "The prestige of the city is at stake," he said.

When John Charles was linked with Italian giants Juventus in April 1957, having scored 39 goals in just 41 appearances that season, the *YEP* had the inside track on his record-breaking £65,000 transfer. Speaking to reporter Phil Brown by what was excitedly described as "trans-European telephone", Juventus chairman Umberto Agnelli said: "We need Charles badly – and we are determined to get him."

Charles would go on to be worshipped in Turin just as he had been in Leeds. And even though his brief return to United five years later didn't work out, his move back to West Yorkshire to run a pub once his playing days were over proved how big a place his adopted home occupied in his heart.

His funeral at Leeds Parish Church in 2004 saw the likes of Norman Hunter, Peter Lorimer, Allan Clarke, Bobby Collins, Sir Bobby Charlton and Dennis Law come together to bid farewell to a man whose huge talent many of them had seen first hand.

Latter-day stars such as Gordon Strachan, Gary McAllister and Gary Speed also filed into church to pay tribute, while both Elland Road's West Stand and the South Leeds Sports Complex were

Jack Charlton plays the city gent outside one of his two clothes shops in Leeds. He also later operated the souvenir shop at Elland Road.

Opposite: John Charles leads the United team through the fire-blackened ruins of the stand at Elland Road, September 1956.

renamed in his honour. Speed himself would be mourned after his sudden death seven years later.

Charles' departure for Italy may have been considered a hammer blow to Leeds, were it not for the fact that a figure who would go on to play an even bigger role in the United story was ready and waiting in the wings.

With the club struggling in the First Division, manager Bill Lambton had decided to sign Don Revie, a 31-year-old who had pioneered the role of the deep-lying centre-forward while at Manchester City.

Revie was soon appointed captain, and when Jack Taylor resigned as manager in March 1961, a year after United had lost their top-flight status, the board gambled on Revie as player-manager.

With director Harry Reynolds, a self-made millionaire, backing him all the way, the appointment would prove to be an inspired choice as Revie proceeded to transform Leeds from a club without major honours to a dominant force in English football and one of the finest sides in the world.

Talking to the *YEP* after making what the newspaper hailed as a "rapid-fire" start to his new role, Revie said: "I shall do my best with United's difficult situation.

"It offers a real challenge, and there is, I know, a tremendous amount of hard work ahead. One and all have to get down to it at Elland Road. I am very pleased with my contract which gives me full power on selection, transfers in and out, training – all aspects of work necessary to get a good playing staff."

Revie quickly showed himself to be a canny operator. He persuaded Bobby Collins to sign from Everton and the pocket-sized Scot became the midfield linchpin of the early Revie years. His battling qualities helped the club avoid relegation, then win promotion to the First Division in 1964.

One of Collins' fellow countrymen would play an even more important role in United's rise. Billy Bremner, from Stirling, had signed for Leeds in 1959.

Handed his debut at outside-right in a 3-1 win against Chelsea at Stamford Bridge at the age

The Don at his desk at Elland Road in March 1971, plotting more success for 'Super Leeds'.

Opposite:
Leeds United parade through the city after winning the Inter Cities Fairs Cup, September 1968.

of 17 years and 47 days, the *YEP*'s Phil Brown noted that Bremner showed "enthusiasm, guts, intelligence, most accurate use of the ball and unselfishness" despite poor weather conditions.

It was Bremner who would prove integral to Don Revie's masterplan. Named as captain in 1965, he would hold the armband for the next 11 years. In all he played more than 750 times for Leeds between 1960 and 1976, becoming the face of the most successful period in the club's history.

"The club was his life," said Eddie Gray, his former team-mate. "He lived for Leeds United and he was an inspiration. He had a great record of coming up with big goals in big games and it says a lot that Don chose him to replace Bobby Collins as captain. You had big Jack Charlton at Leeds, a World Cup winner. But Billy was the one."

"Any captain worth his salt would give his right arm for Billy Bremner's attributes," another team mate, *YEP* columnist Peter Lorimer, recalled. "Heart, bravery, passion and inspiration – wee Billy had it all, in spades.

"You can imagine kids through the years trying to model themselves on him but Billy wasn't a replica of other players. That's what made him such a fine leader. It all came naturally.

"I lost count of the number of times I saw him limping around on a Friday afternoon and thought 'he's not playing tomorrow', only to see him line up as usual and fly into a tackle in the first minute. His levels of commitment were so high that you had no choice but to follow suit.

"I rowed with him from time to time, the same as every player at Leeds. He'd pull you up for mistakes on the field and he'd tear a strip off you in the dressing room if things were going wrong at half-time.

"All he cared about was the success of the club. We'd argue about something or nothing and then I'd go home and think about what had been said. More often than not you realised he was right.

"He and Revie would tangle from time to time too and whenever they crossed words – maybe after Billy had been caught having a few pints on a night when he shouldn't have been out

drinking – Billy would say to him 'you just judge me on how I play'.

"Then he'd have a stormer on the Saturday and Revie would be there with his arm round him at full-time, saying 'Wee man, you were outstanding'. He never failed to put his money where his mouth was. Having someone like that in the thick of your team was a bit like having an extra player. We were lucky to have two of the best midfielders of our generation at Leeds, Billy and Johnny Giles, and while Johnny was the brains of the operation, Billy was the one who carried you."

With Bremner to the fore, the Revie Revolution was soon getting results. Having implemented a youth policy and switched to an all-white strip in the style of Real Madrid, United began the 1964-5 season back in the top flight, winning the Second Division title without losing a game at Elland Road. Expected to struggle, Leeds instead came within a whisker of winning the title, losing out to a George Best-inspired Manchester United on goal average.

There was more disappointment to come in the 1965 FA Cup Final, Leeds going down 2-1 to Liverpool after extra time, although at least they had the pleasure of knocking out arch rivals Manchester United in a semi-final replay. But soon the silverware started coming. In 1968, Leeds netted their first in the shape of the League Cup thanks to Terry Cooper's goal which was enough to sink Arsenal.

Six months later, Billy Bremner was hoisting the Inter-Cities Fairs Cup after a 1-0 aggregate win over Hungarian side Ferencvaros. United would claim it again three years later with an away goals victory over Juventus when the competition – set up to promote international trade fairs and which later became the Uefa Cup – was played for the final time.

Having come so close the previous year, the 1968-9 season was the one when Leeds finally claimed the First Division title. They did so with a gritty performance at Anfield against title rivals Liverpool, but the occasion wasn't without its share of nail-biting moments.

Bremner told the *YEP* after the game: "The team was unusually nervous when it went out. I

Sniffer and the King. Allan Clarke and Billy Bremner share a joke on the pitch.

***Opposite:* Billy Bremner hoists the FA Cup at Wembley as Peter Lorimer inspects his winner's medal, May 6, 1972. *Inset:* Leeds fans show their colours during the 1970 final.**

have never known them like they were tonight. It was worse than our FA Cup final. I couldn't sleep the night before, and that isn't me. I even got up out of bed at four o'clock in the morning and smoked a cigarette to try and stop thinking about the game. There was such a lot at stake, of course, and it nearly beat us."

Nevertheless, the team whose physical approach had seen them dubbed the "Little West Riding Hoods" had finally joined the elite of British football. The following season, strengthened by the signing of striker Allan Clarke from Leicester, a confident Leeds team eyed a treble of league, European Cup and FA Cup.

However, it wasn't to be – the Whites exiting Europe at the semi final stage to Celtic, finishing second in the league and losing the FA Cup final to Chelsea in a replay. Leeds did claim the FA Charity Shield, however, beating Manchester City at Elland Road.

The 1971-72 season saw the introduction of United's famous pre-match routine, which became as much a hallmark of the rechristened 'Super Leeds' as their football. For the home FA Cup quarter final tie against Spurs, the team emerged for their warm-up with trainer Les Cocker clad in tracksuits bearing the name of their wearer, along with numbered and autographed sock tags that would be handed out to fans at the final whistle.

The *YEP*'s Don Warters reported how Cocker then took the players through a choreographed display of exercises. "Billy Bremner, Johnny Giles and Eddie Gray demonstrating ball control; Peter Lorimer trying out his cannon ball shooting power from the halfway line; Gary Sprake testing his reflexes by throwing the ball against a post and saving the rebounds."

Don Revie told Warters: "Obviously we shall change our routine and it is our intention to let the fans see what individual skills we possess in all departments of the game. In addition, we shall continue to give away the autographed stocking tabs after each game.

"In other words, we hope to make the fans feel as important to us as we hope the team are to them. We have a great team here and we have some fine supporters, too, so anything we can do to forge closer links between the two we shall attempt.

"Supporters are very much a part of any club, and it is important that they feel this. After all,

they are the people who pay us our wages, and I think it is important that they associate themselves with the players. It would be great to see us average between 43,000 and 45,000 each home match, for the more support we get the better chance we have of making Elland Road the finest club stadium in the North and perhaps the country."

It was a barometer of the club's confidence and huge ambition and the following year they became the first to sell replica versions of their famous kit to fans.

May 1972 would mark a golden moment in the club's history. Don Revie and his team travelled down to London for the FA Cup final in confident mood, helped by the superstitious Revie spotting a bride outside a church on the journey down, convincing him that Leeds weren't destined to be bridesmaids once again.

Victory over Bertie Mee's Arsenal duly followed, securing the club's first – and so far only – FA Cup in the competition's centenary year. A tight game saw 'Sniffer' Clarke head powerfully past Geoff Barnett in the 53rd minute. The final whistle should have been the cue for mass celebration, with the result and full reports printed in a special late edition of the *YEP*'s Green Post.

But while a city partied, for United's stars the champagne corks stayed in their bottles (except for one plastic cupful and a quick celebratory swig from the trophy) as they quickly found themselves on a coach bound for a Midlands hotel, and preparation for their title-deciding clash with Wolverhampton Wanderers just two days later.

"I remember the elation and the dressing room afterwards, but then it went very, very flat as

Brian Clough gets a mixed response from the home crowd during a game against Queens Park Rangers, August 21, 1974.

we had to leave," Norman Hunter recalled in the *YEP*. "Instead of the gaffer letting us go out Saturday night and have a few bevvies and get up Sunday and then travel up and loosen up on the Monday, he took us away. The first time we win the FA Cup and we were leaving our wives and the cup, as we were straight up to Wolves, getting ready for the Monday."

"I'll never forget it," added Peter Lorimer, the club's all-time top goal-scorer, of perhaps the flattest winners' party of all time. "We stopped at a service station just outside London on the way to Wolverhampton and 'celebrated', in the loosest sense of the word, with a cup of tea and a sandwich in the cafe. One of the lads joked, 'Great winning the cup, isn't it?' It just about summed up the situation."

Needing just a draw against Wolves to be crowned league champions as well, the season would instead end in crushing disappointment for the Whites. Fatigue and injuries – centre-forward Mick Jones was ruled out while Eddie Gray, Clarke and Jonny Giles were all struggling – played a telling hand as Wolves did Brian Clough and Derby County an almighty favour with a shock 2-1 victory that handed them the title. Three penalty claims were waved away and the *YEP*'s Don Warters noted "if ever a team had cause to feel bitter, United have today".

"The hardest league in the world, then the FA Cup final and then they make you play on the Monday," said Norman Hunter. "We had nobody fit. There was a good reception for us when we came home and I remember going to City Square and the Town Hall and it was packed. But having got done for the league on the Monday, we were a bit flat."

If he felt the same way, Don Revie did a good job of hiding it, telling the *YEP* at the celebrations: "I never thought any of us here would live to see a night like this. I was very close to tears at times and so were some of the players, including Billy and Big Jack."

Twelve months later, United were stunned by underdogs Sunderland in the 1973 FA Cup final, but worse was to come in the European Cup Winners' Cup final later that May. It pitted Leeds against AC Milan of Italy, but it was Greek referee Christos Michas who was the centre of attention thanks to some highly questionable decisions.

Norman Hunter was shown a red card and two convincing penalty appeals were turned down as Revie's side lost 1-0 in Salonika. There were claims that Michas had been bribed and his role was later investigated, with Uefa banning him for life for match-fixing.

Really ref? Bremner makes a point on a heartbreaking night in Paris, May 28, 1975.

Below right: **The YEP's newspaper vendors, with Eric Simpson on the far right, set off for the European Cup Final.**

However, Leeds' pleas for a replay fell on deaf ears and it was the same in 2009 when the Yorkshire MEP Richard Corbett unsuccessfully petitioned for the result to be reversed and United awarded the victory.

The end of an era came in 1974, when Don Revie took over from Sir Alf Ramsey as manager of England, ending a 13-year reign that would go down as the most successful period in the club's history and earn him a statue outside Elland Road, not far from the one of his talismanic captain.

Revie went out on a high, with the team he built beating Liverpool to the First Division title by five points. But few could have predicted where United's board would look for his replacement.

Brian Clough had been one of the Whites' most vocal critics. The previous August he had branded the Leeds players "cheats" and called for the club to be relegated to the Second Division on disciplinary grounds.

Perhaps unsurprisingly, Clough would last just 44 days in the job, with one unnamed member of the Leeds squad telling the *YEP* of "considerable unrest" in the dressing room shortly before his exit.

United captain Billy Bremner pulled no punches after the parting of the ways, telling the paper: "People say you cannot get to know a man in such a short space of time, but seven weeks was long enough for me to get to know Brian Clough."

Leeds players mark the sponsorship deal with the YEP by flicking through copies of a specially mocked-up edition, which would end up proving rather prophetic, August 1991.

Jimmy Armfield came in to pick up the pieces, guiding the remnants of Revie's team to the European Cup final. Yet what should have been the crowning glory of the greatest group of players in the club's history instead became a controversy that still rankles to this day.

The *Yorkshire Evening Post* had sent newspaper sales representative Eric Simpson and a team of his sellers all the way to Paris to cash in on the clash between Leeds United and Bayern Munich. But what followed was another refereeing display which immediately raised questions about the official's impartiality. Bayern won 2-0, but not before referee Michel Kitabdjian had ruled out Peter Lorimer's goal and denied Leeds at least one clear-cut penalty when Franz Beckenbauer tripped Allan Clarke.

"As a team at the end of a great era, Paris was our last chance to claim the European Cup and to put the icing on the cake," Lorimer would tell the *YEP* four decades later. "Don Revie had moved on by then, but the squad was his and the one thing Don wanted was for us to be crowned champions of Europe. We'd won the Fairs Cup in 1968 but the European Cup was the one. To be robbed in the way we were robbed by Bayern Munich was incredibly hard to take.

"I can picture the finish clearly – me catching the ball perfectly on the volley and smashing it into the corner of the net. The first thing I did was look at the referee because I wanted to make sure he'd awarded it. He pointed clearly to the centre circle.

"Then Beckenbauer started having words with Kitabdjian and to our total disbelief, the goal was ruled out. We were an hour into the game and it felt like one kick in the teeth too many. They scored on the break with about 20 minutes to go and everything fell apart after that."

The final whistle saw trouble on the terraces that resulted in Leeds being banned for four years, reduced to two on appeal.

"All I'd say is that I don't believe any of the violence involving our fans was premeditated," said

Lorimer. "It was borne out of utter frustration about the fact that we were getting stiffed – just as we had been during the Cup Winners' Cup final in Greece two years earlier."

United were by now a fading force, and even the tenure of former club greats Allan Clarke, Eddie Gray and Billy Bremner couldn't stop the slide. Relegated to the Second Division in 1982, United endured the best part of a lost decade before Howard Wilkinson took the reins, going on to win promotion back to the top flight in 1990 as Second Division champions.

The revival was sparked by a flurry of key signings by 'Sgt Wilko', not least the £300,000 capture of midfielder Gordon Strachan from Manchester United. The Scot would prove the driving force behind a new era of Leeds success, while the club added Mel Sterland, John Hendrie, Jim Beglin, John McClelland and Mickey Thomas too.

Then there was Vinnie Jones. Signed from Wimbledon, with whom he had lifted the FA Cup, the former hod carrier made an instant impression. Boys across the city copied his famous 'V' haircut, many earning a suspension from school for their trouble. By the time he made his debut against Middlesbrough, the Elland Road crowd were baying for him. Jones later said: "The welcome I got from the Leeds fans on my debut made me feel immortal."

Squeezed out by Gary McAllister when United returned to the First Division, the club nevertheless remained close to his heart. "The only picture I have up on my wall in Hollywood is me in a Leeds kit," Vinnie told the *YEP* years later.

The 1991-92 season saw Leeds with a new shirt sponsor in the shape of the *Yorkshire*

Lee Chapman, Eric Cantona, David Batty and Gary McAllister celebrate clinching the league title at Lee Chapman's home, April 26, 1992.

Above: **Gary Speed and McAllister help Rod Wallace celebrate his equaliser during the 3-2 win over Sheffield United which ensured United's top spot finish.**

Vinnie Jones gets into the Leeds tradition of wearing fancy dress for the last away trip of the season ahead of United's game at Bournemouth in 1990 which would see the Whites seal the Second Division title.

Evening Post. To mark the occasion, the players posed with specially printed copies of the paper at their pre-season photo call.

The headline on the front page of the mocked-up edition read 'United set for glory season'. Happily, we got it exactly right, with Leeds seeing off the challenge of Manchester United to claim the title.

Powered by a dazzling midfield of Strachan, McAllister, David Batty and Gary Speed, along with the goals of Lee Chapman and input from leftfield signing Eric Cantona, United held their nerve by securing 13 points from their final five games to United's four.

Key to United's success was the same close-knit atmosphere Don Revie had nurtured all those years before with his trademark indoor bowls matches. "Our squad was like a little family and Gordon Strachan used to arrange regular dinners for the players and wives," recalled Mel Sterland. "It was his way of keeping the camp happy and making everyone feel valued and included.

"But we didn't talk about the title, not until the last seven or eight games – not until we could see the finishing line."

When that finishing line came it was the cue for an open-topped bus parade through the city as Leeds celebrated claiming the last ever First Division title, the Premier League being launched the following season.

An estimated 150,000 people turned out for the party on May 3, 1992 and Sterland was amazed at what he saw. "I won't ever forget those celebrations. You had people up trees and hanging from lampposts. The streets were packed. Young kids, old men – it felt like the whole city came out to see us that day."

"Memories like these can't be bought," Howard Wilkinson told the *YEP*. "There'll never be another day like this."

The mid-1990s saw the unlikely figure of Ghanaian international Tony Yeboah light up Elland Road with a series of wonder goals which got the Leeds faithful chanting: "Who needs Cantona, when we've got Yeboah?"

Not content with winning the BBC's Goal of the Month in August 1995 for a 98mph sledgehammer of a volley against Liverpool, he then went and scored September's, too. That second goal, against Wimbledon, went on to be named Goal of the Season.

Yet Howard Wilkinson's words of "not seeing another day like this" have so far proved all too prophetic for Leeds, although United did become a major force again towards the end of the decade, first under George Graham and then David O'Leary.

Leadership on the pitch came from South African Lucas Radebe, quickly dubbed 'The Chief'. A firm favourite with fans, his previous club Kaizer Chiefs would go on to inspire the name of one of the city's biggest bands. Homegrown talent such as David Batty and academy stars Harry Kewell, Gary Kelly, Jonathan Woodgate and Alan Smith blossomed alongside high-profile signings including Jimmy Floyd Haselbaink, Mark Viduka and £18m man Rio Ferdinand.

O'Leary steered United to a fourth place finish in the 1998-1999 season and the following year Leeds reached the Uefa Cup semi-final – their first in Europe for 25 years – but lost 4-2 on aggregate to Turkish side Galatasaray. The tie was marred by tragedy when two United fans, Christopher Loftus and Kevin Speight, who had travelled to Istanbul for the first leg, were stabbed to death.

Third place in the Premier League saw Leeds qualify for the Champions League and their run to the semi-finals became famous across Europe. Having held European giants Barcelona and AC Milan to draws in the first group stage, they thrashed Besiktas 6-0 on a memorable night at Elland Road and then beat Lazio in Rome to make it to the knockout stage, despite narrowly losing 3-2 to Real Madrid at the Bernabeu.

"The squad O'Leary built for the 2000-01 season had absolutely no fear," defender Dominic Matteo later remembered in the *YEP*. "I genuinely went to every stadium in the Premiership, every stadium in the Champions League, expecting to win. I wasn't bothered who we played or where we were going – the games were ours to lose. It's a sensational feeling and extremely rare."

Lee Bowyer starred in a quarter-final first leg rout of Deportivo La Coruna that saw him become the first player to receive a 10 out of 10 match rating from the paper. At the time he and teammate Jonathan Woodgate were awaiting a second trial over the assault of student Sarfraz Najeib during a night out in Leeds city centre, the story having been broken by *YEP* crime reporter David Bruce. Bowyer would later be cleared but Woodgate was sentenced to 100 hours' community service for affray.

Chairman Peter Ridsdale insisted the club itself had not been on trial, only for manager David O'Leary to pen a book entitled Leeds United on Trial. The episode provided a distraction the Whites could have done without – and some look back on it as the moment things started to turn sour.

In the Champions League semi-final, Leeds lost out to Valencia but the club continued to spend big in the transfer market, leading to that dramatic press conference a couple of years later. United's financial woes were such that even the exotic fish tank in Ridsdale's office was held up as a sign of the club's recklessness. Having sold many of their star names, the Whites were relegated in May 2004 with debts of more than £100m.

YEP football writer Paul Dews wrote that after the signing of Rio Ferdinand for a then record fee in November 2000, money appeared to be no object. "Senior players were handed extended deals on high wages that could only be sustained if the club reached the highest level and stayed there. Young players without first team appearances were put on a long contract with salaries that few could even dream about and a dangerous culture was created. Rewards were being handed out without achievements in some cases and money was thrown around like confetti."

Little did fans who watched the final day defeat at Chelsea suspect that more than a decade later it would remain their last game in the top division, a 4-1 loss at Bolton two weeks before having confirmed the worst.

YORKSHIRE Evening Post

LEEDS EDITION

UNITED STARS' TRIAL OPENS

Student chased and battered, jury is told

BY ROD HOPKINSON AND MIKE HURST

THREE Leeds United footballers and their friends left a teenage student with serious injuries when they chased and attacked him after they had been drinking into the early hours, a court was told today.

LETTERS 12 TV 26-28 BUSINESS 29-31 CROSSWORD, STARS & WEATHER 32 CLASSIFIED 33-42 SPORT 43-52

Lee Bowyer celebrates his winner against AC Milan with Alan Smith, Dominic Matteo and Olivier Dacourt, September 19, 2000.

The YEP reports the start of the trial of Jonathan Woodgate and Lee Bowyer, February 12, 2001.

Opposite:

Left: David Batty and Dominic Matteo salute fans at the final whistle after losing their Champions League semi-final to Valencia, May 8, 2001.

Right: Jermaine Beckford celebrates scoring the winning goal against Bristol Rovers to secure promotion to the Championship, May 8, 2010.

After losing a Championship play-off final to Watford in 2006, it then got worse with relegation to League One the following season, the *YEP* calling it 'The Darkest Day' as Leeds slumped to the third tier of English football for the first time in their history and swiftly entered administration.

"At some stage in the future, a day of painful reckoning will blend itself into the rich tapestry of Leeds United," wrote the paper's Phil Hay. "For now, however, the suffering is real, and United's relegation is the latest punishment inflicted on a club who appear to be trapped in a downward trajectory."

Leeds would eventually bounce back three seasons later with promotion to the Championship, secured in a dramatic last day win over Bristol Rovers in front of a full house at Elland Road.

The winner came from striker Jermaine Beckford, who earlier in the season had secured a place in fans' hearts forever by netting the goal that knocked Manchester United out of the FA Cup.

Off the field, the ups and downs were just as eventful, with the club's ownership changing hands between former Chelsea chairman Ken Bates, Dubai-based private equity group GFH Capital and then Italian tycoon Massimo Cellino. In 2016, Garry Monk became the seventh manager appointed by the latter in just two years with one, Darko Milanic, lasting less time in the job than even Brian Clough as United searched for a route back to football's top table.

In the near 100 years that the *Yorkshire Evening Post* has been covering the club, one thing has become crystal clear. When it comes to Leeds United, another dramatic twist is usually just around the corner.

Leeds Weekly News 1992
L

BEFORE THEY WERE FAMOUS

The offices of the *Yorkshire Evening Post* have received countless high-profile visitors down the years. Members of the Royal family, the nation's Prime Ministers and any number of famous faces from the worlds of TV, film and sport have all dropped in to tour the premises or be interviewed by the newspaper's team of journalists.

Yet some household names went one step further and actually kick-started their careers at the *YEP*. From bestselling authors and Hollywood legends to kings of comedy and pop and rock stars, they all began their rise to prominence at the paper.

Barbara Taylor Bradford, for instance, who penned blockbusting novel *A Woman of Substance*, was a 15-year-old Armley schoolgirl when she landed a job in the typing pool at the *YEP*, much to the dismay of her parents who wanted her to go to Leeds University.

But soon she was writing her own news stories and leaving them on her boss's desk and, when a couple of them appeared in the newspaper, she was summoned to see the editor.

"He said to me, 'Do you want to be a reporter?' she recalled many years later. "I said to him, 'I don't want to be sir, I'm going to be'. After that he took me under his wing and put me in the newsroom as a junior reporter, much to a great deal of grumbling from all the guys for the simple reason that they had to watch their language."

Before long she was editing the paper's women's pages and a move to Fleet Street followed before she turned her hand to writing bestselling novels.

"I loved my time on the *Yorkshire Evening Post* and it's because of that, along with the way my mother and father brought me up, that I am where I am today," she said. "I loved working on the paper and I love Yorkshire."

On a return visit in 2009, Barbara looked through the *YEP* archives with editor Paul Napier where she found a fashion feature she had written in April 1953.

Among the young Barbara Taylor's colleagues was another famous writer-in-waiting. Born in Hunslet, after leaving school Keith Waterhouse became a clerk in an undertaker's office, a job which would later provide inspiration for his most famous work.

Following National Service in the Royal Air Force, Waterhouse became a reporter on the *YEP*, where you could say his career got off to a flying start.

Barbara Taylor Bradford pictured in Leeds, 1981.

Opposite: **Melanie Brown receives the keys to a new car as her prize for being crowned Miss Leeds Weekly News 1992.**

Leeds writing royalty: Kay Mellor, Keith Waterhouse and Willis Hall at the Queens Hotel, 2001.

"The flying ballet in the Leeds Empire pantomime Bo-Peep has been doing very nicely without my help up to now, but I couldn't resist the temptation to see what it's like to go flying through space on the end of a drawn-steel wire," he wrote in one memorable first-person feature which saw him temporarily join the cast of the city's panto.

"So Arthur Kirby, veteran head of Eugene's Flying Ballet, brought from London the harness that Jimmy Nervo used in a *Babes in the Wood* pantomime, and strapped me into it.

"He hooked me on the end of a wire and stood me on a chalk-marked cross in the wings. I felt a slight tugging sensation as though a crane had taken hold of my braces.

"Then stagehand Theo Hancock, all 14 stones of him, took hold of a rope. I didn't realise that the principle of the thing was so simple. Theo pulled and I went up.

"'Go up like a bird,' said Mr Kirby. 'A bird makes a slight curtsy before it takes off, to relieve the strain.'

"I went up like a bird all right. Like an old hen. Arms floundering, legs astraddle, I went up."

Famously fond of a liquid lunch, Waterhouse was a master of the art of a trick well-known in the newspaper offices of yesteryear. Leaving his jacket on the back of his chair to give the impression he would return to his desk at any minute, he would then head out for a long, convivial lunch during which several bottles of wine might be consumed.

Later he moved to Fleet Street, where he became a celebrated columnist and had it written into his contract that he could start early and not have to work after lunch. But it was as a novelist, scriptwriter and dramatist that he truly became a household name. His most famous work was *Billy Liar*, the story of a daydreamer planning his escape from an undertaker's job.

Published in 1959, he adapted it into a hugely successful stage play with close friend and fellow Hunslet lad Willis Hall, the playwright who became a popular columnist in the *YEP* and who himself enjoyed success in his own right, notably with his play *The Long and the Short and the Tall* about British soldiers ambushed in the Malayan jungle.

The pair's long-standing partnership took off when *Billy Liar* hit the big screen as an iconic film with Tom Courtenay playing the title character in what would prove a career-defining role.

The movie is not only considered to be among the pantheon of great British films, but also a trailblazer for the genre of kitchen sink drama.

Waterhouse went on to be awarded a CBE and, as well as writing dozens of works, contributed to a variety of TV shows ranging from the highbrow satire of *That Was The Week That Was* to popular favourites. Together, he and Hall created hits such as *Budgie*, *Queenie's Castle* and *Worzel Gummidge*.

When Waterhouse died in 2009, it was noted that all his work benefited from his roots in Leeds and his background as a journalist in the city and beyond.

Mark Knopfler was 19 when he arrived at the *Yorkshire Evening Post* as a junior reporter in 1968. And even while he was honing his craft with a notebook and pen he was indulging in his love of music. As a young arts correspondent for the paper he profiled Leeds guitarist Steve Phillips, who nearly two decades later would become his bandmate in country rock outfit the Notting Hillbillies, while at office parties he could be found sitting in a corner playing his guitar while colleagues danced along to his strumming.

But not everyone was impressed. The story goes that his news editor, Geoff Hemingway, took him to one side to offer some friendly advice – "Stick to newspapers Mark, you'll get nowhere with that music of yours."

Thankfully he didn't listen. Knopfler

Mark Knopfler is handed a leaving gift by news editor Geoff Hemingway.

4 YORKSHIRE EVENING POST, TUESDAY, SEPTEMBER 16, 1969

Nelson quits Hogline

NELSON FLETCHER, lead singer with Leeds soul band Hogline, has left the group along with two other members.

"It was really a financial disagreement," explained Nelson. "As a band we were all right, but I think the split was the result of mixed personalities as much as anything else."

Now Nelson is looking for a new band, and something different from the Hogline style.

BEAU —a name to remember

By MARK KNOPFLER

A YOUNG Leeds singer - songwriter is one of the first names to record an album on the new Dandelion label — private project of Polydor man Clive Selwood.

The gentleman in question is called Beau, which is also the name of the album. All the songs are Beau's, as is all the accompaniment — on a 12-string guitar.

You may not have heard about Beau yet, but you probably will. He is 23, lives in St. Chad's Avenue in Headingley, works for a building society in Leeds and has been writing songs for as long as he can remember. He says he is quite content, and is not mad keen to turn professional.

... of an opinion on anything the song isn't going to be worth it," he says.

Everything started for Beau when he got in touch with Selwood, manager of John Peel.

"He became my manager. ... everything went from there."

One of the songs on the album, 1917 Revolution was released as a single. It received a lot of air space, got some good reviews, and ... airings behind him, Beau is not itching for the big-time.

"I've got an album out I'm not a professional, and I think the reason I managed to get this far is that I'm not bothered," he told me.

An article on the local music scene by the future Dire Straits frontman, 1969.

Knopfler tries his hand at potholing during his days as a YEP reporter.

Peter O'Toole came face to face with an old friend in Newcastle in 1980 when the photographer taking his picture turned out to be former YEP colleague Arthur Merrill.

formed Dire Straits in 1977 and two years later they were storming the charts with their first hit single *Sultans of Swing*. The group's fifth album, *Brothers In Arms*, is classed as one of the greatest of all time, selling more than 30 million copies around the globe and spawning hit songs such as *Money For Nothing* and *Walk Of Life*.

But despite his fame and fortune, Mark still keeps in touch with Leeds. When the Grove Inn in Holbeck won a Pub of the Year competition in 2008 we revealed that the star regularly travelled from his home in London for impromptu musical sessions in the Leeds boozer.

There may be some uncertainty as to whether he entered the world in Ireland or West Yorkshire, but the *YEP* is pretty sure Peter O'Toole was born at 123 Beckett Street in Leeds. Now part of the site of St James's Hospital, back in 1932 it was known by a different name – the Leeds Workhouse.

Evacuated from Leeds during the war, on his return to the city he entered the darkrooms of the *Yorkshire Evening Post* in Albion Street as a photographic assistant, until he was called up for national service as a signaller in the Royal Navy.

After attending the Royal Academy of Dramatic Art, he enjoyed success as a Shakespearean stage actor before landing his most famous role – that of Captain TE Lawrence in David Lean's 1962 epic *Lawrence of Arabia*.

Melanie Brown was a regular in the pages of the *YEP* while growing up in Leeds. The Spice Girl first honed her performance skills at Leeds' former Intake High School – the city's so-called 'fame school', which later became Leeds West Academy.

Before hitting the big time she also worked briefly for the *YEP*'s former sister paper, the *Leeds Weekly News*, in promotions.

In 1992, 17-year-old Mel was also crowned Miss Leeds Weekly News – as a snap from our archive shows.

"My mum entered me without me knowing and when they asked me to be in the finals I wouldn't let my mum or dad come and watch," she later said.

"I only went and won it though, didn't I! I got a car for a year, even though I couldn't drive, and a trip to Disneyland."

After becoming a member of global pop phenomenon the Spice Girls, her family home in Burley was often an epicentre of attention for the group and when they reunited in 2008, the *Yorkshire Evening Post* chatted with the girls about their memories.

"Leeds has totally made me who I am today," Mel told us. "Apart from being with this lot and travelling the world – your childhood experiences mould you completely."

At this point Geri Halliwell shouted: "Kirkstall!" Gesturing to the other girls, she said: "Do you remember all of us sleeping in your bed in Kirkstall? It must have been 10 or 12 years ago, we were recording up there, we didn't even have a record deal then."

"Oh yes, it was my mum's house," confirmed Mel.

Geri continued: "We were top-and-tailing in this tiny house in Kirkstall, mucking in together, eating chips and, erm, what do you call those things....?"

"Scraps!" laughed Mel.

"That's right, scraps, love those," said Geri.

"Oh and bread cakes!" chipped in Emma Bunton.

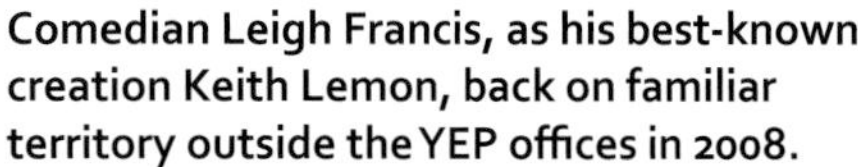
Comedian Leigh Francis, as his best-known creation Keith Lemon, back on familiar territory outside the YEP offices in 2008.

Leigh and his mother Pat have some fun during a book signing at the White Rose Centre.

Successful as he is now with hit shows such as *Celebrity Juice*, a career in comedy didn't seem to be on the cards for funnyman Leigh Francis – better known as Keith Lemon – when he was working at the *Yorkshire Evening Post*.

As a graphic artist his job was to draw the cartoon Page family, who back then appeared in adverts for the paper.

Leigh, who grew up in Farnley, later admitted to the *YEP* that he lied to get the position, telling his interviewer he was a dab hand with computers when he didn't really have a clue.

At weekends he would sneak into the office to make video covers for the short films of sketches he was cobbling together at home.

After a first, disastrous television appearance on a talent show – "I was rubbish, I came last" – he finally plucked up the courage to send his homemade tapes to the Paramount Comedy channel.

They were sufficiently impressed to offer him a job writing skits to appear between programmes. He went on to have his own show in the shape of *Bo' Selecta!* and is now a regular on our screens in programmes such as *Through The Keyhole*, *Celebrity Juice* and *The Keith Lemon Sketch Show*. He even starred in his own movie, *Keith Lemon: The Film*.

Leigh later made a return visit to the *YEP* where he caught up with some of his old mates – all while still in character as Keith Lemon.

The paper can also claim some of the credit for putting together one of television's most popular presenting couples.

After studying engineering at Cambridge University, 20-year-old Carol Vorderman had landed an apprenticeship at a frozen pea factory in Suffolk. But her mother, Jean, was homeless after leaving her stepfather so between them they scraped together a mortgage for a house in Leeds, where Carol had worked out they could just about afford to live.

"The first time Mum came to Yorkshire was the day we moved in – with all our belongings in the back of my car," she later recalled. "We couldn't afford new curtains, so we hung up old ones that didn't fit. At night we'd pin them together with clothes pegs."

Shortly afterwards, Jean spotted an advert in the *Yorkshire Evening Post* which said producers were seeking someone who was very sharp with numbers to co-present a quiz show.

Fiercely proud of her clever daughter, she put her forward for the job at Yorkshire Television without telling her.

"Mum wrote a letter and forged my signature," Carol said. "I was asked to do a maths test and had an interview.

"When I was given the job, I didn't have a clue about TV – for my first week, I didn't even realise that a red light on the camera meant that we were on air."

Four years after joining *Countdown*, the first programme to be shown on Channel 4 when it launched in 1982, Carol added vowels and consonants to her numbers role when the letters hostess decided to leave.

When the producer couldn't face interviewing again, the show's presenter Richard Whiteley said: "Vorders can do it".

She and Whiteley struck up a warm friendship which made them and *Countdown* a huge hit, the programme quickly establishing a cult status which it still maintains today.

The pair went on to present the show for 23 years, until Richard's sudden death in June 2005. When Carol left three years later the story made front page headlines for a week.

Carol Vorderman and Richard Whiteley's partner Kathryn Apanowicz at the memorial service for the late Countdown presenter in 2005. Carol's mum spotted the advert for Carol's big break in the YEP.

Leeds-born celebrity chef Marco Pierre White pictured with his godmother Gilda Porcelli outside her city centre restaurant Pasta Romagna, September 2010.

12-year-old Matthew Lewis from Horsforth celebrates capturing the role of Neville Longbottom in the Harry Potter films.

Yorkshire Evening Post

LEEDS — TUESDAY, JUNE 6, 1944 — No. 16,730

LATEST EDN.

Mr. Churchill Gives Good News of Landings in Normandy

INVASION OF NORTHERN FRANCE GOES ACCORDING TO PLAN

Massed Airborne Landing

Fire of Shore Guns Largely Quelled

WE USE 4,000 SHIPS, 11,000 AIRCRAFT

Heartening news that the Allied invasion of Northern France, which began this morning, is going according to plan, was given by Mr. Churchill in Parliament to-day.

His main points about the scope and progress of the operation were:—

An immense armada of upwards of 4,000 ships, with several thousand smaller craft, has crossed the Channel.

Massed airborne landings have been successfully effected behind the enemy's lines.

The landings on the beaches are proceeding at various points at the present time. The fire of the shore batteries has been largely quelled.

The Anglo-American Allies are sustained by about 11,000 first line aircraft, which can be drawn upon as may be needed for the purposes of the battle.

There are already hopes that actual tactical surprise has been attained, and we hope to furnish the enemy with a succession of surprises during the course of the fighting.

The battle which is now beginning will grow constantly in scale and intensity for many weeks to come, and I shall not attempt to speculate upon its course, but this I may say—complete unity prevails throughout the Allied armies. (Cheers.)

There is a brotherhood in arms between us and our friends in the United States. There is complete confidence in the Supreme Commander, General Eisenhower, and in his Lieutenants, and also in the Commander of the Expeditionary Force, General Montgomery.

The ardour and spirit of the troops, as I saw them myself embarking in these last few days, was splendid.

Nothing that equipment, science and forethought can do has been neglected, and the whole process of opening this great new front will be pursued with the utmost resolution, both by the commanders and by the United States and British Governments whom they serve.

In the early part of the battle I shall endeavour to keep the House fully informed. It may be that I shall ask their indulgence to press myself upon them before we rise to-night.

So far the commanders who are engaged report that everything is proceeding according to plan. And what a plan! This vast operation is undoubtedly the most complicated and difficult which has ever occurred.

General Montgomery is in charge of the Army group carrying out the assault with British, Canadian and United States forces under his command.

"SLASHING INLAND"

The Allies have established beachheads in Northern France and are slashing inland, according to photo reconnaissance pilots back from the landings, says a Reuter message to-day from the 8th U.S.A.A.F. photo reconnaissance base.

First official news of the invasion was given in "No. 1 Communique" issued by General Eisenhower, Supreme Commander, as follows:—

Under the command of General Eisenhower, Allied naval forces, supported by strong air forces, began landing Allied armies this morning on the northern coast of France.

The place of the attack had kept the Germans guessing for months, but their heaviest defences had been prepared at the point of the shortest Channel crossings.

Before our troops could land our minesweepers had to sweep the waters off the coast. Other craft had to deal with underwater obstacles, and bombarding ships had to get into position to engage the coast defence guns.

Value of Bombings

It is hoped that the resistance groups in France will give the Germans an uncomfortable time with

THE KING TO BROADCAST

SUPREME DAY FOR NAVY

Luftwaffe Has Not Yet Appeared

This first day is the supreme day for the Navy (writes a correspondent). They have had to deal with an armada of craft of all types.

"H" hour (time of landing) varied at different places along the invasion area. The timings were adjusted according to the varying natural features of the coast in relation to high water.

Airborne troops were dropped according to schedule.

First reports say that the transport planes returned safely with few losses.

"Going Well"

Gault McGowan, represting the Combined British Press, reporting from an English airfield after watching the second front start from the air, said to-day:

"The situation seems to be going well. The Luftwaffe has not yet put in an appearance in strength, and the masses of manœuvre on both sides are moving into position.

"Before returning I flew for miles inland but saw no German armoured divisions on the move.

"The air umbrella exceeded Dieppe. No outfit seemed without its cover. There was so many of us in the air that we had to get up there by co-ordinated degrees to avoid crossing each others lines."

A Cloudy Day

Another correspondent writes:—

The Allied troops landed in Europe under a blanket of cloud 5,000 feet thick.

In a flight up and down the French coast we could see nothing except clouds, the flash of flak exploding and a pale pinkish glow in the clouds in the area of the heavy bombardment.

Since the invasion began Allied fighter-bombers have been dive-bombing, glide-bombing and strafing German defences and communications. They are hitting any target that has a bearing on the strength of the German armies at the front.

The fly literally into the mouths of guns and dive within feet of the spans which hold bridges together.

IN STRAITS

After a shower soon after daybreak there was sunshine in the Straits, although later more banks of heavy clouds swept up from the north-west.

The wind had blown fairly hard during the night, but it lost some of its strength after dawn. A moderate sea was running, visibility was good and improving further.

The sun shone through broken banks of high cloud this afternoon. The sea was smooth, with a light north-westerly breeze,.

Although the French coast was hidden by haze, visibility was good—13 to 15 miles.

GOEBBELS: Achtung! Achtung! They're coming!

HITLER'S VERSION

A special announcement issued by official quarters in Berlin to-day said:—

"The long expected attack by the British and Americans on the coast of Northern France began last night.

"A few minutes after midnight the enemy landed airborne formations in the area of the Seine Bay, simultaneously making heavy bombing attacks.

"Shortly afterwards numerous enemy landing boats, protected by heavy Allied naval units, approached the coast on other sectors. The German defenders were nowhere taken by surprise. They immediately took up the fight with the greatest energy.

"The parachute troops were partly engaged as they came down, and the enemy ships were taken under effective fire while still on the high seas.

"In Full Swing"

"In spite of constant, violent air battles and heavy bombardment from the enemy ships, the guns of the Atlantic Wall immediately intervened in the fighting. They scored hits on battleships and on landing craft screened from view by smoke.

"The battle against the invasion troops is in full swing."—Reuter.

To-day's German communique says:

Last night the enemy began his long prepared attack on Western Europe, which was expected by us.

Bitter fighting is in progress on the coastal stretches attacked.

INVASION BRIEFS

One of the marshalling areas in England from which the troops were sent to the embarkation points was 300 square miles in extent.

The assembly areas along the British coastline changed to marshalling areas last Sunday, when troops were briefed on their exact missions.

The biggest minesweeping operation in history paved the way for our landing craft and involved 70 miles of sweep wire and 10,000 officers and men.

General Eisenhower spent last night from early evening until dusk paying informal visits to United States paratroop units due to make the landings in France.

About half the smaller types of British landing craft in use are manned and commanded by Royal Marines, and some of the ships carrying the infantry fly the Red Ensign of the British Merchant Navy.

"A BEACHHEAD SECURED"

Tanks Said to be Ashore

Latest reports of the progres[s] of the invasion, received sinc[e] Mr. Churchill's speech, includ[e] the following:

The Allies have secured a beachhea[d] and dug in military circles a[t] Supreme H.Q. heardly early thi[s] afternoon.

The German News Agency say[s] Allied troops are fighting 10 mile[s] inland from the coast of Normandy. Parachute troops and gliders have bee[n] seen in the region of Trouville (jus[t] south of Havre).

Quoting the German High Com[mand's] spokesman the agency said:

"Early to-day Allied airborne for[mations] landed on Guernsey and Jersey. They were at once engaged."

The Channel Islands have bee[n] occupied by the Germans for fou[r] years, since June, 1940. They lie 1[?] to 30 miles off the Cherbour[g] peninsula.

The German News Agency also mad[e] the following reports:

New landings were made befor[e] noon, particularly in the area o[f] Marcouf. Tanks landed in th[e] Arromanches area.

The greatest concentrations [of] invasion forces detected so far ar[e] at Cherbourg and Havre. Obviousl[y] both these towns are wanted by th[e] enemy as his principal ports.

A very strong landing from the ai[r] was made at Harfleur, and also a[t] a point west of Cherbourg.

"I Saw Them"

An Associated Press war corre[spondent], representing the combine[d] United States Press, who flew in [a] Marauder, said to-day:

Allied soldiers have landed i[n] Northern France, and I saw them do i[t].

From the cockpit of a Maraude[r] which participated in the firs[t] bombardment this morning I sa[w] great naval and shore engagement[s] getting under way.

A few miles inland I saw field[s] strewn with hundreds of parachute[s] where Allied airborne forces ha[d] dropped. The fields were dotted, to[o], with aircraft, probably gliders, bea[r]ing the distinctive Allied invasio[n] black and white zebra stripe, whic[h] was hurriedly slapped on the aircra[ft] late yesterday.

An Aerial View

A U.S. photo reconnaissance ba[se] reporter quotes Lieutenant-Colon[el] C. A. Shoop, who has flown over th[e] scene of the initial thrust, [as] expressing surprise at the lack [of] opposition to our air, ground a[nd] naval forces.

"There are lots of burning buildin[gs] and bomb craters," he said. "Tow[ns] are burning all over the area."

"We could see our troops advanci[ng] across ground at one place. Ever[y]thing seemed to be moving very fa[st]

LEEDS THINKS BIG

1940 – 1981

In the first years of the Second World War, British cities suffered horrific damage and huge loss of life in the bombing raids that had come to play such a major role in the conflict.

In Leeds, however, life pretty much carried on as normal. Despite the tempting targets of Kirkstall Forge, the railway marshalling yards and the Royal Ordnance Factory at Barnbow, the city had been left virtually untouched.

Its only real experience of the Luftwaffe had come on August 25, 1940 when three people had been killed by four bombs which fell on Whitehall Road, and six days later when a 60-year-old man died after a bomb hit York House in the Quarry Hill flats.

All that was to change, however, on the night of Friday, March 14, 1941. It was around 9pm when the sirens started to wail. In all, 451 German bombers were over Britain and 40 of them were heading for Leeds.

The first incendiaries – one-pound aluminium cases loaded with fire-raising magnesium – began falling over the Water Lane and Easterly Road areas of the city from 11.40pm with high explosive bombs following at 12.30am in the early hours of Saturday.

Over the next two-and-a-half hours bombs would rain down on civic landmarks including the Town Hall and the City Museum.

Leeds General Infirmary's casualty department had to be moved three times during the night after a bomb fell in front of the emergency entrance. Other buildings hit included Kirkgate Market, the central post office, Richmond Hill Council School and the Metropole Hotel.

But despite the unfolding carnage, the *Yorkshire Evening Post* was bound by the restrictions of the wartime censors, which limited how much could be revealed.

Surveying the rubble after a bombing raid in the Easterly Road area, September 1940.

A semi-detached house is levelled by bombing with just its guttering surviving, 1941.

The newspaper reported that "a number of delayed-action bombs were used by enemy raiders on the central and industrial districts of an inland North-eastern town", but added that a communiqué issued by the Nazi High Command had named Leeds as one of its key targets.

"One of the main hotels in the town received a direct hit from a high explosive bomb," the *YEP* said. "Considerable damage was done to the top floors, but no one was seriously hurt. Early in the raid a high explosive bomb hit the entrance to the emergency receiving department at a hospital. Some casualties were just being admitted when a bomb fell nearby. Doctors and nurses worked throughout the raid, and the matron said afterwards: 'Everyone has been magnificent'.

"Early today rescue parties were working to release a woman and her daughter trapped under the ruins of a house hit by a high explosive bomb. The daughter, it is stated, was to have been married soon, and wedding presents were found by the rescue workers amid the debris."

On the 70th anniversary of the raid, the *YEP*'s John Lynott told how members of the Auxiliary Fire Service tackled hundreds of incidents across the city, among them those at City Square, Wellington Bridge, the City Station, Albion Street and Leeds University.

At the height of the raid, more than 4,000 wardens and 1,845 firemen were on duty, along with 77 ambulance crews. In total, more than 4,500 homes were damaged, 100 of them beyond repair. Gas mains were fractured and 15,000 people were left without water.

But it was the human cost that was hardest to bear. By the time the All Clear sounded at 3.12am that Saturday, 65 people were dead or dying, eight of them children.

Behind those figures were the countless stories of heroism and sheer bad luck that punctuated the Blitz. Four wardens were killed when their post near Union Street Baths suffered a direct hit. Kirkstall Road resident Dr Ernest Donaldson-Sim helped put out several incendiaries but was then killed instantly when he pushed his housekeeper to safety as a bomb exploded at his feet.

Stoker and firewatcher Harry Lee became the first man in Leeds to receive the George Medal for bravery when he directed successful efforts to save New Wortley Gas Works as incendiaries showered down.

John Wilson, a foreman and a firewatcher at a building that received a direct hit, told a *Yorkshire Evening Post* reporter that when the bomb struck he was saved by his steel helmet and a door which was blown on top of him, preventing him from being hit by flying debris.

The next day, Berlin reported that "important war works" had been hit in Leeds and "the dropping of high explosive and incendiary bombs caused big fires".

The first funerals of the 65 victims of the so-called 'Quarter Blitz' – because the tonnage of bombs dropped was about 25 per cent of what constituted a 'major' raid – took place four days later at Harehills Cemetery with a service attended by the Lord Mayor, Alderman Willie Withey.

He told mourners: "When the war is over we have a great responsibility in trying to see that such a happening as this will never occur again."

The *YEP* later published the recollections of those who lived through the raids. Eric Drummond, then a 14-year-old working at J Mays and Son's clothing factory in Holbeck, remembered spending the night in the coal cellar at his home in Oban Street, Upper Armley.

"When we heard the ack-ack guns at Post Hill (a local beauty spot between Pudsey and Farnley) open fire, and then the searchlights joined in, we guessed there was going to be a raid," he said.

Mr Drummond recalled a schoolmate's father having a close shave when a bomb dropped on the local corner shop in Wortley. "He was on fire-watching duty and when it hit the shop he was standing directly opposite. It blew him off his feet and shredded his trousers.

"When the anti-aircraft guns started up I thought that was exciting and shouted 'Go on, give 'em a go!' But my mother quickly told me to shut up.

"The first thing a lot of the lads did when they got up the next morning was to go on the streets to look for shrapnel and any souvenirs. It was the spirit of adventure, I suppose."

Other Loiners' memories of that night were just as sharp. Local historian John Ashbee was 17 and would shortly afterwards join the RAF. On the night of the raid he, his parents and younger sister sought refuge in the converted coal cellar at their terrace in Ash Road in Headingley.

"We had put garden chairs, a table and a gas fire down there so it was quite cosy," he told the *YEP*. "When the air raid sirens went off we all went down there. I wouldn't say we were frightened but there was a certain amount of apprehension.

"We always suspected Leeds would be a target but it was said at the time that the industrial haze over the city made it a difficult target from the air. The smogs were unbelievable, you literally couldn't see your hand in front of you. But then again perhaps it kept us safer than other cities."

John, who at the time was working as a window dresser at a clothes shop, told of there being a funereal air in the city the morning after the attack. "There was glass and rubble around and there was a lot of grief in the city. There was a very subdued atmosphere everywhere and people were very conscious that people had lost their lives. "It made everyone apprehensive that there would be more to come."

Marlene Mann, then Marlene Osborne, was a five-year-old pupil at Ellerby Lane Primary School in Cross Green when the raid took place. "I remember going into the air raid shelters," she said.

Lord Mayor Beatrice Kitson helps unveil the total raised during Wings for Victory Week, July 1943.

Opposite: Activities promote the event, which raised funds to support the RAF, the Fleet Air Arm and the Allied Air Force.

"We had one at the bottom of the street, the fish shop had one in the basement and there were some down Ellerby Lane, near the Bellow Machine Company.

"I was meant to be going on to Richmond Hill School but of course that was cancelled after it was hit by a bomb. "I don't remember being frightened. If anything it was an exciting time, we all took it in our stride. I don't think any of us realised how enormous it was until we started growing up."

Harry Thrush was living in Bridgefield Place and after the all-clear he went down towards York Road and saw flames coming out of the Woodpecker pub that had been hit. "A man nearby shouted at me: 'Get home you silly bugger!'" he recalled. "He must have been an ARP (Air Raid Precautions) man."

There was more tragedy to come. On August 8, 1942, two people died when a bomb fell in the Cardigan Road area. The last bombs to fall on Leeds, three weeks later, killed five people and damaged homes in Armley, Bramley, Stanningley and Kirkstall.

Several theories were advanced as to why Leeds was not subject to further, heavier raids. One was that the city was difficult to find from the air at night, lying in a saucer of land. Another was that the Germans did not want to cause significant damage to Leeds because they wanted to use the city after the invasion of Britain as a regional capital. It was said that Luftwaffe chief Hermann Goering had already picked out Temple Newsam House as his HQ.

In reality, the Luftwaffe didn't have the tools or the will to totally wreck Leeds. Their twin-engined planes couldn't carry the massive tonnage of bombs that the RAF's Lancasters and Halifaxes would later drop with such devastating effect on Germany.

During the war, Leeds took great pride in the heroics of Arthur Aaron, the only serviceman from the city to be awarded the Victoria Cross in the course of the conflict.

Just 21-years-old, the young man from Gledhow had been named after his father's cousin who

was killed at the Somme. He had enlisted in the RAF in 1941 and was promoted to Flight Sergeant two years later. Over the next three months, he flew more than 20 bombing missions over Europe.

On the night of August 12, 1943, Aaron was captain of a Stirling aircraft that came under heavy fire during a mission over Turin. A number of crewmen were killed and Aaron lost the use of his right arm and part of his face.

Despite those injuries, he landed the plane in Algeria, saving the rest of the crew. He died nine hours later and was buried with full military honours at Bone Military Cemetery.

He was awarded the Victoria Cross posthumously, with Sir Arthur Harris, commander-in-chief of RAF Bomber Command, telling his parents: "In my opinion, never, even in the annals of the RAF, has the VC been awarded for skill, determination and courage in the face of the enemy of a higher order than that displayed by your son."

Such were the numbers who wanted to pay tribute that his memorial service was held at Leeds Town Hall. The Lord Mayor was in attendance and there was a parade by the Air Training Corps.

Aaron was a former student of Roundhay School and the *YEP* told how 900 boys there listened to an address by headmaster Mr BA Farrow, who told them his courage should be an example to them all.

The paper would later issue an appeal for the return of his Victoria Cross and Distinguished Flying Medal after they were stolen during a break-in at his parents' home in Thorn Lane. The medals were returned by the thieves, who were "apparently moved by the distress of the dead pilot's father and mother".

Aaron's Victoria Cross is now on display at Leeds City Museum, while a statue of the airman stands on the Eastgate roundabout, despite public calls in 2015 for it to be moved to Roundhay.

Revellers let their hair down outside the Navy, Army and Air Force Institutes club in Albion Street on VE Day.

Leeds also did its bit for the war effort in the form of some astonishing fundraising. Various government-sponsored campaigns were mounted to encourage people to raise money, one of them being to adopt a warship.

In November 1941, Leeds decided to adopt the HMS Ark Royal. But just days later the ship was torpedoed and sunk by a German U-boat in the Mediterranean.

Spurred on by pride and fury, the city's residents raised an incredible £9m for a new Ark Royal, far surpassing the original target of £3.5m.

A huge march took place down The Headrow, led by the Navy and followed by military vehicles and personnel. Contributions included money sent by children to buy nuts and bolts to sums of £250,000 from businesses to purchase Fulmar naval fighter planes, which cost £5,000 each.

The Ark Royal would always enjoy a special connection with the people of Leeds and the ship went on to receive the Freedom of the City in 1973.

The post-war years were a time of rebuilding and also growth. More and more housing estates were built, new schools erected, including the city's first comprehensive school at Foxwood in 1956,

Brisk business for this YEP vendor as the paper announces the German surrender, May 7, 1945.

and public facilities generally improved.

Leeds kept innovating, too. The Hunslet Engine Company on Jack Lane in Hunslet was one of the most famous names in the world when it came to the manufacture of railway locomotives. But in the 1950s the firm decided to branch out and a subsidiary company was formed to produce the Scootacar, a three-wheeled micro-car which legend has it came about because the wife of one of the directors wanted something easier to park than her Jaguar.

Just 87 inches long and 52 inches wide, the Scootacar was nicknamed 'The Telephone Booth' and the deluxe model could reach top speeds of 68mph. Cult classics today, they didn't quite take off at the time and production stopped in 1964 after fewer than 1,000 had been produced.

It was an era of change when it came to how Loiners travelled from A to B. In 1953, John Rafferty, chairman of the Corporation Transport Committee, warned that Leeds trams could be scrapped "in ten years" due to falling passenger numbers.

"I think the people are sick of riding on obsolete trams," the *YEP* quoted him as saying. "Until recently we had trams that were 40 years old. Now a considerable number are 30 years old."

More and more people were opting to use the bus services instead, with a reduction in spending power and the abolition of petrol rationing put forward as reasons for the shift. As it turned out, the Leeds tramway didn't even last the decade Rafferty had predicted, running for the last time on November 7, 1959.

As the final tram rolled into the depot, bedecked with lights and

A 1960 advert for the Scootacar.

The last Leeds tram pulls into the depot, November 7, 1959.

Clockwise:

Shoppers crowd the fruit stalls at Kirkgate Market, December 1951.

Cooling off with a summer swim at Roundhay Park lido, June 30, 1953.

Children from Lower Wortley Infants School hand over donations for the YEP's Toy Appeal, November 25, 1954.

Christmas shopping on Briggate, December 22, 1951.

DEEP WATER THIS SIDE

YORKSHIRE
EVENING POST

Harry Ramsden with twin sisters Wendy Sanford and Mavis Broadbent, who were first in the queue for fish and chips, July 7, 1952.

cheered on by crowds, people laid coins on the track so they would be pressed as it went past and they would have a memento of another chapter in the city's history.

There had been even more astonishing scenes some years earlier when fish and chip legend Harry Ramsden had hung up his white overalls for the final time. Harry's rise to fame had begun on December 20, 1928, when he bought a hut for £150 next to a tram stop at White Cross, Guiseley, near two major roads – Otley Road and Bradford Road – and began selling freshly fried fish and chips to mill workers.

Three years later, he borrowed money to create the famous Guiseley restaurant. It became a stopping-off point for people heading out of Leeds into the countryside and the common-or-garden dish took on a rustic charm which endeared it to a new, more affluent market.

Harry, in turn, did his bit by modelling his new restaurant on London's Ritz Hotel, sparing no expense, decking it out with chandeliers, checked linen tablecloths, silver vases and stained glass windows. The business went from strength to strength and as time went on, the legend grew.

Preparing to sell up and retire, he told the public he would celebrate the restaurant's 21st birthday by turning the clocks back to the pre-First World War days, when a meal could be bought for a penny ha'penny.

On July 7, 1952, the restaurant duly sold a world record 10,000 portions in a single day. The first customers were 20-year old twins Mavis and Wendy Raistrick, from Horsforth, who received a cigarette lighter and a card signed by Harry as a reward for their near six-hour wait.

A total of 635 kilos of fish and 2,000 kilos of potatoes went into six pans, to be devoured by a slow moving queue with three and a half pence at the ready. Crowds came from far and wide in coaches, cars, on motorcycles, bicycles and on foot. Twenty policemen and five patrol cars equipped with microphones were called in to handle the crowds.

To entertain the queues there was Dixieland music played by a band led by Ramsden's nephew, Harry Corbett, who the same year would make his first television appearance with his famous glove puppet Sooty.

Ramsden himself moved among the throng, the 64-year-old happily greeting customers as he signed autographs on their fish and chip wrappers.

An amazing night at Guiseley came to an end at 1am, an hour after the scheduled time, when Harry donned a white coat to serve the last customer, 62-year-old Benny Patrick of Guiseley. "I've been a customer of Harry's ever since he opened up," said Mr Patrick, "and I was determined to be the last customer."

The restaurant continued to be a mecca for fish and chip lovers long after Harry sold up – including famous names such as Jimi Hendrix, Jenny Agutter, Pat Phoenix, Jean Simmons and Margaret Thatcher. Harry died in 1965 at the age of 74.

Four years earlier, the *Yorkshire Evening Post* had introduced readers to a 25-year-old mother from Castleford. She worked as a packer at a local liquorice factory but her life was about to change forever in an astonishing saga that could only have come straight from the Swinging Sixties.

Viv Nicholson's husband Keith, a miner, scooped the jackpot on the football pools in September 1961, his eight score draws netting the couple £125,000 – equivalent to around £3m today. They toasted the win with a couple of halves of beer, but Viv promised to "spend, spend, spend" – and that's exactly what she proceeded to do.

Viv Nicholson won, and lost, a fortune as she lived up to her pledge to 'spend, spend, spend'.

Her first purchase was a green suit the day after TV entertainer Bruce Forsyth handed over the cheque. The Nicholsons then bought a home in Garforth, ate, drank and splashed the cash.

"I'd lived in Castleford all my life and when I got some money I went to Leeds and it was another world," Viv later recalled. "I went in my new suit and I got my money out and said 'keep the change darling' and did all that swaggering about. I didn't know how much it was. I just spent it. We had a fabulous time."

Two months after her win, she estimated that she was spending money at the rate of £1,400 a week. After the £4,000 luxury bungalow came the cars, a silver Chevrolet and a pink Cadillac, along with furs, frocks, shoes – she once bought 14 pairs in one go – jewellery and exotic holidays.

There were lavish parties at the new home they had named the Ponderosa, complete with its own corner cocktail bar and so much champagne that Viv claimed to bathe in it.

But tragedy struck just four years after the win when Keith was killed at the wheel of his Jaguar. Soon Viv was declared bankrupt and back living in a modest terrace in Allerton Bywater, but she remained a regular presence in the headlines, performing on the cabaret scene and battling alcohol addiction and depression.

A West End musical celebrating her life – named *Spend, Spend, Spend* in honour of her catchphrase – premiered at the West Yorkshire Playhouse in Leeds in 1998 before a run at the West End.

It earned her considerable royalties, as did the autobiography that inspired it – but, true to her

SATURDAY, NOVEMBER 23, 1963
No. 22,765
Tel. LEEDS 32701

YORKSHIRE
EVENING POST
COVERS THE COUNTY

Price 3d

…ro-Castro man with a Russian wife faces death penalty ★ Case may go before Grand Ju… next week: No confession

KENNEDY MURDER …HARGE

…NG United States Army … stationed at Menwith … the American installation … Harrogate, kneels in … in the chapel at Menwith Hill, on this day of mourning.

…AKING IN LEEDS

…noch Powell, M.P., former … of Health, was speaking … the Yorkshire Area Conserva… …lf-yearly council meeting at … Theatre, Cookridge Street.

10 hours of questions

DALLAS (TEXAS), SATURDAY.—A CHARGE OF ASSASSINATING PRESIDENT KENNEDY WITH A RIFLE WAS LAID AT MIDNIGHT AGAINST LEE HARVEY OSWALD, 24-YEAR-OLD EX-MARINE AND SUSPECTED COMMUNIST SYMPATHISER.

Captain Will Fritz, of Dallas Homicide Squad, who announced the charge after 10 hours of interrogation of Oswald by police and F.B.I. agents, said Oswald had not confessed and had made no statement.

Earlier Oswald had been charged with the murder of a Dallas policeman shot in the street shortly after a sniper's bullet had killed President Kennedy in his car at his wife's side.

Dallas District Attorney, Mr. Henry Wade, said the case would probably be presented to a Grand Jury before the middle of next week. There was still additional information to be gathered for presentation to the Grand Jury.

Mr. Wade said that his office would ask for the death penalty.

'APPEARS SANE'

Oswald defected to the Soviet Union in 1959 and worked in a Minsk factory before asking to return to the United States.

HE WAS GRANTED AN EXIT VISA BY THE SOVIET AUTHORITIES AND RETURNED LAST YEAR WITH A RUSSIAN WIFE AND CHILD.

Mr. Wade said there was no evidence that anyone was "behind" Oswald or associated with him. "We have no other suspects at the moment."

Asked about Oswald's mental condition and suspected Communist leanings, Mr. Wade replied that "he appears to be sane," and that the police could not say at present if he was a member of any Communist-front organisation. He was, however, a member of the pro-Castro "Fair play for Cuba" movement.

In a brief description of the interrogation of Oswald, Mr. Wade said: "He talked quite a bit. He denied both murders all the way, though."

YOU GO DOWN . . .

HERE IS IS THE SEQUENCE OF EVENTS WHICH LED TO OSWALD'S ARREST, AS GIVEN BY CITY DETECTIVE EDWARD HICKS:

Oswald was working on the fifth floor of the book warehouse—the floor from which the shots were fired—as the President's motorcade was going by.

A man working with him said, "Oswald, let's go to see the President."

"No, you go on down and send the elevator back up," Oswald was said to have replied.

After this Oswald was stopped by police as he left the building. He said he wanted to see what was going on.

About 45 minutes later, a man was seen four miles away, in the city's Oak Cliff district, talking to Policeman J. D. Tippitt.

Mrs Helen Markham, waiting for a bus a few blocks from the cinema, said Tippitt had stopped his police car to talk to the man.

ARREST AT CINEMA

Mrs. Markham said the man walked over to the police car and leaned over to the window to say something. The officer then got out of his car.

"They stopped, looked at each other, and the man pulled his gun and shot the police officer down," she told reporters.

After the man fled, the policeman tried to say something to Mrs. Markham "but he never got it out."

Police said that the landlady of the boarding house where Oswald was living told them that he changed his clothes after going into the house in the early afternoon, then went out again.

Later the cashier of a Texas cinema, six blocks from the scene of Tippitt's murder, called police to say that an usher had told her that a man had just entered the cinema and was behaving in a peculiar manner.

Police surrounded the cinema, where a film called "War is Hell" was playing, and then went in. They began to check the customers.

Police-sergeant Jerry Hill said that when they came to Oswald he jumped up, took out his pistol and pulled the trigger. The gun did not go off. "This is it!" he exclaimed.

Oswald was subdued after a brief scuffle in which he and a policeman were cut on the face. As the handcuffs were snapped on to his wrists he was heard to say: "It's all over."

As he was being taken through the police building, Oswald shouted to reporters: "I did not kill President Kennedy. I did not kill anyone. I do not know what this is about."

MRS. KENNEDY, HER LEGS HEAVILY SMUDGED, ABOUT TO ENTER AN AMBULANCE CARRYING THE BODY OF HER HUSBAND, AT ANDREWS AIR FORCE BASE, NEAR WASHINGTON.

LEE OSWALD'S MOSCOW STORY

LEE HARVEY OSWALD, AGED 24, HOLDS UP HIS MANACLED HANDS IN POLICE HEADQUARTERS IN DALLAS.

SHARPSHOOTER

One report says that Oswald qualified as a sharpshooter when in the Marines.

Police made a wax impression on Oswald's skin to determine if his hands and face bore any powder marks

Oswald's wife Marina, a diminutive blonde, was taken to police headquarters to speak to her husband shortly after he had been held for questioning

She arrived with her two small daughters—a baby in arms about six months old and a girl of five.

President Kennedy was shot at 12.25 p.m.—6.25 G.M.T.

Rifle shots rang out from a fifth-floor window as President Kennedy rode in bright sunshine through cheering crowds in the main business section of Dallas.

The President, hit by two bullets, collapsed face down in the car. Pandemonium followed. Governor John Connally of Texas was also hit and gravely wounded.

MRS. JACQUELINE KENNEDY THREW HERSELF OVER HER STRICKEN HUSBAND, CRYING "OH NO," SHE CRADLED HIS BLOOD-STREAMING HEAD IN HER ARMS AS THE DRIVER SPED TO PARKLAND HOSPITAL.

Oxygen and blood transfusions were used in a desperate bid to save the President. But at 1 p.m (1900 G.M.T.) he died without regaining consciousness.

Half an hour later, in the Presidential plane, before a sobbing

CONTINUED ON BACK PAGE

PRINCE PHILIP AND P.M. FLYING TO U.S.

PRINCE PHILIP and the Prime Minister are flying to America for the memorial service for President Kennedy in Washington.

Travelling by B.O.A.C. charter aircraft, they are leaving London Airport at 5 p.m tomorrow

The aircraft is scheduled to arrive at Washington at 9.30 p.m. (local time) tomorrow

Lady Douglas-Home and senior members of the Prime Minister's personal staff will be accompanying the Premier

PONIES REPRIEVED

Children enjoyed their last rides today on reprieved ponies at the Wayfaring Downs Riding Stables, Jevington, near Eastbourne. They began booking their rides four days ago when it became known that the stables would close tonight, and that under the terms of the will of Mrs. Winifred Macpherson the 18 ponies were to be killed

Last night her partner, Miss Janet Bell, finally agreed to allow the R.S.P.C.A. to take over the ponies next week and find good homes for them.

Told reporter 'How I became a Marxist'

By ALINE MOSBY, British United Press Correspondent in Paris

HE was slight, and looked young and determined and intense, as he sat in Room 233 of the Metropole Hotel in Moscow by the fringed lampshade, and looked out of the lace-curtained window on to Revolution Square.

"Lee Harvey Oswald, Fort Worth, Texas, arrived Moscow, October 15, 1959, applied October 16 for Soviet citizenship," I had written in my notebook that day when I was a British United Press correspondent in Moscow.

Today I found my notebook with the notes of what he said. I had tracked down Oswald in Moscow after he went to the U.S. Embassy on October 31 and asked that his U.S. citizenship be cancelled.

I judged him as a person who was very determined but unsure of himself, naive and emotionally unbalanced.

"I was born in New Orleans and lived for two years in New York. I spent most of my life in Fort Worth. My father died before I was born. My mother works in shops mostly, in Fort Worth.

"I played baseball and football in high school. I had a certain amount of friends, but I don't have many attachments now in the U.S. In my childhood I enjoyed few benefits of American society. I was a bookworm.

'A Marxist'

"I joined the Marine Corps when I was 17 and served in Japan and the Philippines and was discharged, as a radar operator private first class, when I was 20 in Santa Ana, California, last September 11. I won a good conduct medal."

I asked Oswald if he wanted to remain in the Soviet Union.

"I'm a Marxist," he said seriously.

"I became interested about the age of 15. An old lady handed me a pamphlet about saving the Rosenbergs.

"I still remember that pamphlet about the Rosenbergs. I don't know why. Then we moved to North Dakota and I discovered one book in the library, 'Das Kapital.'

"It was what I'd been looking for. It was like a very religious man opening the Bible for the first time.

"I started to study Marxist economic theories. I could see the impoverishment of the masses before my own eyes in my own mother. I thought the workers' life could be better."

Offered help

Reuter reports: Last July Oswald appeared in New Orleans, where he approached an officer of the Miami-based anti-Castro "Cuban Student Directorate," offering his help.

"I was suspicious of him from the start," said Carlos Bringuier, the officer, "but frankly I thought he might be an agent from the F.B.I or the C.I.A.

"A few days later I encountered him distributing 'Viva Fidel Castro' literature."

It was then, after a melee, that Oswald was fined 10 dollars for disturbing the peace.

£200 COFFEE

A coffee morning at Scarborough's Royal Hotel today had as its target £200 for the Mayoress's Benevolent Fund. One of the stalls had gifts presented by young people who on Monday received Duke of Edinburgh Awards from Mrs Irene Smith, the Mayoress.

Premier will lea… Commons tribut…

THE abhorrence which M.P.s on both sides of the … feel at the assassination of President Kennedy … expressed as soon as Parliament meets on Monday (w… Lobby correspondent).

Tributes to the President will then be paid in the House of Lords and in the House of Commons.

The Prime Minister, who knew the President well, will lead the tributes.

The terms of the motion expressing sorrow at the assassination of President Kennedy to be moved in the Commons on Monday were released by No. 10, Downing Street, this afternoon. It will be proposed at the end of question hour and after a statement to be made on the rearrangement of Commons business for the week. The House will then adjourn. The motion reads:

That a humble address be presented to Her Majesty praying Her Majesty to be graciously pleased to express to the President of the United States of America the shock and deep sorrow with which this House has learned of the death of President Kennedy, and to convey their sense of the loss which this country and the Commonwealth have sustained, and their profound sympathy with Mrs. Kennedy and the family of the late President, and with the Government and people of the United States of America.

The House of Lords will meet at 2.30 p.m on Monday to pay tribute to President Kennedy and will then adjourn as a mark of respect.

B.B.C. INQUIRY

An inquiry is to be held by the B.B.C. over the fact that last night's television programmes were allowed to carry on with a comedy show only 24 minutes after the announcement of President Kennedy's death. Many viewers rang to protest when the normal Friday night Harry Worth Show came on the screens—five minutes late. Some said they were appalled by the timing. A B.B.C. spokesman said today: "We are looking into this. The opinions expressed by viewers are always gone into."

FOOTBALL TRIBUTE

The Football Association today asked all clubs under their jurisdiction at today's matches to observe one minute's silence before the kick-off, to fly any flags at half-mast, and to wear black armbands.

U.S. SPORT OFF

From New York it was reported that scores of major sporting events across the U.S. this weekend had been cancelled or postponed. The American Football League cancelled all four scheduled games. The 80th annual football match between Harvard and Yale universities, planned for today, was postponed. Mr Kennedy was a graduate of Harvard

STOCK EXCHANGE

The London Stock Exchange is not open on Saturdays, but is expected to open lower on Monday. There had already been falls on Wall Street before the news of the assassination closed the Stock Exchange in New York

THE CHILDREN

WASHINGTON, Saturday. — Mrs. Jacqueline Kennedy faces the ordeal today of breaking the news to her two children.

Both children have birthdays next week—Caroline will be six on Wednesday, her brother, John, three on Monday.

Several hours after their father's death they were taken quietly out of the White House without being told the news. Officials refused to say where they were.—Reuter

Mr. JOSEPH KENNEDY

Hyannisport (Mass.), Saturday.—Up to late last night Mr Kennedy's father, Mr. Joseph Kennedy, former Ambassador to Britain, who is 75 had

INSIDE . .

They're reel… from the sh… at Menwi…

Evening Post Reporte…

PERSONNEL at Yorkshire's … of America at the 13th U… Security Agency Field Station … with Hill, near Harrogate, w… reeling today from the shock … dent Kennedy's assassination … club and festive activities were … immediately news of their … death came through.

"The men were glued to ra… into the night waiting for … developments to come throug…" Lt.-Col. Robert H. Jackson, w… charge while the Station Com… Col. Charles G. Renfro, is on … tinent on Army duties.

Col. Jackson summed up … ings of more than 800 Amer… sonnel and nearly 100 familie… with when he said: "It is a s… we have not got over it yet."

Plans cancelled

Men cancelled plans for a … trip to an American football … London and others decided … put instead of visiting local …

Said Col. Jackson: "We … opening the gymnasium … Service Club to keep the men … post."

Prayers for President Kenn… family and the American na… be said at the camp chapel … tomorrow

The men and their familie… officially told of the Presiden… at a formal parade on Mond… will be followed by a Mass for … Catholics and a memorial ser… Presbyterians

The Americans were impre… the number of people who h… up to express sympathy. One … came from Col. John North, … Army Apprentice School, Har…

FORECAST

Up to noon tomorrow

WEST AND EAST RIDINGS: … cloudy, with rain at times, … sunny intervals; wind fr… strong; mild.

NORTH RIDING: Mostly clou… rain at times; wind mode… fresh; near-normal temperat…

OUTLOOK: Changeable, with … times in most parts; near … temperatures

LIGHTS ON: 4.18 p.m to 7.…

MEMORIAL SERV…

MONDAY, JULY 21, 1969
No. 24,518
Tel. LEEDS 32701

YORKSHIRE
EVENING POST

LATE NIGHT FINAL

LARGEST CIRCULATION IN THE LARGEST COUNTY

Price 5d.

...e small step for ...an . . . one giant ...eap for mankind

Moonmen rest for 7 hours...

HOME NEXT STOP

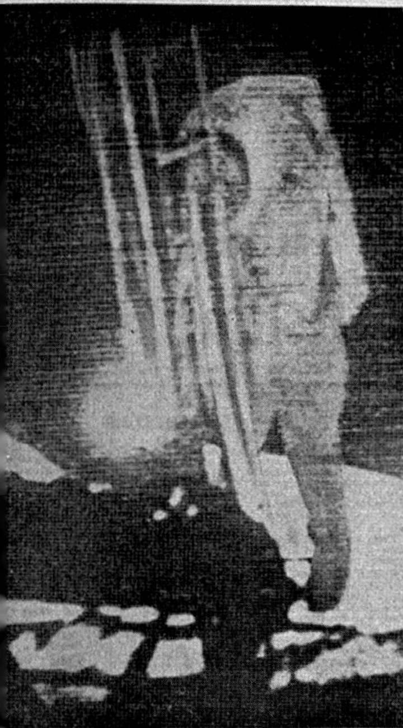

...of Edwin Aldrin ...s towards the ...face as he slowly ...own the ladder ...Eagle spacecraft.

...a 15 ...y be ...earer ...moon

...Bank picked up ...on the Russian ...Luna 15 shortly ...n today, while it ...s 30th orbit. ...picked a second ...signals from Luna ...p.m. ...were indications ...Luna 15 may have ...an even lower ...d the moon. ...Bank reported that ...ans had made a ...ection to the space ...r John G. Davies ...t the correction ...ssibly have put ...to a lower orbit.

All set to link up with Columbia

Apollo II astronauts Neil Armstrong and Edwin Aldrin were all set to lift off from the moon tonight at 6.55 B.S.T.

They had rested for seven hours in landing vehicle Eagle after the triumph of their perfect touchdown and lunar walk, in which they left man's first footprints on the moon, cables Reuter.

Safely aboard their moonship, they awaited a wake-up call before the critical lift-off. It was next stop home after a rendezvous with the command module Columbia piloted by Michael Collins.

The plan was for the rocket motor to burn for just over seven minutes, which should lift the ascent stage into an orbit 10 miles high at its low point and 45 at its high.

Another burn will circularise the orbit at 45 miles, 15 miles below the third astronaut, Collins, in the command ship.

From that it should be relatively smooth sailing to the rendezvous and the transfer of Armstrong and Aldrin back into the command ship for the return to earth.

At 5.57 a.m. B.S.T. tomorrow safely aboard Columbia, they will fire the main engine to start their journey back to earth.

If anything does go wrong with the main motor of the ascent stage then there is some hope that the subsidiary motors, used normally for changing the direction of the craft in flight could take over.

Theme is peace

But they could produce enough work only to put things right in the very final stages of the flight.

The two astronauts sealed themselves into the upper stage of the spidery lunar module after a two-hour television spectacular which clearly showed the two spacemen jumping about and loping light-footed across the clinging, powdery surface of the moon.

"THAT'S ONE SMALL STEP FOR MAN, ONE GIANT LEAP FOR MANKIND," SAID ARMSTRONG WHEN HIS LEFT FOOT FIRST HIT THE LUNAR SURFACE AT 3.56 A.M. TODAY.

Radio contact was restored with Houston about 20 minutes after the two astronauts re-entered Eagle.

After they were aboard, the outdoor television camera kept faithfully transmitting pictures of the ungainly moonship and a United States flag planted firmly in the lunar soil.

The two men performed all but one—and that a minor one—of the tasks assigned to them for their lunar walk, which included collecting soil and rock samples, placing a special laser beam reflector, planting the flag and unveiling a plaque announcing that man came in peace to the moon in July, 1969.

The peace theme was stressed, too, in what U.S. President Richard M. Nixon said "certainly has to be the most historic telephone call ever made."

He spoke to them, via the manned spacecraft centre at Houston (Texas) and the two astronauts replied while standing on the moon surface.

Edwin Aldrin and Neil Armstrong get their "moon legs" by jumping up and down shortly after stepping out on to the surface of the moon.

FORECAST . . . . VERY WARM

Mainly dry with bright periods. Wind south-westerly. Fresh. Very warm.

OUTLOOK: Unsettled w... thundery outbreaks

LIGHTS: 9.50 p.m. 4.25 a.m.

Neil Armstrong uses a scoop to pick up dirt from the surface of the Moon in one of the most important projects connected with the lunar landing . . .

This picture was picked up by the Goldstone Tracking Station and released by the jet propulsion laboratory at Pasadena (California).

Clearly visible are the ...

TONIGHT

More moonday reports—Page 4

Moon landing praised by MPs

Praise for the American moon landing came in the Commons tonight during question time exchanges.

... endorse very strongly what you have said — I am sure it is the wish of all parties in the House to extend to the American Government our warmest congratulations on the tremendous achievements of those men last night."

vow, Viv frittered all that away too and always insisted she had no regrets. She was diagnosed with dementia in 2009 and died six years later at the age of 79.

Conveniently for spendthrift Viv, the UK's largest indoor shopping centre had opened in Leeds in May 1964. Arnold Ziff, owner of Town Centre Securities, unveiled the Merrion Centre on his wife Majorie's birthday and it helped make him one of the region's most successful businessmen.

Marjorie, along with her late husband, donated large sums of money through the Marjorie and Arnold Ziff Charitable Foundation to a string of good causes in the city, including Leeds Art Gallery and Roundhay Park's Tropical World.

In 2011, Marjorie was awarded an MBE at Buckingham Palace for services to the community.

For years the *Yorkshire Evening Post* had faced competition from just down the road. But rival publication the *Yorkshire Evening News* was closed in 1963 – bringing to an end a period of fierce rivalry for scoops, readers and advertisers.

The paper merged with the *YEP*, for a brief time creating a daily circulation of close to half a million copies.

Leeds continued to think big. The idea of building an Olympic-sized swimming pool in the city was first mooted in the 1930s, only for plans to be abandoned because of the outbreak of war. In May 1960, the idea had been put back on the agenda but the *YEP* reported that the council was split over the idea, with many members wanting several smaller pools to be built instead.

The scheme eventually got the go ahead, opening in September 1967 amid a blaze of publicity. The 1,200-seater venue on Westgate was hailed as one of just two Olympic size pools in the North. Yet already there were signs that all was not well as gale force winds almost ripped off the futuristic copper-lined roof.

Worse still, the pool wasn't even fit for the Olympics. Legend has it that it was a couple of inches too short. In fact, it was slightly too narrow for eight-lane Olympic standards.

Its innovative design was by Yorkshire architect John Poulson, but in 1974 he was jailed for his part in a bribery and corruption scandal, which only added to the sense that the whole project was cursed.

That September, Leeds Council claimed more than £278,000 from the bankrupt architect for design flaws in the pool. It also had to spend £82,000 replacing Poulson's copper roof after its wooden frame rotted.

Three years later, ruling Tory councillors suggested selling the pool after it lost more than £400,000 in a year, although there was some light relief in 1981 when members of the International Nudist Federation used it for

A traffic policeman on point duty in City Square, December 1960.

***Opposite:* The inner ring road begins to take shape, 1965.**

their annual knees-up.

However, the pool still felt like a millstone round the city's neck and by 1993 councillors once again suggested selling it so they could afford to build a new sports complex somewhere else. The For Sale signs would eventually go up a decade later and the pool closed its doors for good in October 2007.

Controversy would also stalk another ambitious scheme that came to define 1970s Leeds. Winding its way through the heart of the city, the inner ring road was designed to put the city at the forefront of the dawning age of the motorway.

The *Yorkshire Evening Post* heralded it as 'The Road to the '70s', talking of "a motorway-within-a-city which will one day enable the motorist to drive through the heart of Leeds at 50mph".

It was given the go-ahead in April 1963, but only after a public inquiry presided over by the Ministry of Transport. Council representative Ken Potts was among those who argued in its favour, telling the inquiry: "Leeds is being thrust into the motorway age and should welcome the prospect."

Another fan was long-serving Leeds councillor Bernard Atha, who was on the planning committee when the city's chief engineer CG Thirlwall first mapped out his vision of a major road running through the middle of Leeds.

"It was the post-war era and we were trying to move the city forward because it was in the dark ages then compared to now," he recalled. "The idea of putting in an inner ring road, particularly

Film star Jayne Mansfield and her chihuahuas arrive for an appearance at Armley Jail, April 1967. She was killed in a car crash two months after this photograph was taken.

Right: Cleaners Lily Backhouse and Annie Burke watch the first live satellite television pictures from Australia, November 24, 1966.

Opposite:
The public enjoy the one and only opportunity to walk through the tunnel section of the inner ring road, 1967.

one using tunnels and cuttings, was anathema to many. There were all sorts of stupid objections – people would die of carbon monoxide poisoning and so on – bizarre things advanced as serious arguments.

"But I had seen the same thing in Stuttgart in Germany and it made me passionate about it, because it really was quite revolutionary."

Construction of the motorway section got under way the following year and was carried out in four stages, finishing behind schedule in early 1975. It cost £12.5m – the equivalent today of around £120m – and the first phase saw the removal of 370,000 tons of earth and rock as well as some 2,000 tons of coal.

Underground gas and electricity supplies had to be diverted, while more than 500 homes and business premises were purchased and demolished, sparking complaints that communities were being torn apart to accommodate it.

It was the UK's first urban motorway – hailed by some as an engineering masterpiece, condemned by others as a flawed folly.

Nevertheless, such was the civic pride in the project that on its completion a dinner party was held inside the Woodhouse Tunnel, complete with silver service. Members of the public were also allowed to stroll along the road for the first and last time.

Once it opened there were a few problems to iron out. As completed sections were opened one by one to traffic, drivers blamed confusing junctions for accidents, while the road layout created frequent gridlock. Tunnel pollution was also a problem, with dangerously high carbon monoxide levels causing occasional closures.

Nevertheless the road led Leeds to advertise itself as the 'Motorway City of the Seventies', the inner ring road joining with the M1 and M62 to allow traffic to flow freely to, from and around the city.

There were further plans for pedestrian walkways up in the sky that would leave the road clear for traffic. There was even talk of knocking down the Corn Exchange to make way for a dual carriageway, called the Leeds Approach, running past the Town Hall.

Mercifully, the Civic Amenities Act of 1967, which ushered in a new era for the preservation of existing buildings, along with the passing of clean air and smoke control laws which enabled Leeds' soot-covered buildings to be cleaned up, led to a greater appreciation of the city's architecture and the plans were abandoned.

Despite its critics, few would deny the inner ring road has done its job. It continues to play a vital role in the city's road network, carrying up to 80,000 vehicles a day and linking Leeds to the national motorway network.

By now Leeds was officially a metropolitan borough, with the old county borough ceasing to exist at midnight on March 31, 1974. Knaresborough and Harrogate were lost to North Yorkshire but Leeds gained Rothwell, Morley, Pudsey, Horsforth, Otley, Garforth, and parts of Tadcaster and Wetherby.

The *YEP* wasn't exactly enamoured with the changes, reporting on the front page of April 1: "Today the catastrophically expensive reorganisation of local government comes into force."

The paper had also landed itself in hot water by naming the officials who formed part of the new set-up and their salaries.

However, the Privy Council decided there was no case to answer. "We are not surprised about this verdict," the *YEP* said. "It supports our policy of giving all the facts to the people who put

The height of the blaze at Kirkgate Market, December 13, 1975.

up the money – the ratepayers and taxpayers of this area."

Lord Mayor Jean de Carteret was a little more upbeat, insisting there was nothing that could not be achieved in the new Leeds Metropolitan District.

"It is incumbent upon all of us to be realistic and practical – to work for the benefit of all – and I urge everyone to face up to what I believe is a great challenge in the way that is characteristic of the people making up this new city."

While major shopping chains and department stores have come and gone from Leeds over the last century – Schofields, which operated on The Headrow from 1901 to 1996 being perhaps the best known alongside Lewis's – Kirkgate Market has been a constant presence.

It was opened in 1857 as a response to growing public demand for markets and food halls. The largest indoor market in Europe, it was modelled on Crystal Palace in London. In 1904, a new market hall was completed as part of a grand scheme to improve Leeds's image after it was granted city status. It exceeded the budget by more than £30,000.

The market survived wartime bombing but on Saturday, December 13, 1975, a huge fire caused £7m worth of damage and destroyed many of the modern halls in one of the biggest disasters to ever strike the city.

The cause of the blaze remains unclear to this day – there were suggestions of an electrical fault or an overturned paraffin lamp. Either way, the flames spread quickly and some 150 stallholders were forced to flee for their lives.

The fire came at an important time of year for traders, many of whom had built up their stock for Christmas. All of their hard work was destroyed, along with two-thirds of the market, though miraculously the 1904 hall survived.

Prince Charles chats to a greengrocer in Kirkgate market during his walkabout, December 15, 1975.

Traders march to the Civic Hall to protest against plans to redevelop the Market, November 1985.

The following day, disbelieving crowds gathered to stare at the steaming piles of twisted metal and charred wood.

No lives were lost in the blaze but the city counted the cost to the jewel in its retail crown. Stallholders were left mourning businesses that had served generations of Loiners.

But the fire couldn't kill the fighting spirit of the market or its traders, many of whom were back on their feet within days. Determined not to be beaten, they crammed into whatever space they could find in undamaged sections of the market, mainly on the Vicar Lane side.

Trader Alan Brown summed up the sentiment when he declared in the YEP a few days later: "Kirkgate Market is really a very exclusive club. Its members have a reputation for helping each other and today everybody is doing just that."

Stanley Atack, a fruiterer who had a stall in Top Row, had bravely gone into the burning hall to rescue his day's takings, and the money was immediately offered on loan to other traders who couldn't manage.

Stallholders received a further boost when Prince Charles paid an unannounced visit on Wednesday, December 17, praising their fortitude and resilience.

By Thursday of that week, a temporary market had been set up in the Corn Exchange. The Kirkgate site was cleared and new halls opened in 1976 and 1981.

A few years later, the *YEP* reported plans to spend £120m to increase the market to 400,000 sq ft, longer than the Houses of Parliament, create a new bus station and 2,000 new car parking spaces.

However, there were concerns that it would compromise the historical and unique integrity of the market and Leeds City Council's Compulsory Purchase Order to enable the development to take place was rejected by the Secretary of State for the Environment.

EVENING POST

TUESDAY FEBRUARY 11 1975

TEL LEEDS 32701 — CLASSIFIED ADVERTISING 41234 PRICE 5p

FOWLER PALACE

TV Guide Page 8

HOW THEY RAN IN TONIGHT'S TOP TORY STAKES

1	2	3	3	5
Mrs. Thatcher	Mr. Whitelaw	Mr. Prior	Sir Geoffrey Howe	Mr. Peyton
146	79	19	19	11

It's Thatcher

Blonde bombshell Mrs. Margaret Thatcher, the 49-year-old mother of twins, is tonight the new leader of the Conservative party.

In today's five-cornered vote for the leadership she polled 146 votes.

This was a landslide 67 more than the 79 notched by her nearest rival, Mr. William Whitelaw.

The result was:

Thatcher	146
Whitelaw	79
Prior	19
Howe	19
Peyton	11

There were no abstentions. Mrs. Thatcher had needed only a simple majority—139—to win.

Shares dive

Many share prices fell on the London Stock Market today.

At one time the F.T. share price index was 14.6 points down, but it later recovered to show a fall of 13 points to 262.9.

● Money — Page 20.

RECORDER STOLEN

A stereo recorder, two speakers, and cassettes valued at £60, have been stolen from a car belonging to Mr. R. Thompson, Belvedere Road, Mount Pleasant, Batley, while it was parked outside his home.

'Crisis' hotels for sale

The troubled C. and H. hotel chain is putting all its properties up for sale—including the Grand and the Royal at Scarborough and the Granby Hall, Harrogate.

Suggestions that the group's debt totalled £2m. were "optimistic," said Mr. Nicholas Flynn, assistant to the Receiver appointed to run C. and H. affairs.

The group, which also includes the Norbreck Castle and Blackpool, will be kept running for as long as possible to protect bookings already made, said the Receiver, Mr. Harold Brierley.

But, he said, he was "open to offers for any of the properties.

Property tycoon Mr. Eric Farley bought the Norbreck for £189,000 and spent nearly £1m. on modernising and adding to it but the cash troubles have ended his dream of building up a multi-million-pound hotel group.

MAN DIES IN BLAST

One man was killed in an explosion in a chemical works at Belvedere, near Erith (Kent) today. There were no other casualties.

TOP SHOT

The bronze plaque for Bridlington Photographic Society's Print of the Year has been won by Mr. M. Barnard. There were nearly 400 entries.

Dr. Patrick Nuttgens, Director of Leeds Polytechnic, has a go at tossing a pancake today after presenting a gift token to the winner of a sponsored pancake race held on the Polytechnic campus.

The winner of the race was Mr. Peter Rous (22), left, Blenheim Terrace, a student in the Department of Institutional and Hotel Management.

The proceeds went to the Lord Mayor's Charity.

Entry coupon on Page 6
● Miss Hofbrau contest Page 2.

Pancake cheque pays rates

A cheque made out on a pancake was accepted by Calderdale rates office at Halifax today — Pancake Tuesday — in respect of an outstanding rate bill.

Mr. Norman Green, general secretary of the National Association of Ratepayers' Action Groups presented the pancake cheque for £75.64 after appearing before Halifax magistrates.

Mr. Mohammed Qasim, Calderdale rating officer, explained that Mr. Green, The Old Stones, Ripponden, was one of 1,068 people against whom he was applying for distress warrants because they had not paid their rates in full.

Relief

Mr. Green's total bill was £162 after deducting the special rate relief given last year by the Government.

At first Mr. Green, replying to the deputy clerk Mr. John Slater, said he intended to pay up after he had made a statement explaining why he had not paid in full.

But the chairman, Col. James Crossley, said it was a court of law and not to be used for political speeches and publicity statements.

Validity

Mr. Slater explained that the magistrates could only consider complaints about the validity of the rate demand and the way it was presented.

Mr. Green then said he was not going to pay and started reading his statement but Col. Crossley stopped him halfway through after Mr. Qasim had submitted that the statement was irrelevant.

The statement complained that although the Government had told local authorities severely to restrict their spending, Calderdale was embarking on big capital expenditure.

Revenge killing of milkman

Tit-for-tat killers are believed to be behind the murder of a Protestant milkman in County Tyrone today, after last night's machine-gun attack in a Catholic-owned bar.

The man was gunned down as he was delivering at Galvally, six miles from Pomeroy.

A terrorist last night sprayed automatic fire into Hayden's Bar, again near Pomeroy, killing one man instantly while a second man died in hospital today. Police are convinced today's killing was in retribution for the bar deaths.

ONASSIS RECOVERING

Aristotle Onassis, the 69-year-old shipping magnate, was reported today to be recovering satisfactorily in Paris from an attack of influenza and a gall bladder operation.

Secretary wins £30,000 damages

A secretary who courageously overcame the loss of her right hand only to have her life wrecked in a car crash, was awarded £30,403 damages in the High Court today.

Tragedy first struck when Mrs. Constance Clark was 19. Her right hand was so badly burned that it had to be amputated.

"Such a tragedy would have daunted a lesser woman but she showed courage and determination to overcome it," said Judge William Stabb. Changing to her left hand she mastered shorthand and even typing and became a secretary.

COLLISION

Then, four years ago, her car was in collision with a cement mixer and she suffered multiple injuries. She broke both knees and was left with facial disfigurement, eye damage and serious internal injuries.

Mrs. Clark, now a 40-year-old mother of two, of Wattan at Stone (Herts) was awarded the damages against the cement mixer driver, Mr. John Cooper, of Potters Bar (Herts).

He admitted liability for the crash and the judge had only to decide how much damages to award.

TWO DIE IN BLAZE

A year-old baby boy and his four-year-old sister died today after an explosion and fire at their home at Leigh (Lancs). The children's mother, Mrs. Lynda Mulcrow, and two more children, escaped.

Queen's pay: Wilson delays statement

By JOHN EGAN

The Prime Minister abandoned plans to make a Commons statement today announcing an increase of £420,000 to the Queen's official pay.

Mr. Wilson decided on this after speculative reports alleged he was making his controversial announcement today in the hope that Parliament's preoccupation with the Tory leadership would divert the attention both of MPs and the media.

After consulting colleagues gathered for a Cabinet meeting he let it be known he would make a statement tomorrow or after his return from Moscow early next week.

The delay will not diminish the impatience or anger of many Labour MPs who have been distressed by forecasts that the Queen would get a 40 per cent. addition to her present Civil List allowance of £980,000 a year.

WHAT THEY GET

Civil List allowances for other members of the Royal Family are not expected to be increased with any new allocation for the Queen.

They were fixed in the 1972 Civil List as:

The Queen Mother £95,000;

The Duke of Edinburgh £65,000;

Princess Anne £15,000 raised to £35,000 on her marriage to Capt. Mark Phillips in November 1973;

Princess Margaret £35,000;

Princess Alice, Duchess of Gloucester £20,000.

There is no separate Parliamentary provision for the Prince of Wales, who retains a part of the services of the Duchy of Cornwall.

Silent gunman kills two

A "silent" gunman shot dead

NEW LESLEY MYSTERY

Why did kidnapper come to Leeds?

Britain's most wanted criminal – wanted for the ruthless killing of three sub-postmasters and the kidnapping of heiress Lesley Whittle – was in Leeds at the end of last year, police have revealed.

They say he visited a Leeds store to buy a pair of trousers, found in the car in which he drove away with Lesley.

Today police in Leeds were trying to establish what "The Black Panther" was really doing in Leeds on Wednesday, November 20.

On that day he visited the C. & A. store in Boar Lane and bought a pair of brown, needlecord cotton trousers for £3.50.

The trousers and a store receipt were found in a bag in the car.

Lock of hair

A spokesman at C. & A. said today they had verified that the receipt came from their store. "It was a receipt for just one item—the trousers—which cost £3.50," the spokesman added.

Also in the car—a Morris 1300 found at Dudley where a security man was shot — was a lock of hair similar to Lesley's.

The hunt took a second new turn today when the "Panther" was reported as being seen in the Sedgley area of the West Midlands.

Police said yesterday that the man who kidnapped Lesley, heiress to an £82,000 legacy, from her home at Highley (Shropshire), on January 14 was also the raider who has killed three sub-postmasters, including Mr. Donald Skepper, at Harrogate, last February.

Police forces investigating the murder, shooting and kidnapping have now combined into a 300-strong team to hunt the killer.

Yorks pit strike call is rejected

By MAGGIE BRITTAIN

Hopes of peace in Britain's pits got a boost this afternoon when miners' leaders threw out a £25-a-week pay claim and rejected a strike call from the militant Yorkshire coalfield.

A move headed by fiery Yorkshire president Arthur Scargill to press the £25 demand, backed by an all-out strike call, was rejected when the NUM national executive met in London.

Voting was 15 to 11 — with one abstention.

Breaking point

But trouble is still rumbling among Britain's 246,000 mineworkers — for the union chiefs agreed on new wage targets that would mean rises of up to £20 a week — which they are putting to the Coal Board this afternoon.

The rejigged figures — £64.50 for coalface men, £50 for underground workers and £44 for those on the surface — will stretch the social contract to breaking point.

Mr. Scargill, looking disgusted as with the other leaders he went on to the Coal Board for further talks, refused to say anything except: "My credibility is intact — and a lot more than me have got their credibility intact."

'Ridiculous'

Communist leader of the Kent miners Mr. Jack Colins put it bluntly: "It's the beginning of Lent, we know, but this is ridiculous."

And Eric Clarke, of the militant Scottish coalfield, commented: "So the Stock Exchange will have another good day."

Careers service needs staff

A report to Leeds Careers Advisory Committee says the difficulty of attracting trained careers officers, or staff suitable for emergency training, is making it hard to maintain the service at the level operated by the former Leeds and West Riding authorities.

Group discussions and group interviews by careers officers had been used, but the school-leaving periods at Easter and in the summer

Bosanquet divorced

Reginald Bosanquet (41), the housewives' favourite television newscaster, offered no defence in the London Divorce Court today when a decree nisi was granted to his wife, Felicity.

Judge Callman held that their marriage had irretrievably broken down because of Mr. Bosanquet's intolerable conduct.

Mrs. Bosanquet, Cedar House, Marloes Road, Kensington, is a public relations consultant. She was formerly Press officer

REGINALD BOSANQUET

daughter was granted to Mrs. Bosanquet, and her husband was given reasonable access.

POPC

LIVE AT LEEDS

On November 3, 1963, a police escort accompanied a car carrying four young musicians into Leeds. Their route into the city had been lined with adoring fans and the police's presence was considered necessary to ensure their safe arrival at the Odeon Cinema on The Headrow.

As they pulled up outside the venue, The Beatles found yet more of Leeds City Police's finest straining to hold back the screaming crowd of 8,000 who had gathered to greet them.

"It's fantabulous!" the 20-year-old George Harrison told a *YEP* reporter who had chosen – voluntarily or otherwise – to brave the hordes. "Crowds lined the route and waved to us. We felt like royalty.

"Our hire car broke down and they (the police) brought us another and escorted us to the theatre. It was just like James Bond treatment – without the guns."

Once inside the Odeon, the 2,500-strong audience developed a case of mass hysteria.

"For 27 ear-splitting minutes I tried to listen to The Beatles," wrote the *YEP*'s reviewer. "It was as if the whole audience had been sprayed with an infectious screaming virus. Three minutes after the curtain fell they were still yelling."

The band were captured in all their youthful glory by young *YEP* photographer Paul Berriff. Having made it his job to seek out good contacts such as the local theatre and cinema managers, it soon paid off as he found himself up close and personal with The Beatles on their first UK tour.

"I was 16 years old and had just left school," Paul recalled. "We had no idea how famous The Beatles were soon going to be. It was this tour that started Beatlemania.

"When they came on stage you knew straight away there was something different about their music. The audience, mainly girls, started screaming and jumping up and down on the theatre seats. The noise from the audience got so loud that you could hardly hear the music.

"Their lyrics and melodies were amazing and captured the imagination of the young audience. This new pop scene was something we seemed to have been searching for."

Paul, who went on to photograph many more rock icons, including a 21-year-old Jimi Hendrix, resplendent in a crushed velvet suit backstage at the Odeon, was still learning his art and keen to experiment.

"I wanted to capture The Beatles in a natural situation," he said. "I very rarely used a flashgun on my camera and preferred to use available light. It meant I could capture shots which would make the background go darker – which was quite artistic for the time.

Paul Berriff was a junior photographer for the Yorkshire Evening Post when he started shooting the biggest pop stars of the day, gaining intimate access to the likes of The Beatles when they played at the Leeds Odeon in October 1964.

"I took pictures of Paul using this method which resulted in some very atmospheric images. I also think Paul knew I was learning my profession and he would often pose for me. There were never any forbidden areas where I couldn't photograph the group.

"They were always very amusing backstage. They would joke around all the time. I didn't like traditional poses for my photographs and always looked for something different. On one occasion John lined up four chairs for me in the dressing room and pretended it was a train. He wanted to be the engine driver and he asked Paul to be the guard. You could never get a straight answer from any question you asked them. John would always answer with a jokey comment and the others would then follow.

"Looking back at the images I cannot believe how good they are," he said. "But if I had produced them for the newspaper in 1963 I think Donald Futrell, the picture editor, would have rejected them as underexposed and not suitable for publication."

Though it has not always responded with quite the same level of delirium reserved for Beatlemania, Leeds has always loved its music.

In the late 19th and early 20th centuries workers let their hair down at music halls such as the City Varieties, later home to popular BBC show *The Good Old Days* and still going strong today.

While the Grand Theatre had strict regulations about who could sit where and what they were allowed to wear, the music hall was for everybody and standing tickets cost just a couple of pence.

Lovers of classical music meanwhile looked forward to the Leeds Triennial, a music festival usually held every three years from 1858, when it celebrated the opening of the Town Hall by Queen Victoria, to 1985.

The Leeds Festival Chorus, which was founded for the first festival, became independent in 1976 and continues to perform, broadcast and make recordings to this day.

The city is a proud home to the world famous Leeds International Piano Competition, spearheaded for five decades by the redoubtable Dame Fanny Waterman, which first brought such celebrated names as Radu Lupu and Murray Perahia to global attention.

The biggest names in jazz have also found a ready audience here. In the mid-1950s the likes of Humphrey Lyttelton, Ronnie Scott and Tubby Hayes could be seen at swinging jazz club Studio 20, now Sela Bar, on Upper Briggate.

The same era saw the rise of dance halls, with the Mecca in the city centre a hugely popular night out along with several others that quickly sprung up in the suburbs. Meanwhile, homegrown stars such as glamorous singer Marion Ryan and Ronnie Hilton, a former fitter in a sewing machine plant, enjoyed chart and TV success.

Shirley Bassey, Tina Turner, Roy Orbison and The Everly Brothers were just some of the top performers who beat a path to Batley Variety Club during its glory years of the 1960s and 1970s.

And the club celebrated a famous coup in 1968 when it secured the booking of Louis Armstrong for a two-week residency, at a cost which the *YEP* reported to be "a record fee in excess of 60,000 dollars". Our cameras captured the magical moment when Armstrong was met at Yeadon airport by seven-year-old Enrico Tomasso, of York Road, who greeted the great Satchmo with a rendition of Basin Street Blues on his trumpet.

Four years earlier, The Beatles had returned for what would be their fourth and final visit to the city, their only non-Odeon performance being at the Queens Hall, that draughty, but much-loved, converted tram shed at the junction of Swinegate and Sovereign Street. If anything, this

Beatlemania hits The Headrow for the arrival of the Fab Four, November 3, 1963. (photo: Paul Berriff).

Louis Armstrong is greeted with a tune from seven-year-old Enrico Tomasso at Leeds-Bradford Airport, June 15, 1968.

time the scenes at the Odeon were even more chaotic.

'Beatles under siege – fans under treatment' ran the *YEP*'s headline on a story which told how "six girls broke through a strong cordon of usherettes and attendants to climb over the organ on to the stage.

"The first to break through got within inches of Paul McCartney, the bass guitarist, before being dragged offstage and ejected. One of the Beatles was struck in the face by a cigarette lighter thrown onstage, along with pounds of jelly babies, letters, coats and gifts."

Among the audience that day was Betty Westwood. The 14-year-old successfully secured the autograph of her idol John Lennon – and the added bonus of a world exclusive.

John kindly used the back of her prized photo to sketch ideas for the group's next album, *Beatles For Sale*, making her the first person outside the band's inner circle to know its title.

More than four decades later the *YEP* reported how Betty, from Colton, was enjoying a windfall of £5,640 after putting Lennon's doodlings up for auction.

"I was obsessed with The Beatles in those days and I liked John the best because of his character," she recalled. "I always had a thing for him. I kept the photograph in an envelope in a plastic carrier bag in the loft and thought that one day my kids would throw it away."

Similar scenes of pandemonium accompanied another boy band, The Bay City Rollers, when they came to Leeds at the peak of what had been dubbed 'Rollermania'. Warren Smith, former manager of The Grand, shuddered at the memory of the Tartan-clad pin-ups' visit to the theatre in May 1975.

"We had police horses down the street by mid-afternoon, two barriers on Briggate to hold back the crowds... I've never seen anything like it," he said. "The kids only had one ticket between them but they were tying themselves together with tartan scarves. We set up a pen to separate the ones without tickets but it got so full we had to let them go, otherwise we'd have had a riot on our hands." After the show the group were smuggled out via the basement, through a secret back door and into a waiting truck on Vicar Lane.

Warren also remembered a young Elton John leaping off the stage and strolling casually along the narrow rail of the orchestra pit when he appeared at the famous venue, recalling: "He had the audience in the palm of his hand."

Another outpouring of teenage over-enthusiasm greeted heartthrob Rod Stewart when he appeared with The Faces at Leeds Town Hall in December 1972 – the concert being hit by a stage invasion 15 minutes from the end of the band's set.

"One girl led the rush and the others followed until there were hundreds of fans at the stage screaming to be near their hero," the *YEP* told readers the next day. "The police were called when several youths tried to climb on the window ledges outside the Town Hall to get in."

A year later, Rod was back for a gig at the Queens Hall, where crush barriers in front of the stage had to be hastily reinforced after giving way.

Rod Stewart rocks the tartan look at Leeds Town Hall, December 1972.

Pete Townshend and Roger Daltrey of The Who unveil a Civic Trust blue plaque in honour of their legendary 1970 concert in the Refectory at Leeds University, June 17, 2006.

The Starman has landed. David Bowie on stage at the Rolarena in Kirkstall, 1973.

The Who immortalised their gig at Leeds University's refectory on Valentine's Day 1970 in the form of the only live album they released with their best known line-up. It would go down in rock history as one of the most celebrated live recordings of all time, selling millions of copies worldwide and putting the city on the international musical radar.

In June 2006, the newspaper was with Roger Daltrey and Pete Townshend as they returned to the scene of their triumph to unveil an official blue plaque commemorating the event, the band later turning back the clock with another rollicking performance at the venue.

In the summer of 1973, David Bowie put on two shows in the unlikely surroundings of the Rolarena, a roller skating hall on Kirkstall Road, in his incarnation as interplanetary rock god Ziggy Stardust. Reviewer Derek Ogden came away suitably impressed, writing: "He ended the first half with Space Oddity, during which the whole place was bathed in specks of light reflected from one of those mirror-covered balls that used to be standard accompaniment to the last waltz at the local palais."

The gig had originally been planned for Leeds University but was rescheduled for the Rolarena after Bowie decided the stage at Leeds University was too small. It was to be his penultimate show performing as Ziggy. Ian De-Whytell, who owns Crash Records on The Headrow and saw Bowie in concert more than 40 times, recalled that he walked out of the concert "with my mouth wide open".

"It was amazing. I had never seen anything like it before. I felt as if I was in the presence of something unique, someone head and shoulders above anyone else in terms of talent."

Bowie would return in 1997 for an intimate show in front of just 500 devotees at the city's legendary Town and Country Club. The *YEP*'s review lavished praise on his renditions of classic tracks such as *The Jean Genie* and *Fashion*, adding that he "seemed so comfortable with the size of the T&C, as his grin confirmed, and it was great to be able to watch him at such close quarters."

Less impressed were the *YEP*'s Steven Kendall and Howard Corry when confronted with the brash face of the burgeoning punk phenomenon in the form of one Johnny Rotten in December 1976.

The Sex Pistols' arrival in Leeds as part of their *Anarchy in the UK* tour had been making headlines for days – not least as it had quickly become the opening date due to bans slapped on the group elsewhere in the country.

Norwich, Derby and Newcastle had all stopped them from playing after the Pistols had turned the air blue during their infamous appearance on the *Today* show with Bill Grundy the previous week.

Union vice president Ian Steele told the paper that the group had been told to cut the swearing from their performance at Leeds Polytechnic. But although reports of the Pistols trashing plant pots in the lobby of the Dragonara Hotel, now the Hilton, on Neville Street were rubbished by the hotel's management, they still weren't exactly flavour of the month.

Councillor Bill Hudson said Leeds would be "far better off without them", while his colleague Patrick Crotty added that he felt it a pity "people studying higher education found it necessary to listen to such rubbish".

Lead singer John Lydon duly responded by dedicating the gig's opening number to "Councillor Bill Hudson of Leeds, and Bill Grundy and the Queen", followed by a string of obscenities.

The next day's scathing report in the *YEP* claimed a large proportion of the 500-strong crowd

John Lydon of the Sex Pistols, pictured during the group's infamous gig at Leeds Polytechnic, December 6, 1976.

Opposite: Madonna at Roundhay Park , Leeds August 15, 1987

had walked out before the concert had finished, saying that "a vile, disgusting show was met with derision, scorn and hoots of laughter".

Photographer Steve Riding, who was taking pictures at the front, later recalled: "All I can remember was everybody was jumping up and down, spitting and throwing beer and generally causing mayhem. I'd done other bands like Bowie and Roxy Music, but I'd never seen anything like this in my life. I thought 'Christ, what's this all about?'"

The post-punk movement spawned local bands the Gang of Four, whose political stance and risque lyrics delighted fans and troubled the establishment, and The Mekons.

The Sisters of Mercy were formed in Leeds in 1980 by Andrew Eldritch and Gary Marx, two regulars at the F-Club, an alternative music night run at Leeds Polytechnic and other venues across the city.

Taking their name from a Leonard Cohen song, they played their first gig – with a drum machine called Doktor Avalanche – at Leeds University in 1981.

The band would go on to enjoy chart success, their high point coming with the release of second album *Floodland* in 1987 and were at the forefront of the goth rock scene which flourished in the city in the early 1980s, focused on clubs such as The Phono in the Merrion Centre.

Leeds began to be referred to as 'Gothic City' after the *YEP* ran a story in September 1983 around the annual Futurama 5 festival at the Queens Hall. The paper headlined the piece 'A Day In Gothic City' and described the line-up as sounding "a bit gothic horror".

The Wedding Present, formed in 1985 by Leeds local David Gedge, were initially influenced by punk and went on to become darlings of the independent music scene. Their popularity peaked in the early 1990s when they made a string of appearances on Top of The Pops and matched Elvis Presley's record of having 12 top 40 UK hits in one year, putting out a single a month. The group are still going today despite having seen a succession of line-up changes involving more than 20 different members, with Gedge the only ever-present.

In May 1982, Leeds was graced by rock royalty when Queen, led by the incomparable Freddie Mercury, lit up Elland Road. Hits like *We Will Rock You* and *Another One Bites The Dust* blasted out of a PA system that cost a cool £1m.

In fact that summer proved to be a very special one for the city's music fans with the Rolling Stones becoming the first household names to stage a huge concert at Roundhay Park. Resplendent in a series of bright bomber jackets and headbands, Mick Jagger strutted across the stage in front of 80,000 fans. A triumphant show was book-ended by classics *Under My Thumb* and *(I Can't Get No) Satisfaction*.

Genesis followed the Stones' lead in June 1987 on the home leg of their 10-month *Invisible Touch* world tour. An astonishing 160 labourers, 100 plumbers and electricians, plus the band's own 120-strong road team all worked to get the Roundhay stage set up. The light show alone cost £3m.

Then, that August, pop royalty came to town with Madonna landing by private jet at Leeds-Bradford Airport for the first British show of her *Who's That Girl* tour. One of the hottest music stars on the planet, rumours swirled that she ate in the kitchen of her hotel to protect her

Mick Jagger of the Rolling Stones struts his stuff on stage at Roundhay Park, July 25, 1982.

privacy and even installed her own gym to avoid public health clubs.

"It looks like the whole of Britain is here!" she said when she hit the stage in front of the 73,000-strong crowd at Roundhay, who were treated to hits including *Open Your Heart* and *True Blue*. They responded by singing *Happy Birthday* to mark her turning 29 the next day.

'Teasing Madonna sets the park alight' was the *YEP*'s headline the next day, with the paper's review noting that "before she even took to the stage 40 youths had to be stretchered away after a huge crushing surge – the first of many as fans battled for a prime view of the star in her scanty black basque.

"She did not disappoint them – teasing with kisses before going into an energetic work out which featured innumerable costume changes."

It's not often that the Mayor's official duties include meeting the planet's biggest star but that was the case when the King of Pop followed the Queen of Pop to Leeds. Michael Jackson performed to 90,000 people at a packed Roundhay Park on August 29, 1988, a Bank Holiday Monday, which also happened to be his 30th birthday.

Before the two-hour concert, the city's Deputy Lord Mayor, Bill Kilgallon, met the singer in his dressing room and took delivery of a cheque for £70,000, the share of the show's takings which Jackson had pledged to the council's Give For Life campaign to raise £1m for communities in Africa.

The *YEP* was also invited along, but we didn't get much out of the late superstar. The paper's Anne Pickles told how Jackson's inner sanctum was an elaborate blue and white marquee in the heart of a sprawling backstage area. "From its rouched ceilings hung chandeliers and in its corners fountains played at the feet of white statues in small, perfectly tended miniature gardens," she wrote in a special souvenir supplement.

"Awaiting his visitors, the star was displaying more chains than the combined Civic party. 'Oh hello,' his little voice repeated, as each of his guests was introduced. He gave the impression of a tiny nervous kitten, ready to cower at any sudden move."

On stage, however, it was a different story. Gusting winds may have made it hard to hear every word, especially for those at the back, but reviewer Howard Corry said that "not even that could detract from a superhuman performance from the man they call, with some justification, the greatest performer in the world.

"From the moment he appeared on stage to a pulsating explosion of sound, smoke and flame, to his last, echoing 'I love you all', Jackson had given a two-hour, non-stop display of music, dance and illusion that defied the imagination.

"He rose high across the crowd on a moving hydraulic platform for the opening of *Beat It*... he disappeared in a puff of smoke at one end of the stage to reappear instantly at the other... he

One of the stranger cheque presentations the YEP has covered. Michael Jackson does the honours.

wore the famous hat for a breathtaking version of *Billie Jean*... he was magnificent, moody and magical."

Four years later, on August 16, 1992, Jackson was back at Roundhay as part of his *Dangerous* world tour. The next day's *YEP* review told how "when the opening fanfare reached a climax he shot out of the stage in a Jack-in-a-box and stood motionless in front of a sea of adoring faces for a full two minutes.

"One regal turn of the head brought a mighty roar from the crowd and he was off." At the end of the concert he left the stage on a jetpack, or at least a lookalike did.

Having played at Elland Road in July 1987, Irish rockers U2 also enjoyed triumphant dates at Roundhay in 1993 and 1997. The first concert was part of their *Zooropa* tour and the *YEP* published a special pull-out guide, suitably becoming the *ZEP* for the occasion.

The stage set for the second of those concerts in August 1997 boasted a massive state-of-the-art LED screen, giant revolving silver-lemon-cum-spaceship and extensive sound systems, as well as spectacular lighting and laser effects. As Bono said from his mid-crowd podium: "Hope you're enjoying the show – because you paid for it."

Throughout the 1980s, a band calling themselves Chumbawamba were residents at South View House, a large, damp, dilapidated property in Armley which would serve as an unlikely launchpad even for an anarchist pop group.

The crowd for the visit of U2 to Leeds, August 14, 1993.

U2 singer Bono stops to take a look from behind his orange glasses while on stage at Roundhay, August 28, 1997.

One day they stumbled across an article in the *Yorkshire Evening Post* entitled 'How to Get Your Band on Television' and decided this wasn't merely a guide to ignore, but one they should turn inside out.

They duly stuck to their guns, even when their song *Tubthumping* became a huge hit in 1997, peaking at number two in the UK and breaking into America's top 10. After performing their anthem at the Brit Awards in 1998 they tipped a bucket of water over then Deputy Prime Minister John Prescott in retaliation for New Labour's refusal to back the Liverpool dockers' strike.

"We'd get offered money by a company, usually about £40,000, just to use it in a Ford truck advert in South Africa," Alice Nutter, one of the group's founder members told the *YEP*. "Then we'd give all the money to South African anti-capitalist groups."

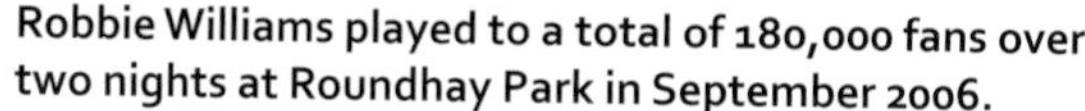

Robbie Williams played to a total of 180,000 fans over two nights at Roundhay Park in September 2006.

Noel Gallagher of Oasis on stage at Leeds Festival, August 28, 2000.

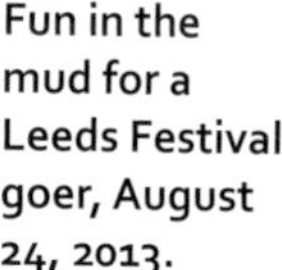

Fun in the mud for a Leeds Festival goer, August 24, 2013.

In 1999 Leeds made music history once again when it was chosen to become the second leg of the world famous Reading Festival. The extravaganza started life at Temple Newsam Park, which had hosted the V Festival for the previous two years.

Oasis headlined in 2000 and took the opportunity to inform the 70,000-strong crowd that, despite the rumours, they weren't splitting up. In a rare show of cross-Pennine solidarity, Liam Gallagher dedicated the band's hit *Live Forever* to Chris Loftus and Kevin Speight, the two Leeds fans who had been fatally stabbed the night before the first leg of Leeds's Uefa Cup semi-final against Galatasaray some months earlier.

The following year US rapper Eminem arrived at the festival with a reputation as one of the world's most controversial acts. In the event, however, the show passed off relatively calmly, with the *YEP* reporting: "Eminem delivered most of his hits, interjected with tales of pistol-whipping and his own cartoon on the big screen featuring the characters from TV's South Park."

The festival was witness to a triumphant return to live performances by a new-look Guns 'N' Roses in 2002, with the group coming back in 2010. This time, however, the Leeds crowd were kept waiting over an hour for an apparent Axl Rose tantrum to pass. He eventually emerged but, after running over by 30 minutes, the band's sound was cut and after a rendition of *Paradise City* the members staged a sit down protest. Many of the crowd had already gone home.

With violence and riots having marred the festival's stay at Temple Newsam, in 2003 it moved up the A1 to Bramham Park. With a daily audience of festival goers that has now swelled to 75,000, the likes of Arctic Monkeys, The Killers, Red Hot Chili Peppers, Metallica and Morrissey have all delivered barnstorming sets there.

There was a minor row in 2013 though when revellers on their way home from the festival turned the area around Leeds train station into a sea of mud. The *YEP* revealed that around £50,000 was subsequently spent installing 1,000 metres of piping to improve drainage at Bramham in a bid to prevent future mudbaths.

Local bands appearing at the festival have included The Cribs, The Music, The Sunshine Underground and The Pigeon Detectives. In 2012, Pulled Apart By Horses had the honour of becoming the first Leeds band to open the festival.

But it was a group fronted by former Leeds Grammar schoolboy Ricky Wilson, the Kaiser Chiefs, which became the most successful band to emerge from the city since rock band the Sisters of Mercy in the 1980s.

Having been featured in the pages of the *YEP* in their previous incarnation as Parva, we gave the new-look Kaisers – named after the home club of former Leeds legend Lucas Radebe – a rave review when they supported the Ordinary Boys at the tiny Blank Canvas in October 2004.

The original line-up featured drummer Nick Hodgson, from Cookridge, who was classmates with keyboard player Nick 'Peanut' Baines, from Horsforth, and bassist Simon Rix, from Guiseley, at St Mary's School in Menston.

He then met Ricky Wilson, from Ilkley, plus guitarist Andrew White, from Garforth, at various music nights around Leeds. Hodgson revealed to us that their breakthrough single *I Predict A Riot* was inspired by a Friday night in Leeds when he was a DJ at The Cockpit and would drive past the Majestyk nightclub.

As well as a string of appearances at Leeds Festival and the US leg of Live 8, the lads packed out concerts at Leeds Town Hall and Millennium Square. Then, in May 2008, they saw a dream come true when they played at Elland Road, home to their beloved Leeds United. It was the first concert at the ground since the Happy Mondays in 1991, but the band were more concerned about the result of Leeds United's play-off final against Doncaster 24 hours earlier.

Nick Baines told the *YEP*: "I'll be pretty nervous when it comes round to kick-off time. The gig – well, we're musicians, it's what we do. Saturday is a one-off, obviously, and it's a big deal to us, but we'll be in control.

"We've been planning this for so long, it's something we've always wanted to do. We're going to be pulling out all the stops."

Our review told how "the setting sun cast a magical glow over the packed pitch as frisbees and beach balls floated above a sea of nodding heads and fists punched the air.

"Thousands roared along with Ricky on choruses like *Ruby* and *Na Na Na Na Naa* and the frontman's energy was infectious, refusing to let anyone stand still.

"Youngsters bounced around on their parents' shoulders while grey-haired businessmen shuffled their feet and screeching girls jumped up and down in excitement."

Nearly a decade after it hosted its last major concert, a combined total of 180,000 fans flocked to Roundhay Park to see former Take That star Robbie Williams belt out hits such as *Millennium* and *Kids* at two gigs in September 2006.

The *YEP* reported how Robbie, having heard that 11 schools in Leeds had been closed because of the concerts, informed the crowd: "How great am I? That never happened when I was at school. Michael Jackson never came to Stoke-on-Trent."

Over the years, the city has lost a fair few of its legendary smaller music venues, including the Queens Hall, the Duchess of York, The Warehouse and the Town and Country Club.

Between them they hosted the then little-known likes of Nirvana, Stone Roses, The Jam, Duran Duran, The Police, Oasis, Blur, Coldplay, Radiohead and, in the case of The Warehouse, witnessed the first ever live performance of Soft Cell's all-time classic *Tainted Love*, sung by its then cloakroom attendant Marc Almond. The frontman had performed a series of theatre pieces during his time at Leeds Polytechnic and one, Zazou, had been panned by a YEP critic as "one of the most nihilistic, depressing pieces that I have ever had the misfortune to see", prompting Almond to later refer to it as a "success" in his autobiography.

Another keeper of coats would rise to prominence a quarter of a century later. Corinne Bailey Rae, from Moortown, worked in the cloakroom at The Wardrobe club in St Peter's Square while studying at Leeds University. Her self-titled album, released in 2006, sold millions of copies and was a major hit in America.

But by the dawn of the Noughties, there were calls for a proper arena that would bring the biggest acts in the world to Leeds – and the *YEP* shouted louder than most.

Our Leeds Needs an Arena campaign won the backing of the likes of the Kaiser Chiefs as well as local businesses and residents. It was praised in Parliament and credited with helping to secure the go-ahead for the 13,500-capacity venue.

In an editorial comment in 2009, the *YEP* said an arena would "galvanise Leeds", "add to the city's flourishing cultural scene and mean the millions of pounds gig-goers spend in Manchester and Sheffield stay here instead."

It was Bruce Springsteen who had the honour of performing on the opening night of the brand spanking new First Direct Arena in July 2013.

Handing the gig a five-star review, the *YEP* said: "After 29 songs and a set which stretched for three hours and four minutes, Springsteen left the stage and paid tribute to the newest venue

Top: The Kaiser Chiefs check out the changing rooms ahead of their gig at Elland Road.

Left: The Chiefs' Ricky Wilson on stage at the concert, May 24, 2008.

Above: Leeds lass Corinne Bailey Rae made the journey from cloakroom attendant to international singing sensation.

in Yorkshire, saying: 'This is a great building, and a great place to play'."

For the venue's official opening night that September, the honours fell to Elton John, who arrived on stage with the words: "Good evening Leeds, it's great to play this wonderful new place."

For the next two hours the Rocket Man had the audience in the palm of his hands – just as he had at the Grand Theatre all those years ago.

Sir Elton John performs on the official opening night of the First Direct Arena, September 4, 2013. However, rock legend Bruce Springsteen (below) beat him to it by appearing at the venue six weeks earlier.

INSIDE › The Ripper's trail of fear — Pages 2 and 3

Yorkshire EVENING POST

GARDEN LANE.

MONDAY JANUARY 5 1981 TEL LEEDS 32701 — Classified Advertising 441234 WEATHER PAGE 14 PRICE 12p

Secluded Melbourne Avenue in Sheffield.

WHERE VICE-SQUAD OFFICERS POUNCED ON COUPLE IN CAR

Reporters: ROY HOLLAND, NICOLA GOULD, BRIAN KAY and MALCOLM HAIGH. Pictures: STEVE RIDING and ERNEST BROOK.

Police today guard the detached home in [Garden] Lane, Heaton, Bradford, of Peter Sutcliffe.

Ripper: Bradford man, 35, due in court today

Bradford lorry driver Peter William Sutcliffe was due to appear before magistrates later this afternoon in connection with the Yorkshire Ripper murders.

Sutcliffe, a 35-year-old married man of Garden Lane, Heaton, Bradford, was appearing at Dewsbury Court.

Ripper Squad Press liaison officer Superintendent Frank Morritt said: "The precise nature of the charges has not yet been decided and discussions are taking place between senior officers.

"One charge will relate to the Ripper series of incidents and one to suspected stolen car number plates."

Asked if the Ripper charge would be concerned with the actual murders, Mr. Morritt said: "Probably, yes. But I can't say for definite."

Wife

Today Sutcliffe's wife, Sonia, and another woman were also still helping police with their inquiries.

Mr. Morritt said Mrs. Sutcliffe was a "material witness" but was not in custody.

The other woman was with the man in a parked car near Sheffield city centre on Friday night when they were seen by two vice squad officers.

They detained the man over the alleged theft of number plates on his dark - coloured Rover car.

He was brought to West Yorkshire and after discussions between detectives from the West and South Yorkshire forces further inquiries were made.

The hearing is at Dewsbury because it is believed a missing number plate was taken from a Dewsbury scrapyard.

Delighted

An ebullient West Yorkshire Chief Constable Ronald Gregory told a packed Press conference at Dewsbury last night.

"This man is now detained in West Yorkshire and is being questioned in relation to the Yorkshire Ripper murders.

"I can tell you we are absolutely delighted with developments at this stage."

Extra police were called in to control a crowd of over 1,000 people outside Dewsbury Courthouse today.

One demonstrator held a noose aloft and another called for the death penalty.

People going into the court were searched.

By George! Top police trio take time for a smile

Smiles all round from Assistant Chief Constable Mr. George Oldfield (left), Chief Constable Mr. Ronald Gregory (centre) and Assistant Chief Constable Mr. Jim Hobson in Dewsbury last night.

WALKER DIES
Post-mortem examination being held on Mr. Eric Smith, 56, of Silcoates Lane, Wrenthorpe, Wakefield, who collapsed and died while walking in Derbyshire Peak District.

CAMERA STOLEN
Thief stole camera and equipment worth £516 from van parked in Follifoot, near Harrogate.

UNION LEADER HELD
Mr. Ken Ashton, general secretary of National Union of Journalists, questioned for five hours by immigration officials at Johannesburg and then put on plane back to London. Mr. Ashton in South Africa to advice black journalists union on union affairs and training.

M-WAY STRETCH CLOSED
Ten-mile stretch of the M62 between Liverpool and Manchester, near Burtonwood Service area, closed because of toxic fumes from burning tanker. No-one injured.

M1 VEHICLE BAN
Heavy vehicles over 32 tons or more than 9ft. 6ins. wide to be banned from using stretch of M1 for ten miles between junction 29 at Heath, Derbyshire and junction 30 at Barlborough, Derbyshire because of subsidence from nearby collieries. Ban starts on January 11 until mining in area has ended.

HOUSE RAID
Thief broke into house in St. George's Road, Harrogate, taking cash and cheques worth £500.

ANTIQUES TAKEN
Antiques worth £3,000 stolen from house in Scholes, near Huddersfield.

HOUSE FIRE
Extensive damage caused to house in Priestman Street, Manningham, Bradford. Cause of fire being investigated by police.

PRISONERS CAUGHT
Two escaped prisoners, Alan John Baines and Derek Bull, recaptured in Bradford at weekend after absconding from Kirkham Prison, near Preston, before Christmas.

Devoted coup[le] say neighbou[rs]

Stunned neighbours today des[cribed] Peter and Sonia Sutclife as a "de[voted] couple" who have lived in [a] spacious detached home in G[arden] Lane, Heaton, for the past three ye[ars].

Mr. David Bowman

Mrs. Barbara Bowman

Neighbour Mr. Anthony O'Callaghan.

They said M[r. Sut]cliffe was a [long] distance lorry [driver] and was away [from] home quite a bit.

Mr. David B[owman], 46, a wool me[rchant], and his wife, B[arbara], 39, spoke of th[e time] when they invit[ed the] couple into their [home].

It was when [the Sut]cliffes had first [moved] into the house [a] few yards on th[e oppo]site side of [Garden] Lane.

"They were very quiet," sa[id Mr.] Bowman. "She i[s a] good-looking gir[l. I] think she is a teacher in som[ething] like pottery or a[rt].

"She was inte[lligent] and intellectua[l. She] spoke about fi[ve lan]guages. She sa[id she] was of Uk[rainian] origin."

Mrs. Bowma[n des]cribed the Sutc[liffes as] a "pin-up couple[. He] was handsome [and she] was attractive [with] long, brown hair.

"We saw he[r] yesterday morni[ng and] she looked serio[us. She] got into a green car and was [driven] away."

The couple ha[d been] trying to sell [the] house to set [up a] pottery business [else]where, sai[d the] Bowmans.

"They paid [... for the house [three] years ago and i[t was] put on the ma[rket at] £37,000," sai[d Mr.] Bowman.

Mrs. Bo[wman] thought Mr. S[utcliffe] had previously [...]

Continued on P[age ...]

Big jobs boost

One thousand new jobs are set to come to Leeds, it was revealed today by the city's Deputy Planning Chairman, Coun. Brian North.

He said a firm was seeking planning permission to build a factory on land at Millshaw, Beeston, that would create 1,000 new jobs next year, and the firm expected to double its workforce in less than five years.

Coun. North said the firm had requested its name be kept secret, as negotiations were taking place with the Government for special grant-aid to build the factory.

EXPORT

These negotiations could, said Coun. North, be completed by the end of the month.

Yorks boss tells of 1977 . . .

Police quizzed our workers

The managing director of the Bradford firm where Peter Sutcliffe works told today how Ripper Squad detectives had interviewed a number of employees, including Sutcliffe, three years ago.

Mr. William Clark, 35, said the interviews took place after the death of Manchester mother-of-two Jean Royle, 21, whose mutilated body was found in Manchester in October, 1977.

Sutcliffe has worked as a long distance lorry driver at T. and W. H. Clark Holdings Ltd., Hillam Road, Bradford, since October, 1976.

Mr. Clark said: "Detectives interviewed several men, including myself, at the firm after that murder.

"Detectives asked us where we had been on certain dates and wanted

Today's picture of Mr. William Clark.

Mr. Clark said Sutcliffe was "very quiet - a bit of a loner."

"He spoke slowly. He did not speak without

CRIME AND PUNISHMENT

On June 29, 1961, Hungarian-born miner Zsiga Pankotia left his cell at Armley jail for the last time. Waiting for him was Harry Allen, who had already done his homework. The hangman had measured 31-year-old Pankotia at five feet six inches tall and a weight of 10 stones and eight pounds. Allen calculated he would need a long drop of seven feet and six inches to get the job done.

Pankotia had been tried, convicted and sentenced to death at Leeds Crown Court for the murder of market trader Eli Myers, who had scooped £1,275 on the football pools shortly before dying in a struggle with Pankotia during a break-in at his home in Roundhay. The 91st prisoner to be hanged at Armley, Pankotia would also be the last. Four years later, the death penalty was suspended and in 1969 it was abolished completely.

Like any major town or city, Leeds has had its fair share of stories of horrific crimes down the decades. It has been the duty of the *Yorkshire Evening Post* to report them, to issue the countless police appeals designed to catch those responsible, and to detail how justice was duly delivered.

MRS. SWANN.

Emily Swann calmly chatted to her lover John Gallagher before the pair were hanged in 1903.

Many of those convicted of murder in the first decades of the *YEP*'s existence shared the same fate as Zsiga Pankotia, meeting their end within the confines of the grim and forbidding Victorian prison at Armley, built in 1847 at a cost of £43,000.

In 1903, the paper reported on the execution of Emily Swann, the only woman ever to be hanged at the prison. The 42-year-old mother of 11 children was believed to be having an affair with miner John Gallagher, who lodged at the home she shared with husband William in Wombwell, near Barnsley. Suspicious of her closeness to Gallagher, William gave Emily two black eyes, which a jury at Leeds Assizes decided was the trigger for Gallagher to murder him. He and Emily were found guilty after just an hour of deliberations and were hanged together at 8am on December 29.

Normally not a word was spoken in the moments prior to execution, for the simple reason that the condemned were usually too paralysed by fear to utter a word. But as Emily entered the execution room she saw John on the gallows. "Good morning John," she said to her hooded lover. "Good morning love," he replied. As the noose was placed around her neck, Emily added: "Goodbye. God bless you."

Years later, young killer Arthur Osborne would have the unfortunate distinction of being hanged on his birthday. His crime was to murder 70-year-old Ernest Westwood in the course of a robbery. At the end of his three-day trial in 1948, the jury recommended that Osborne be shown mercy, but the Home Secretary refused. He was duly hanged on December 30 – the same day he turned 28.

Leeds Prison, better known as Armley Jail, has housed some of the city's most dangerous criminals.

Opposite:
A prisoner stages a one-man protest on the roof, 1911.

Demonstrators in City Square protest against the death penalty. Just under a hundred prisoners were hanged at Armley Prison before it was abolished.

One of the more famous hangmen who served at Armley was Thomas Pierrepoint, uncle of the well-known executioner Albert Pierrepoint. Thomas carried out 32 executions at the prison, including three double hangings.

Prior to the 1950s, prisoners awaiting execution at Armley were said to face one of the longest walks to their death of any inmates in the country. It was a full 40 yards from condemned cell to noose through what was dubbed the Hangman's Tunnel. Little wonder then that one prisoner struggled so much it took guards 15 minutes to get him to the gallows.

Two gunmen sent shoppers diving for cover as they fired warning shots while fleeing a raid at a jewellery store on Albion Street on the morning of November 16, 1949. Jeweller Harry Levine was shot during the robbery and died the following day. The gunmen, teenagers Walter Sharpe and Gordon Lannen, had months earlier lost their Leeds factory jobs. Sharpe, who was 19, was hanged at Armley on March 30, 1950. Lannen was also found guilty of murder but as a 17-year-old he escaped the death penalty, serving eight years before being released.

Among the countless murders reported by the *YEP*, one of the most heartbreaking unfolded in March 1986, when 10-year-old Sarah Harper disappeared after leaving her home in Morley to buy a loaf of bread from the corner shop 100 yards away. A huge search was mounted but no trace of her could be found.

At a press conference a week later, her mother Jackie told the *YEP* and other assembled media that she feared the worst. She made a direct appeal to her daughter's abductor to reveal the whereabouts of Sarah's body, which was later found in the River Trent near Nottingham.

Leeds detective John Stainthorpe quickly linked the murder to those of Scottish schoolgirls Susan Maxwell and Caroline Hogg. He would be proved right – delivery van driver Robert Black

was subsequently arrested and convicted of the kidnap, rape and murder of four girls.

Fifteen years later, another Leeds girl would tragically go missing. Leanne Tiernan, from Bramley, disappeared in November 2000 after a shopping trip in Leeds city centre with her best friend Sarah Whitehouse. The 16-year-old's body was found nine months later in undergrowth at Lindley Wood, near Otley. In 2006, the *YEP* reported that her murderer, John Taylor, who lived a short distance from Leanne's home, would have to serve a minimum of 30 years behind bars.

Barry Prudom was an electrician from Leeds who also happened to be a former member of the territorial SAS. In the summer of 1982 he put his skills to use in what was then the largest armed police operation Britain had ever seen, involving no fewer than a dozen forces. It was launched after Prudom, trying to evade arrest for jumping bail on an assault charge, shot dead PC David Haigh at the Warren Point picnic area near Otley on June 17.

Days later he shot electrician George Luckett, 52, in a village near Newark, Nottinghamshire, before returning to North Yorkshire and going to ground in Dalby Forest. His astonishing ability to escape capture by the police officers who flooded the area saw him dubbed 'The Phantom of the Forest'.

The following day Prudom shot at police dog handler Ken Oliver, but he managed to get away and survived. Then, on June 28, North Yorkshire Police took the unusual step of naming Prudom as the man they needed to find. That same day saw Sergeant David Winter become Prudom's final victim after he challenged him in the centre of Old Malton, North Yorkshire, and was shot dead on the grass – 200 yards from the police station.

The police threw a cordon around the town as the 1,000-strong manhunt for the killer

Armed police in Malton during the hunt for Barry Prudom *(above)* in the summer of 1982.

continued. On July 3, Prudom got into the home of Malton pensioners Maurice and Bessie Johnson and their 43-year-old son Brian, holding them hostage throughout the Saturday night. He finally left their home at 3.30am and limped 50 yards to the Malton Tennis Club, hiding in undergrowth beneath a plastic bag.

The Johnsons freed themselves and alerted the police. Former SAS man Eddie McGee, a survival and tracker expert who had written the book on which Prudom was basing his evasion tactics, then managed to track him to his hiding place. In a bid to take Prudom alive police used stun grenades, but the killer refused to surrender. When he fired at them, they shot back, but an inquest later found that Prudom died from a self-inflicted wound.

In July 1991, Leeds sex worker Julie Dart was picked up from the city's red light area by Keighley tool repairer Michael Sams. She was abducted, forced to write a ransom note and then murdered when she tried to escape.

Sams would go on to kidnap estate agent Stephanie Slater, keeping her imprisoned in a 'coffin' made from a wheelie bin. After receiving the £175,000 ransom he had demanded, he dropped her outside her home. A nationwide manhunt was launched after the kidnap was linked to Julie's murder.

Sams was eventually caught following an appeal on the BBC's *Crimewatch* programme. He enjoyed taunting the police but made a crucial mistake. On one of his telephone calls to negotiate the ransom he forgot to disguise his voice. The tape was played on *Crimewatch* and his ex-wife Susan recognised the voice instantly. She tipped off detectives and Sams was arrested, being sentenced to life behind bars in July 1993.

A decade later there would be fresh tragedy for the police at the hands of another fugitive. Traffic officers Ian Broadhurst and colleague Neil Roper were on patrol in Leeds on Boxing Day 2003 when they spotted a car parked suspiciously at the junction of Grange Park Avenue and Dib Lane in Oakwood.

Little did they know that the man reading a copy of the *Racing Post* at the wheel was David

Bieber, a former US Marine from Florida who was on the run after the murder of a love rival. He had been living in Leeds under the alias Nathan Coleman, working as a nightclub doorman. After confirming the car's licence plates were false, the officers attempted to arrest Bieber, who quickly produced a handgun and opened fire.

PC Roper was shot twice but managed to escape. PC James Banks, who had arrived to provide support, remarkably survived being shot as the bullet lodged in his police radio. PC Broadhurst was hit twice. The first shot to his chest may well have proved fatal, but Bieber ensured he had no chance of surviving by shooting him in the head as he lay pleading for his life on the ground. The gunman then calmly left the scene, threatening a couple who were out shopping and stealing their car to make his getaway.

"It was a black evening for the police and the city," wrote the *YEP*'s chief crime reporter David Bruce a few days later. "Gun crime that has stalked Leeds with increasing ferocity in recent years had claimed the life of a man dedicated to doing his bit for the community."

The murder sparked a five-day manhunt for bodybuilder Bieber. He was eventually cornered in a guesthouse in Gateshead. Convicted of murder and told he would spend the rest of his life in prison, his sentence was subsequently reduced to a minimum of 37 years.

Three years later, the *YEP* revealed that Bieber had been foiled in a plot to break out of the top security jail where he was being held. He and two other inmates planned to take hostages with a gun smuggled into Whitemoor Prison in Cambridgeshire.

In 2008, Ian Broadhurst's widow Eilisa unveiled a memorial stone at the scene of his death. Thanking the Leeds public for the messages of support she had received since the killing, she told the congregation: "I know Ian will be looking down on us with great delight.

"As you all know the police force was a big part of who Ian was. It was one of the great loves of his life and it allowed him to do what he liked best: fast cars, helping people and getting paid for it."

The *Yorkshire Evening Post* has received countless visits down the years from readers armed with stories they want to be told in the pages of the newspaper. One of the more unusual came in 2007, when Colin Norris, a nurse from Kirkstall, turned up at reception and asked to speak to a reporter.

Glasgow-born Norris informed the journalist that he was being investigated over the deaths of a number of patients in his care and pleaded his innocence. The following year, a jury convicted him of murdering four elderly patients with secret shots of insulin.

Doris Ludlam, 80, Bridget Bourke, 88, Irene Crookes, 79, and Ethel Hall, 86, had all died at Leeds General Infirmary and St James's Hospital in 2002. Norris was also found guilty of the attempted murder of Vera Wilby, 90, and told he must serve at least 30 years behind bars.

Suspicions had first been raised when he predicted the death of Ethel Halls, saying she would die at 5.15am. Her condition worsened badly around 5am that same morning and she passed away some weeks later.

However, campaigners later claimed fresh evidence cast doubt on his conviction and insisted there were logical explanations for all the deaths. Paul May, who has visited Norris in prison and fought for his release, told the *YEP*: "I'm confident that Colin is not a murderer.

"For anybody to commit the crimes he is convicted of they would have to have a severe personality disorder. In other words, they would have to be a psychopath. Colin is nothing of the kind." At the time of writing, the Criminal Cases Review Commission was considering new

Michael Sams murdered teenager Julie Dart, pictured, before kidnapping estate agent Stephanie Slater.

PC Ian Broadhurst was shot dead on Boxing Day 2003 as he investigated a car with suspicious number plates being driven by fugitive David Bieber, who was living in Leeds under the alias Nathan Coleman.

Ian Broadhurst's widow Eilisa is joined by Michael Winner, chairman of the Police Memorial Trust, to unveil a memorial to her husband at the scene where he died, October 2, 2008.

scientific evidence to determine whether the conviction was sound.

Mystery stalks many murder cases that have unfolded in the city. On the night of February 16, 2004, businessman John Luper was out walking his dog when he was ambushed by up to five men and dragged back inside his luxury Alwoodley home.

His wife, Iyican, daughter, Liza-Rose, and their au pair were tied up while the gang ransacked the house before making off with a £100,000 haul of jewellery and cash. After they left, the women managed to free themselves and found 57-year-old Mr Luper collapsed in a downstairs room.

Paramedics battled to resuscitate him but their efforts proved in vain, a post mortem revealing he died of asphyxiation. A jar of marmalade was found next to him, suggesting the gang had fed some to him in the belief he was diabetic and had lapsed into a coma. Despite exhaustive investigations at the time and in the years since, the culprits have never been found.

Len Farrar, a former merchant seaman and coach driver, was found stabbed to death at his home in Cardinal Road, Beeston, in May 2002. His body was discovered by two police officers who called to tell him his stolen lilac Fiat Panda car had been found burned out nearby.

Though his killer has never been identified, a prime suspect in the inquiry has been Gary Bradley, who was handed a life sentence for stabbing to death retired solicitor Christopher Scholey in the area's Cross Flatts Park in September of the same year.

Four years after his death, Mr Farrar's adopted sister, Christine Willans, told the *YEP* that the hardest part for them was not being able to tell Len that the police had caught his killer. "We go to his grave in Harrogate and talk to him," she said. "We want closure and just hope that one day we will be able to tell him the person who murdered him has been caught."

The shooting of Adam Chadwick is the subject of another long-running riddle that police are still desperate to solve. He was visiting his sister at Clifton Mount in Harehills on the night of June 24, 2008 when a woman and three men came to the door.

Following a disturbance, 20-year-old Adam was shot. The attack happened the day after his daughter, Ruby, had turned three. He died two days later. Police told the *YEP* they believed Adam, a carpet fitter who lived in Seacroft, could have been mistaken for another man, but his killers have never been caught. His family set up The Adam Chadwick Fund for Sport in his memory, staging an annual football tournament for primary schools in West Leeds.

One of the grisliest murders reported by the *Yorkshire Evening Post* came in 2008 when chef Anthony Morley was found guilty of murdering lover Damian Oldfield. A former Mr Gay UK, Morley had invited Mr Oldfield to his home in Bexley Place, Harehills, and cooked him a meal. He later cut his throat and sliced off chunks of flesh from his chest and leg which he fried in olive oil before chewing.

After the killing, Morley walked into the Desi Khan takeaway on Roundhay Road wearing only a blood-stained dressing gown and flip flops and told stunned staff what he had done. The 36-year-old was jailed for life, with a minimum term of 30 years, at Leeds Crown Court.

But the most infamous killer to ever stalk the streets of Leeds was undoubtedly the man dubbed the Yorkshire Ripper – Peter Sutcliffe. No detective, let alone a reporter, could have predicted a single murder in the 1970s would herald one of the most infamous and long-lasting series of sadistic killings Britain has ever endured.

The first evidence of a spree that would terrorise Leeds and the rest of the region for half a decade emerged on a misty morning at the tail end of October 1975. A partially-clothed body

Det. Chief Supt. Denis Hoban

Savage and sadistic sex attack on Leeds 'mother in fear'

30 OCT 1975

Murder in fog

A police photographer prepares to take pictures of the body—indicated by arrow—as police officers erect canvas screens round the area.

Mrs. Wilma McCann—stabbed to death.

A young Leeds mother of four was stabbed to death

HEARTBREAK OF 5 A.M.

the playing field. I think it was because she didn't want people to know what time she was going out and

BODY FOUND HERE

The murder of Wilma McCann in October 1975 began the most horrifying chapter in Leeds' history.

found on Prince Philip Playing Fields in Scott Hall belonged to Sutcliffe's first murder victim. Prostitute and mother-of-four Wilma McCann, 28, had been brutally stabbed and mutilated 150 yards from her home in Scott Hall Avenue.

That morning Wilma's son Richard and daughter Sonia, aged five and seven, had gone looking for their mother when she failed to return home. They had spotted a "bundle" on the fields not realising it was their mother and instead waited at a bus stop in the hope she would soon be getting off there. After 10 buses they went home.

Eleven weeks later, *YEP* crime reporter Bruce Smith was at the scene of another grim discovery. The body of a second prostitute, 42-year-old Emily Jackson from Churwell, had been found in an alley of Manor Street in Sheepscar. She too had been brutally stabbed.

Soon Leeds CID boss Detective Chief Superintendent Denis Hoban was linking both killings and the city's "working girls" were warned off the streets and urged to come forward with information. Police released an artist's impression of a suspect not dissimilar to Sutcliffe – with a moustache but no beard – and 10 days later appeal posters featuring the victim were everywhere.

A year passed during which Sutcliffe stabbed and left for dead a 20-year-old Leeds woman who survived, before reporters were once again gazing across playing fields towards a covered body on February 7, 1977.

This victim was another 28-year-old mother of two. She was called Irene Richardson and was a former chambermaid and would-be nanny. She was found stabbed and with her throat cut on Roundhay Park's Soldiers' Field. Then, that April, prostitute Patricia Atkinson was found battered to death in a bedsit in the Manningham area of Bradford.

"This was the pattern," Bruce Smith, who was part of the *YEP* team which covered the story, later recalled. "New victims, frequently not prostitutes, and new detectives and their squads, hunting the same killer."

A call on a sunny Sunday nine weeks later – June 26, 1977 – sent him back to Chapeltown, where 16-year-old supermarket worker Jayne Michelle McDonald had been found bludgeoned to death in a children's adventure playground off Reginald Terrace – grabbed on her way home to Scott Hall Avenue after a night out with friends.

At a press conference the man then in overall charge of the Ripper Inquiry, Assistant Chief Constable George Oldfield, revealed his mounting frustration.

Replying to a tricky question, he snarled at the reporter concerned: "What is it about me you don't like?"

The case was then clouded by a letter and tape sent direct to Oldfield by a man with a Sunderland accent claiming to be the Ripper. It was a hoax, revealed decades later to have been the work of labourer John Humble.

But Oldfield was convinced this was the man they were after and a £1m publicity campaign was mounted by a local agency to help police put a name to the voice.

"There were so many shocking moments and images," said Bruce. "I recall watching spellbound faces in a working men's club as the so-called Ripper Tape was played by police to drinkers.

"There was the darkened timber yard in Huddersfield where a prostitute and twin Helen Rytka was found naked and the face of building society clerk Josephine Whitaker, 19, – Sutcliffe's 11th victim – just visible from beneath the sheet covering her body where it lay on Saville Park, Halifax, on April 5, 1979.

A dark coloured Ford Escort saloon similar to the one seen in Halifax last Wednesday night.

Moustache link with Leeds attack in 1977

HAVE YOU SEEN THIS MAN?–RIPPER PLEA

9 APR 1979

Today's photofit picture of a man the Ripper police want to see.

Victim's £1,500 payment 'is not enough'

Mrs. Maureen Long

A £1,500 compensation pay-out to a woman who survived an attack from the Yorkshire Ripper has been described by her solicitor as too low.

Mr. Desmond Joyce, head of the firm of solicitors repre-

Police hunting the Yorkshire Ripper who killed for the eleventh time last week today issued this photo-fit picture of a man they want to interview.

Mr George Oldfield, Assistant Chief Constable, said they wanted to interview the man who was the driver of the dark-coloured Ford Escort saloon seen in Halifax the night 19-year-old Josephine Whitaker was savagely murdered.

"If anyone thinks they can help us to trace him or identify him we would like them to come forward," he said.

He said the man had been seen in the car, registered between 1968 and 1975 (G to N inclusive) in the centre of Halifax soon after 9 p.m. last Wednesday. The car was described as "dirty."

Park Road at five minutes after midnight.

Meanwhile detectives ... the Ripper has made his big mistake.

Until his latest killing, mass murderer, who ... Britain's most wanted ...

Blood-crazed killer keeps promise . . . and student dies

A briefing for police officers in Ash Grove, Bradford, today, close to the murder scene.

4 SEP 1979

THE RIPPER CLAIMS HIS 12th VICTIM

By DAVID BRUCE, TONY HARNEY and BRUCE SMITH

THE YORKSHIRE RIPPER *HAS* CLAIMED HIS 12th VICTIM, POLICE CONFIRMED TODAY.

She was named as Barbara Jane Leach (20), of Kettering, a student at Bradford University.

Det. Chief Supt. Jim Hobson, leading the hunt for the blood-crazed killer, said during the night he held discussions with pathologist Prof. John Gee — who has carried out post-mortems on all Ripper victims.

He said: "We are now satisfied this murder is linked with other unsolved murders in Yorkshire and Manchester."

And he said police were now in a better position than ever to catch the Ripper. Preparations were being made to trap him — but he refused to disclose them.

The full-scale Ripper inquiry was launched after a patrolling police officer found Barbara's body in the back garden of 13, Ash Grove, a terrace house, on the edge of Bradford's red-light district.

Police said Barbara, a social-science student, apparently went for a walk on her own. And it was then she met the Ripper...

Within an hour of her bloodied body being found over 100 police officers were drafted into the area.

The victim

Barbara Leach . . . the dark-haired 20-year-old who became the 12th victim of the frenzied Ripper.

Never walk alone, warns university

The pro vice-chancellor and vice principal of Bradford University, Mr. Robert McKinlay, this afternoon described Barbara as an extremely good student and said the whole university was horrified and sho...

The YEP reports student Barbara Leach has become the Ripper's twelfth victim, September 1979.

"After a tip about a body found in Bradford late on September 4 1979, I remember calling a police press officer to ask whether we had "another Ripper victim" and him discreetly replying: "Well, I can't tell you to go home".

"It was the 12th victim, talented student Barbara Leach found in a back garden on Ash Grove near a popular student pub.

"Then there was the shocking picture we would never use of the face of the Ripper's final victim, Leeds University student Jacqueline Hill, 20, found on wasteland behind Headingley's Arndale Centre on November 19, 1980."

There was a lengthy period early in the run of murders and assaults when police did not openly link all of the crimes.

When, with the murder of teenager Jayne MacDonald, George Oldfield finally acknowledged her killer was probably responsible for other murders, it inevitably heightened the pressure to catch him. Various specialist detective groups were formed, including the team immediately dubbed the 'Ripper Squad' in 1978.

The squad evolved over three years as the murders mounted and public and Home Office pressure grew to catch the Ripper. Rewards were offered, including one by the *YEP*, but all to no avail. Ordinary women and young girls were frightened to go out alone and prostitutes made it a duty to keep a watchful eye on colleagues, checking punters' faces and recording registration plates.

There were frequent police checkpoints, particularly in North Leeds, and husbands, boyfriends, friends and relatives would pick up their loved ones from work or from a night out as no street seemed safe. The pressure to catch the killer took its toll on officers of all ranks and their families. The impact on Oldfield was marked by his heart attack in August 1979 and ultimate replacement by Acting Assistant Chief Constable Jim Hobson following the final killing of Jacqueline Hill in 1980.

Such was the weight of paperwork connected with the case that the floor of the incident room at Millgarth Police Station in the heart of Leeds, the epicentre of the Ripper Inquiry, had to be reinforced to cope. A quarter of a million names were individually filed on cards and more than 30,000 statements were taken. But none of it led to the Ripper's arrest.

The best chance of a breakthrough seemed to come when a £5 note was found with the body

Lorry driver Peter Sutcliffe makes his first appearance at Dewsbury Magistrates' Court, January 5, 1981.

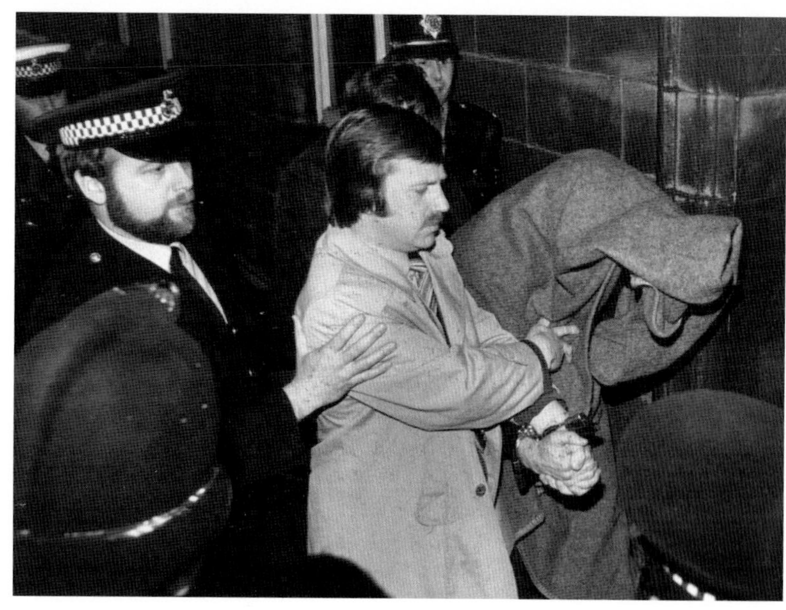

Opposite:

Left: A huge advertising campaign was launched during the Ripper Inquiry on the back of the messages from 'Wearside Jack', later found to be a hoax.

Right: Painter and decorator John Holmes joins the YEP's poster campaign to catch the Ripper, November 1980. Such was the terror caused by the murders that women were frightened to be out alone at night.

of victim Jean Royle. It had been handed over by the Ripper before he killed her. Checks were launched to find others from the same bank wads which had been distributed in payrolls. Peter Sutcliffe was interviewed, one of nine occasions when he was quizzed by police, but his alibis once again helped him escape detection.

Instead it was a chance spot-check that saw him caught. When PCs Robert Ring and Bob Hydes moved in on prostitute Olivia Reivers as she sat inside Sutcliffe's car on Sheffield's tree-lined Melbourne Avenue on the evening of January 2, 1981 they were simply anticipating a vice arrest and saw her punter merely as a witness for the prosecution – not Britain's most wanted man.

They duly discovered he had put false number plates on his car and found weapons in the boot. Once arrested, Sutcliffe, a Bradford lorry driver, quickly admitted he was the Yorkshire Ripper and spent 15 hours giving the police graphic details of his crimes.

"I remember getting a call on the Sunday afternoon telling me to go to Dewsbury as they had 'caught the Ripper'," recalled long-serving *YEP* photographer Steve Riding. "The press conference scene wouldn't happen today – three senior police officers delirious with relief telling the media they had caught the Ripper. At this stage he hadn't even made an appearance at court, but they knew they had their man.

"I still remember that night well. I had to go to Bradford afterwards to photograph his house, finishing about 3am and then back at work four hours later on the Monday as the newsroom was buzzing. Everyone wanted to be on this story."

Sutcliffe's capture and subsequent conviction triggered a wave of relief in Leeds and across Yorkshire as a whole. But there was horror too that he had been able to kill so many women for so long in what ranks as the darkest chapter in the city's history.

CONSTRUCTIONAL ENGINEERS & STEEL STOCKHOLDERS
PEARL

SPORTING HEROES

With all the drama that has unfolded at Elland Road in recent decades it's easy to forget that Leeds was traditionally considered to be a rugby town. And while their football counterparts have languished outside the top tier of the English game for over a decade, the same period has seen Leeds Rhinos enjoy unprecedented success.

In 2015 a golden era culminated in the Rhinos, led by skipper Kevin Sinfield – or 'Sir Kev' as he's known to the Headingley faithful – completing the treble of Challenge Cup, League Leaders' Shield and Super League title.

But Leeds haven't always been the number one rugby team in the city. Formed in 1883, seven years before the first edition of the *Yorkshire Evening Post* rolled off the presses, Hunslet Rugby Club was created by joining together local teams Albion and Excelsior.

Their first major trophy came after the move to their Parkside ground – which had been created by clearing 2,000 tons of rubble from a piece of land owned by the Low Moor Iron and Coal Company at Hunslet Carr. Hunslet triumphed over Leeds St John's, later to become Leeds RLFC and then the Rhinos, to clinch the Yorkshire Cup.

The club was known for its passionate following – and sometimes those passions spilled over. In April 1895 a cup tie defeat to Brighouse Rangers ended with 21 police officers having to rescue a match official, a Mr Rayner of Batley, from the crowd.

Antagonism between Hunslet and Leeds – as well as the rival sets of supporters – was spelled out in a flurry of letters to the *Yorkshire Evening Post* following an ill-tempered match between the two sides in March 1913.

One correspondent wrote: "Everything suggests that the scenes at Parkside were caused solely by the failure of Leeds' strongest team to romp round Hunslet's weak team to the tune of 40 points. To place all the blame on Hunslet is absurd. The fact of three Leeds players being sent off and only two Hunslet players is evidence that Leeds were chief offenders."

Right: **Hunslet's Albert Goldthorpe was one of the first sporting superstars to feature in the pages of the YEP.**

Opposite:

Top: **The Lord Mayor of Leeds Albert Wilkinson welcomes Challenge Cup winners Hunslet to the Civic Hall, May 1934.**

Bottom: **Through cheering crowds, a coach brings the Leeds players and the Challenge Cup they won at Wembley to Leeds Town Hall, May 1957.**

Another reader took a very different view. "I am a former member of the Hunslet club and followed them for several years," he wrote. "My reason for severing my connection was that I could not reconcile myself to the conduct of the Hunslet players and spectators."

What isn't open to debate is the fact that Hunslet produced one of the city's first sporting superstars to ever appear in the pages of the *YEP*. Albert Goldthorpe captained the club's 1897/98 League Championship winning team and the 1905 Yorkshire Cup champions. He was also at the helm and at half back for Hunslet's greatest ever season in 1907/8 when the team won all four cups, including the Challenge Cup and Championship trophy.

Keen to go out on a high, Albert, one of five rugby-playing brothers and also a fine cricketer, officially retired at the end of the season. He would go on to serve the club as a committee member and as secretary before his death in January 1943 at the age of 71. He was buried at Woodhouse Hill Cemetery, not far away from the old Parkside ground where his talents had shone so brightly.

Hunslet endured some lean times until the 1930s, when they regained the Yorkshire League trophy and reached the final of the Yorkshire Cup. They then celebrated their 50th anniversary season in style, beating Widnes 11-5 at Wembley in the Challenge Cup final. Four years later, they defeated arch rivals Leeds to clinch their second, and to date last, Championship title.

One of Hunslet's stars in the 1950s was winger Alan Snowden, who had switched codes for the then-considerable sum of £500 – around £12,000 in today's money – which was enough to help him buy his first house. Alan scored 151 tries in 213 games, and his 1956/7 record of 34 tries in a single season still stands. He combined his on-field heroics with his job as a compositor on the *Yorkshire Evening Post*, one of the highly-skilled crafts in pre-computer newspaper production, and later became production controller.

Hunslet narrowly lost to Wigan at Wembley in 1965 in what is still regarded as one of rugby league's greatest Challenge Cup finals. They left Parkside in 1973 when it was sold to developers and were nomads for years before finally coming home in 1995, moving into the purpose-built South Leeds Stadium.

Denied entry to Super League in 1999, despite winning the Northern Ford Premiership Grand Final against Dewsbury, the re-christened Hunslet Hawks struggled to stay afloat before moving to a more stable footing. Now playing in Kingstone Press League One, Hunslet remain one of the most famous names in the sport.

But it's Leeds who have been the city's premier club over recent decades. Founder members of the Northern Union when it broke away from the Rugby Football Union in 1895, their roots date back a quarter of a century earlier to the formation of the Leeds St John's club which played at Cardigan Fields, near Headingley.

In 1888 the Cardigan Estate was sold at auction and Lot 17a was purchased by a group of Leeds citizens, who intended to form the city's leading sports club. Lot 17a would become what is now Headingley Stadium, one of only a handful of venues in the world to have staged international matches in three different sports – rugby league, union and cricket.

Leeds St John's played their final season under that name in 1889-90, before becoming the football section of Leeds Cricket, Football and Athletic Co Ltd. With Headingley still being completed, Leeds' first game was staged at Cardigan Fields, the home side defeating Otley.

Kevin Sinfield and the rest of the Leeds Rhinos celebrate winning the Grand Final, October 16, 2004.

TETLEY'S
SUPER
Rugby
TETLEY'S
TETLEY'S
TETLEY'S
TETLEY'S

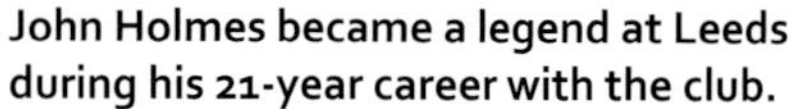

John Holmes became a legend at Leeds during his 21-year career with the club.

Leeds captain David Ward with the Challenge Cup after the classic 1978 final.

The first game at Headingley was played on September 20, 1890, just a few weeks after the *YEP*'s first edition hit the streets, when Manningham were beaten by a try and drop goal to nil.

Leeds' debut in the Northern Union was a 6-3 success at Leigh on September 7, 1895 – the inaugural day of the new competition. The club's first major trophy triumph came in 1910, when they won the Northern Union Cup, after beating Hull in a final replay.

Blue and amber ribbons have been tied on the Challenge Cup another 12 times since then, including wartime successes in 1941 and 1942 and victory over London Broncos in the last final staged at the old Wembley in 1999. That game saw winger Leroy Rivett become the first player to score four tries in a Challenge Cup final and the 52-16 triumph was also a record.

The club reached the Championship final for the first time in 1915, but were beaten 35-2 by a Huddersfield side who are remembered as one of the greatest of all time. Leeds had to wait until 1961 to be crowned champions, the great Lewis Jones leading them to an emotional victory over Warrington in the title decider at Odsal.

In a career spanning from 1968 to 1989, Burley-born John Holmes became a club legend with a record 625 appearances for Leeds. He played in 19 major finals for Leeds, winning all but five, including the 1978 Challenge Cup. That year's final is regarded as his finest hour, his vital drop goal edging Leeds ahead of St Helens. When the Rhinos lifted the 2009 Grand Final they dedicated it to Holmes, who had died from cancer a fortnight earlier.

The Championship trophy returned to Headingley in 1969 and 1972, but Leeds fans then endured an agonising 32-year wait before coach Tony Smith's side claimed the Super League title with a Grand Final triumph over arch-rivals Bradford Bulls in 2004. It meant Leeds had now won every available domestic honour, including the Yorkshire Cup a record 17 times from 21 finals, and it was a victory that would mark the dawn of a golden decade at the club.

Between 2004 and 2014, the Rhinos chalked up six Grand Final wins, two League Leaders' Shields, three World Club Challenges and a Challenge Cup victory. The honours served as proof, if any were needed, of the club's dominance over their Super League peers. It got even better in 2015 as Kevin Sinfield captained the Rhinos to a seventh Super League Grand Final triumph at Old Trafford and went on to be runner-up in the BBC *Sports Personality of the Year* as Leeds captured the treble.

"If it wasn't a comparison so liable to stick in the throat this side of the Pennines," wrote the *Yorkshire Evening Post*, "it would be tempting to dub them the Manchester United of rugby league. Fittingly, Wayne Rooney is a Rhinos fan."

It proved the perfect farewell for three of the players who had been the bedrock of so much of the club's success – Sinfield, local lad Jamie Peacock and New Zealander Kylie Leuluai, who later revealed he had been diagnosed with an irregular heartbeat earlier in the season, leading coach Brian McDermott to thank him for "putting his life on the line" for the team.

A former roofer and once fond of a pint, Bramley-born Peacock sometimes spent entire weekends drinking while he was trying to establish his rugby career. Some of it contributed to his mixed fortunes on the pitch. But a big influence was his late father, Darryl, who encouraged him to trust his raw talent even when he began to doubt it.

He once told of how he almost blew his career before it had even started. As a car-less 18-year-old off for his first trial with Bradford he caught the bus.

But as it got nearer to the ground he "bottled it" and didn't get off. He phoned his dad, who in turn called Bradford coach Brian Noble. "Dad said he believed in me and that Brian Noble believed in me," he later recalled. He got back on the bus and the rest is history as he and fellow Leeds-born stars including Danny McGuire, Jamie Jones Buchanan and Ryan Hall helped the Rhinos to such unprecedented success.

As for Kevin Sinfield, he left the club after their treble triumph to spend a year at union side Yorkshire Carnegie before announcing his retirement. Having become one of the most recognisable figures in his sport around the world, he once told the *YEP* that it brought him some interesting requests. "I've not had any underwear in the post," Sir Kev said, "but I once had a bloke write to me asking for my jockstrap. I haven't a clue why."

Before the visit of the Tour de France kick-started Yorkshire's cycling craze, Leeds' own Beryl Burton was one of the sport's iconic figures. A remarkable sportswoman, Burton was crowned world champion over 3,000 metres, was named British best all-rounder champion for 25 successive years and out-cycled the opposite sex by holding the men's world 12-hour time trial record for two years in the 1960s.

Beryl Burton, from Morley, became a cycling world champion and icon of the sport.

Born in Halton but living most of her life in Morley, childhood illness had kept Beryl out of school for two years and an irregular heartbeat led doctors to warn her

Jamie Peacock, Kevin Sinfield and Kylie Leuluai celebrate the 2015 Grand Final win at Old Trafford.

she should avoid strenuous exercise.

Incredibly, she turned down a contract with the Raleigh Bicycle Company, meaning she remained an amateur cyclist with no financial backing or professional training throughout her career, though her husband Charlie provided constant support.

Her sizeable achievements finally got the recognition they deserved 18 years after she died of heart failure aged 58. In 2014 Leeds City Council unveiled plans to celebrate the cyclist with a posthumous civic honour, weeks after a blue plaque was placed at Beryl Burton Gardens, the street named after her in Morley.

In all, Burton won seven world titles and more than 90 domestic titles in her career. Her story was told in a special production at West Yorkshire Playhouse, which Maxine Peake, the acclaimed actor-turned-writer, based on her own Radio 4 play, *Beryl: A Love Story on Two Wheels*.

"It's not just that she was an incredible athlete, but that she achieved so much on a shoestring," Peake told the *YEP*. "Beryl didn't have a great big support team. All she had was a supply of rice pudding and an incredible determination to succeed."

An intense sibling rivalry would go on to spark Olympic glory for two brothers from Bramhope. The sons of doctors who encouraged their hyperactive sons to burn off their energy outdoors, the young Alistair and Jonny Brownlee could usually be found doing just that on the lanes and fields of West Yorkshire.

After finishing 400th out of 450 in the Leeds Schools Cross Country Championships, nine-year-old Alistair promptly vowed to give up "pies and chips" to get fitter. Introduced to triathlon by their uncle, the brothers soon found their calling. Alistair was the first to excel – chosen to represent Great Britain at junior level. The day he brought home his Team GB kit and plonked it on the kitchen table was the day the brothers' rivalry was truly born.

"I was 12," Jonny recalled in an interview with the *YEP*. "I looked at that bag of GB kit and

Jonny and Alistair Brownlee have helped make Leeds the unofficial triathlon capital of Britain.

Right and far right: Paralympians David Stone and Kadeena Cox.

Boxer Nicola Adams celebrates with her gold medal during an Olympic homecoming event at the Merrion Centre, August 2012.

Future Olympic champion Adrian Moorhouse poses with silverware won for City of Leeds Swimming Club, September 1980.

thought, if he can do it then so can I." Although to be fair, it had been that way for as long as the Brownlee boys could remember. Born two years apart, their competitive instinct had been ever present. Badminton in the back garden, monopoly at Christmas – everything became a competition, even the tidying up. A game of crazy golf was liable to implode in violent acrimony.

"There have been times where we've thrown balls at each other," Jonny admitted. "I think having a brother – especially one who's almost exactly two years older – means that you're going to be competitive. It's good because I've never shied away from competition. He's always been there, it's just always been a part of my life."

At London 2012 their rivalry was played out in front of billions around the world as Alistair claimed Olympic gold to Jonny's bronze. They would then win gold and silver respectively at the Commonwealth Games two years later.

The first brothers to share an Olympic podium in an individual sport since 1908, it was an astonishing family achievement in one of the most gruelling sporting tests – a 1,500m swim followed by a 40km bike ride, finished off with a 10km run. Their success has helped make Leeds a world renowned centre for triathlon training.

Nicola Adams became a world and Olympic champion by accident. Her mum Dee used to do aerobics classes in the evening but one night couldn't get a babysitter for 12-year-old Nicola and her brother, so she dropped them off at an after-school boxing class.

"I can still remember my first fight as a 13-year-old," recalled Nicola, from Burmantofts. "It was at East Leeds Working Men's Club and I boxed three one-and-a-half-minute rounds. I won on points."

But it was only when she won the National Championships at 18 that she realised she was going to pursue a professional career in the sport. At London 2012 Nicola won the nation's hearts with her ready smile and down-to-earth manner outside the ring, coupled with her clinical performances inside it. The combination took her all the way to a gold medal and a postbox painted in the same colour next to the Henry Moore Institute in Leeds city centre.

Along with silver medal-winning cyclist Lizzie Armitstead, the Leeds contingent were part of a staggeringly successful Yorkshire team which on its own would have finished twelfth In the medals table. They were welcomed back to the city with a civic reception which saw a massive crowd packed into Millennium Square to greet them. The celebrations capped a memorable Olympic summer for Leeds, more than 200,000 people having lined the streets during the 2012 torch relay's visits in June.

The Rio Olympics in 2016 would bring further success for the city's athletes with Alistair and Jonny Brownlee claiming gold and silver in the men's triathlon and Leeds-based Vicky Holland taking bronze in the women's race. Cyclist Katy Marchant and rower Paul Bennett won bronze and gold respectively.

Gymnast Nile Wilson, from Pudsey, swung his way to a bronze medal in the men's horizontal bar, while Jack Laugher and Chris Mears, who live and train together in the city, earned a sensational gold in the men's 3m synchronised diving.

Len Hutton and his son Richard go out to bat.

Nicola Adams, meanwhile, retained her Olympic flyweight title, becoming the first British boxer to win back-to-back gold medals since 1924 and declared herself "the most accomplished amateur boxer Britain of all time". Perhaps mindful of her hefty right hook, few disagreed.

Back in 1988, City of Leeds Swimming Club had also celebrated Olympic success when one of its number, Bradford-born Adrian Moorhouse, won gold in 100m breaststroke at the Seoul Olympics.

The city's Paralympians have also done us proud in recent times, most notably Rawdon cyclist David Stone, powerlifter Ali Jawad and golden girl Kadeena Cox, from Chapeltown, who triumphed in both cycling and athletics in Rio.

As well as witnessing greatness in the sizeable shape of the Leeds Rhinos, Headingley has played host to some of the most memorable games in cricket history. The ground hosted its first match in 1890 and Yorkshire won the Championship in 1893, 1896 and again in 1898 under legendary captain Lord Hawke. Although hailing from Lincolnshire rather than the Broad Acres, Hawke fiercely advocated that all players should be born in Yorkshire, a rule that would finally be revoked in 1992.

Hawke would captain Yorkshire for 28 years and lead them to a further five Championship titles. Brian Sellers managed six either side of the Second World War, and Brian Close four with 1960s teams featuring the likes of Ray Illingworth, Fred Trueman, Jimmy Binks, Ken Taylor and Bryan Stott.

In 1924, the *Yorkshire Evening Post* described a 19-year-old Hedley Verity as "one of the most promising cricketers in the Leeds district". As far as hype goes it was hardly over the top, but the billing would prove spot on as the Headingley-born slow left-arm bowler went on to take nearly 2,000 first-class wickets. The outbreak of the Second World War ended his career and Verity, a captain in the Green Howards, died of his injuries after being wounded and taken prisoner during the Allied invasion of Sicily in 1943.

Verity played in four Ashes series, including the infamous 'Bodyline' tour of Australia in 1932-33 when England resorted to short-pitched bowling. The second Test of the 1934 series became known as 'Verity's Match', after he took 15 for 104, including 14 wickets in a day and the scalp of the great Don Bradman in each innings. Against Nottinghamshire two years earlier he had taken all 10 wickets for just 10 runs – still the greatest bowling performance ever recorded in first class cricket.

Sir Len Hutton, from Pudsey, opened the batting for Yorkshire from 1934 to 1955 and for England in 79 Test matches between 1937 and 1955. Described as one of the greatest batsmen in the history of the game, he set a record in 1938 for the highest individual innings in a Test match, scoring 364 runs against Australia. The milestone stood for nearly 20 years and remains an England Test record.

Yorkshire legends Ray Illingworth, Geoff Boycott, Brian Close and Fred Trueman celebrate winning the 1967 County Championship.

He was also involved in one of cricket's more unusual incidents. In June 1946 the *YEP* reported that Yorkshire's match against Derbyshire was disrupted when the wicket was discovered to be two yards too long. Doubts raised by players were passed to the umpire, who duly investigated the matter and discovered the error. By that time, Derbyshire already had nine runs on the board.

While the players were forced to retire to the pavilion so the wicket could be re-marked, the runs were removed from the scoreboard and the game started again. Len Hutton, who was fielding in the gully, told the *YEP*: "I hadn't noticed anything but Ellis Robinson mentioned it and so did Bill Bowes. Then, after the second over, we decided to do something about it."

Bowes, the tall, bespectacled fast bowler who had also played on the 'Bodyline' tour, would later bring his expertise to cricket writing in the *YEP*. He was remembered by colleagues as a genial giant, with a quick sense of humour and an unforgettable deep, gurgling laugh. The only advice was never to whistle in the great man's company. Apparently, everyone had whistled all day during the years Bill had been incarcerated in a prisoner of war camp and the sound of even a few bars brought back unhappy memories.

When the Prince of Wales came to Leeds to open the paper's new headquarters, Bill was introduced. "I've met your father a few times," he told the Prince. "He's not a bad bowler."

Then there was Geoffrey Boycott. His relationship with the Yorkshire committee may have been tempestuous at times but the adoration of his legions of supporters was obvious in August 1977 when an elegant on-drive brought up his century against the old enemy Australia. It was the hundredth first-class hundred of his career and the ovation lasted for six ecstatic minutes. A pitch invasion followed and when police cleared the crowds Boycott emerged from the ruck minus his England cap. He signalled to the pavilion he needed another one but then, out of the crowd, a spectator emerged bearing the one he had lost. Boycott walked across, shook the cap bearer's hand and quipped: "A good Yorkshireman, he brought it back."

Boycott was the third Yorkshireman to achieve the century of centuries after Herbert Sutcliffe and Len Hutton but was the only one to achieve this landmark score during a Test match. The fact that it was on his home ground made it all the more special.

Four years later, Headingley was witness to more amazing scenes as England pulled off a victory against the odds in one of the greatest turnarounds the game has ever seen. The performance of Ian Botham in the match has entered cricket folklore and the match – which started just under a fortnight before the Royal Wedding of Prince Charles and Lady Diana – was the stuff of true fairytales.

The drama started with the visitors on the verge of going 2-0 up in the series. Following on, England were all but out for the count at 135-7 – 92 runs short of an innings defeat. Then lion-hearted Botham hit one of the most savage knocks in Test history, his 149 prompting Richie Benaud to utter one of the most famous commentary lines ever.

Beefy had just whacked Terry Alderman straight over his head into the Football Stand for six, when the legendary Benaud mused: "Don't bother even looking for that, let alone chasing it – it's gone straight into the confectionery stall and out again."

With the seeds of doubt now well and truly sown an inspired Bob Willis swept through the Australian batting line-up, claiming eight wickets for just 43 runs. It sealed a remarkable 18-run win and turned the series, which England went on to win 3-1, on its head. Years later, the *YEP* asked Botham if he ever tired of people asking him about the match. His response? "How can you get bored about it?"

Sadly, however, it's an Australian who holds the record for the highest Test innings at Headingley. But then Don Bradman was no ordinary player. His innings of 334 not out at the ground in 1930 was also the highest of his Test career. Incredibly, Bradman made a second triple century in LS6 four years later.

For Yorkshire, the good times have returned with back to back County

Yorkshire captain Andrew Gale with cricket's County Championship trophy, September 12, 2014.

Ian Botham leaves the Headingley pitch after his heroics had helped England beat Australia, July 21, 1981.

Championship titles, while the likes of Joe Root and Jonny Bairstow have put in some match-winning performances for the national team.

It is fairly widely known that the first ever playing on British soil of golf's Ryder Cup – the biennial clash between golfers from either side of the Atlantic – took place at Moortown Golf Club in Leeds in 1929. Less well-known, however, is the role played by the *Yorkshire Evening Post* in bringing pay and play golf to the city.

Bert Baker, then golf correspondent at the *YEP*, campaigned long and hard for the introduction of municipal golf to Leeds. His efforts paid off when the first golf course at Temple Newsam, designed by Dr Alistair MacKenzie who also created the Masters course at Augusta, was opened on July 20, 1923. Fittingly, Bert became the club's first chairman.

First spotted as an eight-year-old playing in tournaments at the Northern Snooker Centre on Kirkstall Road, the good looks and blond locks of snooker's Paul Hunter saw him dubbed the Beckham of the Baize. Paul, from Moortown, went on to become a three-time Masters winner and was tipped as a future world champion.

He recorded one of his greatest triumphs at the 2001 Masters at Wembley. Finding himself 6-2 down, he retired to his hotel room where he and his future wife, Lindsey, put "Plan B" into practice. Paul later admitted that, although he hadn't been in the mood, "I had to do something to break the tension".

"I had a kip and then played like a dream," said the former Cardinal Heenan High School pupil.

Teeing off at Armley Park, later known as Gotts Park, with Kirkstall Power Station as a backdrop, April 1950.

"I reeled off four centuries in six frames. I won easily." Tragically, Paul would die five days short of his 28th birthday after being diagnosed with neuroendocrine tumours. His funeral at Leeds Parish Church in October 2006 was attended by hundreds of mourners, including greats of the game such as Stephen Hendry, Steve Davis and Ronnie O'Sullivan.

Courage in the face of adversity was the defining feature of another Leeds resident who captured the hearts of the nation and the world. Told in August 2000 that she had terminal cancer, Jane Tomlinson was given just months to live.

A lesser person's spirit might have been broken but for Jane the news signalled the start of an epic adventure. "I just refuse to get depressed," she told the *YEP*. "If I start feeling sorry for myself I would end up doing nothing at all and that's not how I want to spend the time I have left.

"Nothing can stop me from dying, I know that will happen. I just want to be remembered as someone who was happy." While still receiving treatment, Jane signed up to run Cancer Research UK's Race for Life in Leeds in May 2001. The event was meant to be a one-off but Jane found comfort and strength from taking part.

She took part in the Abbey Dash that December and then came to national attention when she

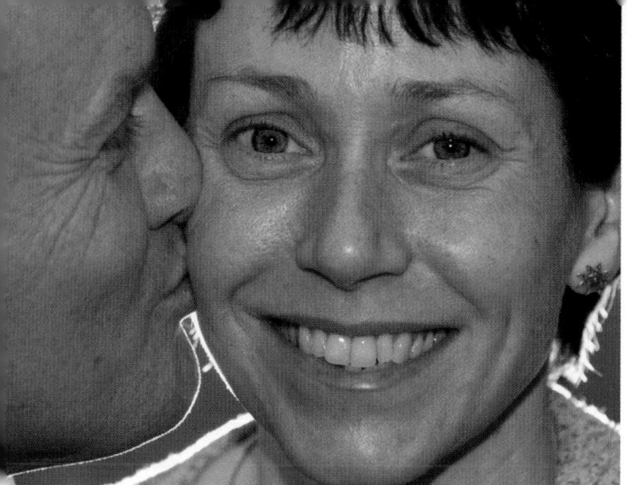

Jane Tomlinson receives a congratulatory kiss from husband Mike on the day she announced raising more than £1m for charity, January 28, 2005.

Paul Hunter was dubbed 'The Beckham of the Baize' for his good looks and huge talent.

ran the London Marathon in April 2002, becoming one of only a handful of terminally-ill patients to complete the 26 miles. She finished in a respectable time of 4hrs 35 mins, though she was by this time coping with agonising pain. Her courage and determination propelled her on and in May she was awarded the *YEP*-backed Yorkshire Woman of Achievement 2002. In July she presented the Jubilee baton to the Queen at Temple Newsam. She then became the first terminally-ill athlete to complete the London Triathlon, in August 2002, coming 20th in her age group.

Later that year she announced she would be stepping down from her fundraising work to spend more time with her family. But after heartfelt chats with her children and husband, she was back on the road in 2003, cycling from John O'Groats to Lands End on a tandem with brother Luke Goward. She was forced to stop along the way for life-saving chemotherapy sessions. The day after the three-week ride in April ended, she ran the London Marathon for the second time, becoming the first person ever to have completed a marathon while still on chemotherapy.

The mother-of-three from Rothwell carried on entering longer, tougher races including a 2,500-mile cycle ride from Rome to Home in just 36 days. She became the only cancer patient to complete a full Ironman contest – 2.4 miles of swimming, 112 miles of riding and a full marathon. Then there was her final challenge, an exhausting 4,200-mile bike ride across America.

Along the way she smashed her target of raising £1m for cancer and children's charities, won the Helen Rollason award at the BBC *Sports Personality of the Year* awards in 2002, became one of only six Freemen of the City of Leeds and was awarded the CBE.

In 2007 she and husband Mike launched the 10K Run For All in Leeds, which she hoped would become an annual event. Unable to

Vinnie Jones walks Josh Warrington into the ring ahead of his win over Dennis Tubieron for the WBC International Featherweight title, April 11, 2015.

take part herself, she watched as 8,000 runners took to the city's streets that June, telling the *YEP*: "The reality is that this will probably be the last summer that I get to spend with my family. That's quite difficult to live with and it's quite difficult to stay positive, but you have to put that at the back of your mind so that you can enjoy the summer and that's what I'm going to be trying to do... spending the summer with my family."

She died three months later at the age of 46, her Requiem Mass conducted by the Bishop of Leeds, Arthur Roche, at St Anne's Cathedral. Thousands lined the streets outside to pay tribute and watched the service on the big screen in Millennium Square. Mike told mourners: "If there is a story of what could be achieved by an indomitable human spirit, this was it."

He and the rest of Jane's family have since continued her work, adding to the near £2m she raised in her lifetime with their hugely successful Run For All events. It is a fitting legacy to a remarkable woman.

In more recent times Leeds has drawn pride from the achievements of boxer Josh Warrington. Having previously held the English, British and Commonwealth featherweight titles, the Garforth-based fighter claimed the WBC International and European belts. His victories have lit up Elland Road – home of his beloved Leeds United – and the First Direct Arena, not least when former Whites legend Vinnie Jones carried his belts into the ring to the strains of *Marching on Together*, followed by the Kaiser Chiefs' *I Predict a Riot*.

HOME FROM HOME

It's said that while every building has its stories, newspaper offices are filled with the stories of everyone. For the first eight decades of its life, home for the *Yorkshire Evening Post* was a smoky warren of offices on the junction of Commercial Street and Albion Street.

The clatter of manual typewriters filled the newsrooms above, while the printing hall below thundered with the sound of printing presses the size of houses running off thousands of copies an hour.

Long since redeveloped, former *YEP* editor Malcolm Barker recalled the cluster of Victorian buildings, which had housed the Yorkshire Conservative Newspaper Company since 1866, as a unique environment.

"We used to joke that newcomers would get lost and never be seen again," he said. "The trouble was there were too many little offices and the noise and smell of hot metal was always around you and, if you wanted to move between different places, you were in and out the whole time."

All that changed on September 28, 1970 when the official switch to a new nerve centre on Wellington Street took place. Led by managing director Gordon Linacre, the £5m purpose-built block was built on the site once occupied by textile magnate Benjamin Gott's Bean Ings Mill on the banks of the River Aire and next to what would eventually be the inner ring road.

Housing both the *Yorkshire Evening Post* and sister paper *The Yorkshire Post*, the five-storey building was filled with 1,300 staff and produced eight editions of the *YEP* a day.

"When we shifted to Wellington Street you were struck by the space and great layout which meant that all the editorial departments were together in one place," recalled the late Mr Barker. "I must admit we were very nervous about the shift, but it was so well designed that everything worked beautifully.

"One of my most important roles," he joked, "was testing the newly installed sprinkler system when I accidentally dropped a cigarette in my wicker basket and set fire to my office."

The design of the building saw all the editorial staff now working in one open-plan hall, with the presses located far enough away to ensure the sounds and smells of hot metal weren't as invasive as they had once been.

But although the transition was relatively smooth and painless, there wasn't much affection for the architectural style of the new HQ. When the *YEP* ran a survey in 2005 asking readers to tell us which of the city's buildings they disliked the most, they voted for the paper's then home on Wellington Street.

"We just referred to it as 'The Building'" admitted Mr Barker. "It wasn't very well liked by many people, it was so brutal and undecorative. But it was very much the fashion of the day – at the same time there were all these tower blocks going up all over the place.

"On the other hand, the one stroke of real genius was the addition of the clock tower because it made the place so distinctive. Everyone knows the *Yorkshire Evening Post/Yorkshire Post* clock

Opposite: **The original Yorkshire Evening Post building on Albion Street.**

1
2
3
VISCOUNT
4
5
GOSS
EVENING POST
6
7
8

Opposite:

1. An early printing method sees YEP staff mount curved plates of type onto the cylinder of the press.

2. Journalists work by candlelight during a power cut caused by the 1972 Miners' Strike.

3. The typesetting department at the paper's Albion Street offices.

*4.*Printing press at the Yorkshire Evening Post building.

5. Linotype machinists in the 1930s hard at work compiling plates of text ready for printing in the YEP.

6. The first editions of the Yorkshire Evening Post to be printed at the new Wellington Street headquarters roll off the presses.

7. The last page to be made in the Albion Street building is hammered down, September 1970.

8. Inside the YEP newsroom, September 2007.

tower on Wellington Street – it's become an intrinsic part of Leeds."

The architect behind the building was John Madin who, from his practice in Birmingham, created many of the modern concrete structures in the Midlands city. He designed the Pebble Mill TV studios, Birmingham Central Library and the Birmingham Post building – the latter securing him a recommendation for the Leeds job.

Many of his concrete buildings were intended to be clad in marble. Some actually were, but the Wellington Street landmark was always meant to sport the natural, grey look. And it wasn't just because it was fashionable at the time.

"What you have to remember was that when we started designing the building in the mid 1960s materials were actually still difficult to get hold of and expensive because, as strange as it might sound, the construction industry was still suffering from the effects of the war," Mr Madin recalled in 2011. "So concrete was relatively inexpensive and relatively easy to use.

"The site itself was rather difficult and everything was crammed in. We needed a lot of space for the printworks which included a mix of old and very new technology – it was around the printworks that everything else was centred really. Another key criteria was accessibility but also they wanted all the editorial departments in one large area."

The end result was the rather large concrete bulge on the corner of Wellington Street which staff dubbed 'The Bunker' due to its size and lack of windows. This housed the newsrooms of both the *Yorkshire Evening Post* and *Yorkshire Post*.

The unusual design had its roots in logic. Because the editorial hall was so vast, placing windows in the walls would mean some areas would be very bright, others rather dim. Instead a huge skylight ensured the room could be illuminated from dawn till dusk with the sun's rays being spread as evenly as possible.

The only downside for those who worked within was the complete absence of views. Someone coming in from a trip outside would invariably be met with the query: "What's the weather like out there?" from colleagues keen to know if they might need a coat or umbrella.

There was another hall installed underneath which served as the main area for welcoming people into the building, the whole point of which, said Mr Madin, "was to add a sense of importance to the place, a kind of modern grandeur".

"And that was the thinking behind the clock tower too," he added. "It was our modern version of a church's clock tower – something which told everyone what the building was. And I think that's just what it did."

The move from Albion Street to the new premises came in a carefully planned and coordinated operation on the last weekend in September 1970. It began immediately after the printing of the Saturday night's *Yorkshire Evening Post* and was achieved in time for the *YEP* to be printed at Wellington Street on the Monday.

The unashamedly modernist building was officially opened that December by Prince Charles, who toured the editorial floor talking to journalists.

A noisy hive of activity, there was still a fug of cigarette smoke in many corners until smokers were banished to a smoking room some years later. Stories came in via phone, letter and in person, with readers walking in off the street to the large reception area to speak to reporters, order photographs from the archive and insert adverts and announcements.

During what many veteran journalists refer to as "the glory days", leisurely visits to the pub in the afternoon were almost expected. Reporters justified these outings with the countless newsworthy tip-offs and stories that emerged from them, which had the added bonus of allowing them to put at least some of the drinks on expenses, listed under "entertaining contacts".

Indeed, many only revealed the true depth of their creative talent when it came to filing their expenses, with some even boasting that they were enough to live on while they banked and saved their pay cheques.

In 2008 it was the end of an era when printing of the *YEP* moved to Dinnington in South Yorkshire. The press had been built by the paper's parent company Johnston Press two years before as part of a £60m project. One of the most advanced newspaper presses in Europe, it boasts the latest colour technology and can print up to 86,000 copies an hour, more than twice as many as the press in Leeds.

Then, in August 2012, it was announced that the *YEP* would be leaving its Wellington Street headquarters for new offices on Whitehall Road. There were mixed feelings among staff at the move. Sadness to be leaving a building containing so many memories but excitement too at the prospect of at least being able to enjoy views of the outside world after decades spent in 'The Bunker'.

The building was demolished to make way, at the time of writing, for a planned block of offices and apartments, but the famous *YEP* clock tower was left where it stood – nostalgic Loiners not quite ready to see the back of an unofficial city landmark just yet.

The famous illuminated sign is hoisted into place, November 1970.

BBC

A NEW LEEDS
1982–2015

At an editorial conference in the *Yorkshire Evening Post*'s offices one June morning in 1982, an idea for a new fundraising campaign was under discussion. The city's hospices for people with terminal illnesses – Wheatfields in Headingley and St Gemma's in Moortown – had been open for just four years, but were already both heavily in debt.

Running costs at St Gemma's had rocketed to £40,000 a month and so desperate was the situation that one floor had to be closed to avoid incurring more costs.

"We'd raised money for an all-body scanner and it was our managing director at the time, Sir Gordon Linacre, who asked if there was anything we might do for the hospices," recalled then editor Malcolm Barker. "We mulled it over in conference and decided we would have a go.

"Fred Willis, who was on newsdesk at the time, piped up and said: 'So we're splitting the money 50-50?' I said yes. And then he said: 'Half and half?' and we thought, 'Aha, we have a title!'"

Wheatfields' home, a former headquarters for a Royal Auxiliary Air Force Squadron during the 1950s, had been chosen by Leeds-born philanthropist Sue Ryder to provide more much-needed hospice care in Leeds. After a *YEP*-backed public appeal to raise funds, it was opened to patients in the August of 1978. Two years later, the people of Leeds once again sprang into action to help rescue the hospice from near bankruptcy when it finished the year £60,000 in debt.

As it now launched this new appeal, the paper quoted a list of the essential work that was required. More single bedrooms were urgently needed and the kitchen which originally catered for 22 patients and 15 staff was now "too small for both patients' needs and those of 60 staff and volunteers". It added: "The medical director has no room of his own to interview relatives", a paid part-time social worker was "badly needed" and the hospice had no laundry, which "may well be a future requirement".

YEP editor Malcolm Barker, on the far right, at the opening of a ward named in his honour. St Gemma's Hospice, 1982.

Opposite: **A worker helps ready the new Trinity Leeds shopping centre ahead of its official opening, February 2013.**

June Hancock outside the former JW Roberts factory in Armley after receiving news of her court victory.

As soon as news of the Half and Half Appeal appeared in print, the people of Leeds and beyond rallied to donate as much as they could. Malcolm Barker's son Patrick was among the early fundraisers, collecting £1.56 through a pen sale. On the appeal's first anniversary the *YEP* published a supplement highlighting the fundraising achievements of the appeal's supporters, with activities including knitting and running with a sack of potatoes.

Within two years, the original target of £250,000 had been reached – and the money kept coming in. Donations passed the £1m milestone in 1990 and the £2m mark by 2003. By 2015 the total stood at almost £3m.

Now believed to be the longest running newspaper charity campaign in the country, *YEP* readers continue to keep the cause close to their hearts and in so doing continue to play a sizeable role in safeguarding the future of the city's two hospices and the wonderful work they do.

By the early 1980s, the manufacturing which had helped forge the city in the early part of the century and contributed to so much of its wealth and success was on the decline. Yet in one part of Leeds it had also left a deadly legacy.

For decades before its closure in the 1950s the J W Roberts factory in Armley had spewed out blue dust which settled on the rooftops and window sills of surrounding houses. Children played in the dust in the streets, making 'snowballs' which they threw around, oblivious to the danger they faced.

The dust was asbestos and hundreds contracted mesothelioma, a cancer of the lining that covers most of the body's organs, not only as a result of working at the factory but also simply living near it. The link was discovered by *Yorkshire Evening Post* reporter Richard Taylor. In 1987 he began checking through the coroner's court reports, examining death certificates and interviewing relatives and neighbours of the deceased. It allowed him to show there was a pattern "of an incredibly high incidence of mesothelioma deaths in Armley around the Roberts factory".

The coroner, Philip Sanderson Gill, agreed with the findings, saying: "I have very few other cases from other areas of Leeds. It is significant that virtually all the cases we have come from that area." The *YEP* produced a series of articles about the ongoing contamination and disease, which it dubbed the 'Armley Asbestos Tragedy'.

Richard Taylor met with John Battle, then the MP for Leeds West, to present his findings and Mr Battle raised the matter in a House of Commons debate. Along with Leeds City Council, he called for a public inquiry into the deaths at Armley, but the Government refused. Undaunted, the *YEP* continued to reveal the horrifying scale of the problem and in 1994 June Hancock became the first resident to launch a legal fight for justice.

June had been a little girl when she was first exposed to the deadly dust. She had lived 250 yards away from J W Roberts and, along with her classmates at Armley Park School, her lunch-times had been filled with carefree fun playing with the dust that flew over from the factory. She was diagnosed with mesothelioma in 1994, the disease having killed her mother a dozen years earlier.

Sculptor Anthony Gormley pictured with a maquette of his controversial Brick Man.

Despite knowing she didn't have long to live, she sued Roberts' parent company, Turner & Newall. Against all the odds, June survived long enough to win compensation in a case which set a precedent for thousands, dying in July 1997, two years after her landmark victory. Since then, more than £25m in damages has been paid out to victims and a charity, The June Hancock Mesothelioma Research Fund, has been set up to raise money for research into the disease.

His Angel of the North near Gateshead has undoubtedly become an iconic national landmark, but acclaimed sculptor Antony Gormley's first choice of site for one of his giant creations was right here in Leeds. In 1988 he wanted to build a 120ft tall Brick Man on Holbeck Triangle, unused scrubland near Leeds city station which the council had long earmarked for a sculpture park. The sculpture was to be hollow inside, with a door at one heel and two tiny windows where the ears were, so people would be able to wander in and peer up into the empty gloom.

The idea had its supporters, but the *Yorkshire Evening Post* wasn't among them. In fact, the paper actively campaigned against the £600,000 project after a phone poll revealed 800 readers

Crowds gather outside the new Harvey Nichols store on Briggate for the long awaited official opening, October 1996.

Above: YEP street vendor, Joe Haigh MBE.

Opposite: The stunning restoration of the Victoria Quarter, which dates back to 1900, was completed in 1996.

Above: Developer Kevin Linfoot with a scale model of Lumiere, which would have been the tallest residential building in Europe, October 2006.

Below: An artist's impression of the Supertram, which would never be made reality.

were for it but more than 2,000 against. Then council leader George Mudie said of the result: "I am delighted but not surprised with the formidable common sense of the Leeds public (which) contrasts sharply with the airy-fairy views of celebrities who don't live within 100 miles of the city." Councillor Richard Hughes-Rowlands, meanwhile, said the figure reminded him of King Kong. "If Mr Gormley is talking about it going elsewhere," he added, "my eyes won't exactly be weeping tears."

The council duly rejected the proposals and Gormley did go elsewhere, swapping his Brick Man for an Angel overlooking the A1. The only evidence of his bold vision for the city now stands just 6ft tall in Leeds Art Gallery in the form of a scale replica, a reminder perhaps of a missed opportunity.

By the mid-1990s there was a sense that Leeds, having endured its time in the economic doldrums, was once again on the up. It was an optimism reflected in the changing face of the city. The Corn Exchange, designed by renowned architect Cuthbert Broderick and opened in 1864 as a bustling centre for the exchange and sale of corn wheat, barley, hops and other foodstuffs, had been given a grand makeover and resurrected as a shopping centre.

Quarry Hill, site of that failed experiment with modern European-style social housing, was on its way to becoming modern Leeds' cultural quarter. It is now home to Leeds College of Music, the West Yorkshire Playhouse, Yorkshire Arts and BBC Leeds. The imposing Quarry House, meanwhile, housed the offices of the Social Security in the North – and was nicknamed 'The Kremlin' for its trouble. Down by the river, the crowning glory of the redevelopment of the rundown waterfront was the new Royal Armouries, a northern branch of the London museum, which opened in 1996. And that same year saw another institution make its way up the M1.

When upmarket fashion store Harvey Nichols decided to open its first shop outside the capital, few expected it to choose Leeds. But its arrival in the historic Victoria Quarter on Briggate in October 1996, complete with top hat-sporting doorman, was to be a game-changer for the city – even if a relatively small percentage of the population could actually afford to shop there. It helped change the city's image, raised its profile and paved the way for much of the investment and other big names that followed. It even led some to dub Leeds the 'Knightsbridge of the North'.

There were big ideas when it came to public transport, too. Plans for a new tram system were first proposed in 1991 – more than three decades after Leeds had scrapped its original tramway. In 2003 preliminary construction work finally began on the so-called Supertram, a 17-mile tram network which would incorporate three lines. One would run to Stourton and Tingley via Hunslet, Belle Isle and Middleton. A second to Weetwood via Leeds University, Hyde Park and Headingley. The third would terminate at Whinmoor with stops at St James's Hospital, Harehills and Seacroft.

The routes were to be the start of a wider system which included plans for other tram lines from Leeds city centre to Bradford via Armley, Bramley and Stanningley and to Alwoodley via Chapeltown, Chapel Allerton and Moortown. All three of the initial lines were to meet in the city centre in a loop line running along The Headrow, Park Row, Boar Lane, Kirkgate and behind Kirkgate Market. Artist's impressions printed in the *YEP* showed sleek, futuristic vehicles gliding along the streets.

Work was due to begin in earnest in 2004, ready for trams to start running within a few years, only for the scheme to be halted as projected costs doubled to around £1bn. The following year, Transport Minister Alistair Darling said he wouldn't give Supertram the go-ahead, despite £40m having already been spent on its development.

Plans for an alternative trolleybus system, known as NGT, were put together. Powered electrically by overhead wires, it was slated to serve destinations including Lawnswood to the north and Stourton to the south of the city. Nick Clegg, then Deputy Prime Minister, arrived in Leeds in July 2012 to give the green light to the £250m scheme, telling the *YEP*: "What we are doing is something that Labour failed to do for 13 years."

Leeds, though, still needed formal permission to build and operate the system, permission that could only be granted after a public inquiry. It took place over the course of 72 days in 2014 and heard claims from objectors that trolleybus would damage the environment, affect 3,000 homes and offer poor value for money.

NGT's promoters – the council and the West Yorkshire Combined Authority – insisted it would create up to 4,000 new jobs and generate £175m for the economy each year. But when the Government subsequently scrapped the scheme it became clear that the objectors, rather than the city's civic leaders, had won the argument.

Among the small army of street vendors who have sold the YEP down the years, Joe Haigh stands out. He regarded his job as the best in the world and became something of a city institution, selling the paper from his regular spot outside what was the Lewis's store, later Allders, on The Headrow. He was such a fixture there that the store put up a plastic booth to keep him warm.

Born in Middleton, he began selling newspapers in 1924 when he was 14. Over the years he sold hundreds of thousands of them, with his record being 12,000 copies of the YEP in one day when US president John F Kennedy was assassinated in November 1963.

When he retired in 1998, Joe said: "I get to meet people from all walks of life and it's a great feeling to think that you're keeping them informed." A year later he was awarded an MBE in the New Year Honours' List for services to the newspaper industry.

On the morning of July 7, 2005, Britain was still celebrating the previous day's announcement that the 2012 Olympics would be held in London. Then came reports from the capital of a series of "power surges" on the Underground. Fears that this was more than an electrical fault were proved to be well-founded – suicide bombers had detonated explosives across the city's transport system.

It soon transpired that the men responsible were from Leeds. Mohammed Sidique Khan and Shehzad Tanweer had both grown up in Beeston, while Hasib Hussain was from Holbeck. The three men travelled from Leeds and with a fourth man, Germaine Lindsay, triggered the bombs that were hidden in their backpacks in an attack staged in support of terrorist group Al Qaeda. A total of 52 people were killed in what was the worst terror attack on British soil.

The world's media swiftly descended on the city and satellite trucks seemed to be stationed on every street corner. A bomb factory was discovered in Burley where the plotters had put together their explosive devices before leaving for London. The overwhelming emotion in Leeds was one of shock, not least as there was little inkling that those responsible were radicalised to such a degree to commit an atrocity on this scale.

Khan worked at Hillside Primary School in Leeds as a learning mentor, helping the children of immigrant families who had just arrived in Britain. The 30-year-old had a wife and young child. Known as 'Kaka' (little one) by his family, Tanweer was remembered as a talented all-round sportsman by former classmates at Wortley High School. The 22-year-old, who worked in his father's fish and chip shop, then attended Leeds Metropolitan University where he studied sports science before leaving for Pakistan in 2004 to attend a course in Islamic studies. Hussain, the youngest of the trio at 18, had been a student at South Leeds High School, where teachers remembered him as a "gentle giant", and then Thomas Danby College.

The younger bombers attended the Hamara Youth Access Point, where Khan worked as a volunteer. It was an offshoot of the Hamara Healthy Living Centre in Beeston, a popular community hub running various youth and public health and education initiatives. Those who ran it had no idea that the trio were secretly plotting.

In the wake of the bombings, the area's multi-cultural community refused to be divided and on the 10th anniversary of the attacks they held a vigil on Tempest Road, organised a trip to London to lay a wreath at Kings Cross and staged a peace march into Leeds city centre. Gill Hicks, who lost her legs in the 7/7 attacks and is now a global peace campaigner, travelled to Beeston to meet Hamara Centre chief executive Hanif Malik, who told the *YEP*: "This community is so much more than just three individuals. As huge as it was in scale, it should not be allowed to take away from the huge amount of good work that happens here."

Reflecting on the bombings a decade on, Leeds imam Qari Asim said: "7/7 was a particularly horrible day for people of Leeds. When we heard the news that the perpetrators had come from Leeds we were in a complete sense of shock and disbelief. Never in a million years did we think that something like that would happen on our soil, in our country. But I'm really pleased to say the communities really came together, the people of Leeds came together and I think they came together because they did not want the terrorists to win."

The setback Leeds had suffered over the Supertram scheme was followed by fresh disappointment for this newly ambitious city, which had become one of the boom towns of Europe on the back of its burgeoning reputation as a leading centre for finance, law, accountancy and the communications industry.

In 2006 the *YEP* profiled property developer Kevin Linfoot, who was estimated to have built almost a third of all the new apartments in the centre of Leeds as people embraced the trend for city living. Despite his huge success, he told the paper that he wasn't interested in money. "It doesn't light my fire at all," he said. "It's just the commodity which allows me to do what I like doing, which is building things and doing something different."

And Mr Linfoot certainly wanted to do something different in the heart of Leeds. It started with his creation of the towering Bridgewater Place, at 367ft the tallest building in Yorkshire when it opened in 2007. "My goal is to build another one or two iconic buildings in Leeds," said Linfoot at the time. "And believe me, we will do it."

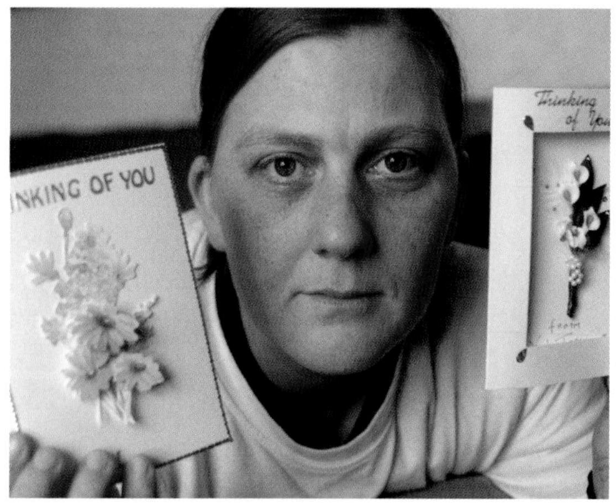

Karen Matthews was jailed for faking the disappearance of her daughter Shannon in March 2008.

Opposite:

Top: **A two-minute silence is held in Millennium Square in memory of the victims of the London suicide bombings, July 14, 2005.**

Bottom left: **England fans watching on the big screen in Millennium Square celebrate a World Cup goal against Slovenia, June 2010.**

Bottom right: **The late Jane Tomlinson's son Stephen carries the Olympic Torch through Beeston as part of the nationwide relay, June 25, 2012.**

ISLAM IS AGAINST
SUICIDE BOMBING

TERRY

018
London 2012

His landmark creation was to be Lumiere, twin skyscrapers that were set to dominate the city's skyline. Launched with a lavish party featuring fire-eaters and fireworks, the £225m development on Wellington Street was to stand 54 and 32 storeys high on land next to the former Royal Mail building, itself now transformed into apartments.

At 560ft at its highest point, Lumiere was set to become the UK's tallest structure outside London and the tallest residential building in Western Europe. Construction work on the much-trumpeted scheme began in December 2007, but by the summer of the following year it had stalled due to the crippling effects of the credit crunch.

In February 2009 it was announced that the developer's firm KW Linfoot had entered administration as the funding dried up. And his weren't the only bold ideas to bite the dust. In July 2008 the *YEP* revealed that the 377ft tall 'Kissing Towers' scheme at Criterion Place – the site surrounded by Neville Street, Sovereign Street, Swinegate and Leeds railway station which was previously home to the Queens Hall – was among the victims of the property slump, the plug being pulled after it was deemed to be no longer commercially viable.

And the problems didn't end there. Nicknamed 'The Dalek' because of its distinctive design, it was soon discovered that Bridgewater Place caused the acceleration of winds around it, leading to the death of Dr Edward Slaney, a 35-year-old from Sowerby Bridge who was killed by a lorry which flipped over in high winds in 2011. It led Coroner Melanie Williamson to recommend that Leeds City Council close the road when wind speeds reached 45mph. Remedial measures to counter the effect were also drawn up.

Thankfully, many of the missing person appeals issued in the pages of the *YEP* end with the individual concerned being found safe sooner rather than later. But that wasn't the case in March 2008, when the search for a missing schoolgirl would become the biggest investigation undertaken by West Yorkshire Police since the hunt for the Yorkshire Ripper 30 years earlier.

Shannon Matthews had reportedly failed to return home after a school swimming trip. The nine-year-old, from Dewsbury Moor, would be missing for a total of four weeks, her mother Karen and partner Craig Meehan making a series of television appeals urging the public to come forward with information as to her whereabouts.

The *Yorkshire Evening Post* provided daily updates on the search, with many fearing the worst. So it was an enormous relief when the paper reported that it had been told by a local resident: "I've just seen Shannon being taken out of a house in Batley Carr. She is safe and well."

The news prompted a huge outpouring of joy and by that evening impromptu street parties were in full swing. But one word in the official statement issued by the police hinted at a different story: the circumstances of her disappearance, it said, were "complicated".

Shannon had been discovered hidden in the base of a divan bed at the home of Meehan's uncle, Michael Donovan – and it transpired that the plot had been orchestrated by her own mother, Karen. The idea had been for Donovan to come forward and claim to have found Shannon, collecting the £50,000 reward for her safe return. He and Karen would then split the cash between them. Matthews had apparently come up with the idea after seeing a similar storyline in Channel 4 show Shameless.

She and Donovan went on trial at Leeds Crown Court that November and were both found guilty of kidnapping, false imprisonment and perverting the course of justice. They were each given eight-year prison sentences. Shannon and her brothers and sisters were put into care with new identities.

For decades Leeds' own Jimmy Savile had been a much-loved celebrity and an internationally-recognised philanthropist. He was one of the nation's favourite sons, a figure who had generated £42m for a host of good causes through a seemingly never-ending series of fundraising stunts.

There had always been rumours about his behaviour with women - particularly a fondness for young girls – but he had always laughed them off, saying it came with the territory. "If you are odd, people want to know why you are odd," was his stock response. Allegations were dismissed and accusers ignored or disbelieved. Police investigations left him in the clear.

When he died at the age of 84, thousands turned out to pay tribute. Part of the city centre was brought to a standstill as he did a final lap of places that held personal significance for him – his hearse passing the modest house where he grew up and the hospitals he had raised money for as it made its way to Leeds Cathedral. Inside there were prayers along with fond memories and laughter. But some of the tributes would also prove prophetic. "None of us really knew the real Jimmy," mused fellow DJ Mike Read. "Maybe he didn't even know himself."

Soon the late presenter's home city, and the rest of the nation, were having to come to terms with the real Jimmy Savile. Now those who had been silenced for years came forward to tell their own stories of their encounters with the DJ. Hundreds of allegations of sexual abuse were made against him, leading detectives to the conclusion that Savile was possibly one of Britain's most prolific and predatory sex offenders.

Among those who had known him there was an enormous sense of shock.

Sylvia Nicol, a trustee of his charity and long-time friend since the 1970s told the *YEP* she saw "no inappropriate behaviour ever" by the star, who she worked with raising funds for Stoke Mandeville Hospital: "From the time he came to Stoke Mandeville I only saw him do good," she said. "It takes away 40 years of very happy, very good memories." Savile's devastated family were forced to make the decision to remove and destroy his Scarborough headstone after it was defaced by vandals.

The story of the last few years leading up to the 125th anniversary of the *Yorkshire Evening Post* has been one of major building projects. The 13,500-capacity First Direct Arena means Leeds at last has a world class music venue that attracts the planet's biggest stars. Work on the spectacular £350m Trinity Leeds shopping centre began in 2008 but was stopped for more than a year as the economic storm swept the UK. When it finally opened in March 2013, shoppers swarmed through the doors.

Within just over six months a staggering 12 million had shopped inside the one million sq ft centre, named after the Holy Trinity Church it stands next to. Meanwhile, over on Eastgate, finishing touches were being put to the £165m Victoria Gate development, which would be anchored by another new arrival to the city in the shape of upmarket retailer John Lewis. Buoyed by such investment and the success of the Tour de France's Grand Départ, Leeds City Council announced in March 2015 that it planned to mount a bid for Leeds to be named European Capital of Culture 2023.

To look at Leeds now is to see a city transformed. To the likes of Alexander Paterson, the young editor who launched the *Yorkshire Evening Post* back in 1890, it would be all but unrecognisable. Once familiar buildings have been torn down and shiny new ones put up in their place. Shops that had become household names are now long gone. Even the trams no longer trundle along the city's streets. But some things haven't changed. There are still countless stories to be told of this city and its people, its triumphs and setbacks, its celebrations and key events. And here's hoping the *Yorkshire Evening Post* will continue to tell them for many more years to come.

Top: The First Direct Arena has given Leeds a first-class music venue that attracts the world's biggest names.

Bottom: The Victoria Gate development on Eastgate will further enhance the city's reputation as a leading retail destination.

Opposite: The sun rises behind Leeds' tallest building, Bridgewater Place.

BMB

AFTERWORD

While it has spent the last 125 years charting the changing face of Leeds, the *Yorkshire Evening Post* has had to move with the times too. The digital revolution ushered in by the inexorable rise of the internet has transformed the way news is read and reported.

For many the laptop computer, tablet or mobile phone is now their means of getting their daily diet of information, rather than unfolding the evening paper on their way home from work.

News has become a 24-hour a day, seven-day a week business and the *YEP* operation has changed to reflect this exciting new frontier. And while the result has been a drop in the number of newspapers being sold, this has been accompanied by an incredible rise in the number of people visiting the *Yorkshire Evening Post*'s website.

As many as 100,000 people access news, sport and other content from the site each day, collectively reading in the region of a million or more articles a week. And the numbers are rising all the time. It enables the *YEP*'s team of journalists to ensure that those who come to us for their news and sport are always kept up to date, whether it be a serious fire somewhere, the latest comings and goings from Elland Road, play by play reports from a crunch Rhinos game, or a review of a major concert at Leeds Arena just minutes after it finishes.

The value of having such rolling coverage at your fingertips was illustrated only too recently in what were truly tragic circumstances. Around lunchtime on June 16, 2016, the *YEP*'s Twitter account relayed reports of someone being violently attacked in the street in Birstall.

The breaking news duly appeared on the *YEP* website, the story being constantly updated as reporters phoned police and other contacts to get the full picture. It soon transpired that the victim was Batley and Spenborough MP Jo Cox, who had been holding a monthly constituency surgery at Birstall Library to meet and talk to local residents.

The 41-year-old mother of two young children had been shot and stabbed, dying a short time afterwards. The *YEP* published ongoing developments as they happened, with eyewitness reports and video from the scene all being quickly uploaded to the website. Meanwhile, tributes to Jo and words of sympathy and support for her husband Brendan and their two children poured in from readers and duly appeared on the site alongside the stories.

It was a heartbreaking event to report, but the rolling coverage now made possible by the internet age meant readers were kept up to date every step of the way as it unfolded. Where once there were several editions of each day's *YEP* to keep the news up to date, all it takes now is for a new version of the story to be typed out and, with a few clicks of a mouse, it is sent out to the public.

It is a far cry from the days of typesetting by hand and big, clanking printing presses. But just as the story of Leeds shows that nothing stands still, so must the *Yorkshire Evening Post* continue to evolve in order to meet the changing demands of readers in the 21st century.

After all, only by doing so can the *YEP* expect to continue to tell the story of this great city and its extraordinary people, to play a part in the future of the Leeds it loves.

LOYAL LOINERS

Mr C J Abbott
Joyce Appleton
Jayne and David Armitage
Jonathan R Armitage
Vic Atkinson (In Loving Memory of)
Brian Baker
Lindsay Barlow
Keith Barran
Colin Bateson (Late Husband of Mary)
Stephen Baxendale
June Bell
Frank Bickerdyke
Gwen Blackburn
Simon Bowman
Gary Boyes
David Brearley
Martin Brennan
Dorothy Brook
Marjorie Broom
Martin Bullock
Michael A Busby
Malcolm Butler
Rowland Bywater
Derek Chadburn
Micheal Colledge
Richard Colledge
Jennifer Cooke
Jeremy Coulson
Kym Cox
Ivy Coyle
CJ Cusworth
John Dalton (PC42)
Selina Jane Darler
Sabrina Rita Davies
Neil Murray Devlin
Dorothy Dixon
Danny Dutson
Michael Dutson
Patricia Edwards
Barry David Evans
Patricia Evans
Florrie Fawcett
Maureen Forbes
Reginald French
Thomas Fryer
Brendan Gallagher
Neil & Patricia Garrick
James Edward Gill
Anthony Stuart Gomersal
Irene Gordon
Rose Green
Caroline Gruen
Anthony Grundy
Paul Michael Grundy
Alan Hall
Susan Harris
Brenda Hartley
Ian Mark Hartley
Janet Hawden
Mike Hayes
Tony Hector
Catherine Henderson
David Henderson
Jane Heyes
Eric A Hill
Pauline Hill (In Loving Memory of)
Gordon Hird
Shirley Hodgson
Michael Hogg
Robert Desmond Howe
Jean Hutchinson
John Hutchinson
Peter Jenkins (Builder)
Andrew Johnson
Richard Johnson
Jeffrey Jones
Kay
Barry Kitchen
Robert Fred Lawrence
Alex Lawson
Brian Leaf
Evelyn Leonard
Lillian Ida Leonard
Martina Leonard
Craig Philip Levelle
Colin Lightfoot
Edwin Myers Lockwood
Graham Lunn
Craig James Malcolm
Michael Marsh
Colin Martin
Gregor McIntyre
Clifford Basil Metcalf
Peter Milner
Elizabeth Naylor
Elizabeth Robinson Naylor
The O'Brien family - Rothwell, Leeds
Kevin J O'Connor
Mark Palmer
Bill Park
Muriel Parkin
David Pegden
Richard Pegden
Robert Pickles
Julie Playforth
Jean E Poole
Gloria Potter
Eric Precious
Jack Quarmby
Big Kev Quinn
Audrey Rains
Brenda Saunders
Matthew Neil Scholey
Martin Scott
Matthew Scott
Jane Sharp
Jean Shaw
Kathryn Smith
Norman Christopher Smith
Katherine Somers
Billy Spence
Gary Spence
Eileen Spencer
Carl Stanley
Pat Startek
Dale Stones
Fred Summers
John E Sutcliffe
Barry Taylor
Kathleen Thompson
Brian Leslie Tudor
Tyler James Warnford Turpin
Ian J Ward (Thorner)
Tom Warnett
Stuart Watkins
Barbara Wells
Neil Whitaker
Paul Whitaker
Stephen Whitaker
John White
Valerie White
Trevor Whitehead
Jose Whitney
Robin Wight
George Lewis Wilby
Hazel Doreen Williams (nee Hart)
Malcolm Wilson
Roland Winn
David M Wood
June M Woodhead
Rory Woodward
Skye Woodward
Arthur Wormald
Mark Wormwell
Christopher David Wright
John & Christine

YORKSHIRE Evening Post

YORKSHIREEVENINGPOST.CO.UK #championingleeds MONDAY, SEPTEMBER 12, 2016 72P (58P TO SUBSCRIBERS)

REVEALED: THE YEP CHIPPY OF THE YEAR WINNER!

Chippy of the year

TURN TO PAGE 3

MEDALS JOY FOR OUR KADEENA

FULL STORY: PAGE 5

GARRY MONK : WE'RE ENTERING 'MUST-WIN' TERRITORY: BACK PAGE

LEEDS: BRITAIN'S BEST CITY

Study will be read by millions across world

Georgina Morris
georgina.morris@jpress.co.uk
@ReporterGeorge

LEEDS HAS been named as the best city in Britain when it comes to quality of life, beating the likes of London, Manchester and Edinburgh in a new global ranking.

It placed 26th out of 100 cities around the world when leading infrastructure consultancy Arcadis measured factors including health, education, income inequality, work-life balance, crime and living costs.

The city was also in the top quarter for economic sustainability, but struggled to compete in the economic rankings where it came in at 69th.

The Sustainable Cities report, published today, highlighted poor transport, high unemployment and skills gaps as factors holding the city back.

Nick Kealey, cities director for Leeds at Arcadis, said: "In an era of devolution of powers, the city needs to do more to push its own regional agenda, to avoid getting left behind."

Full story: Page 4